The Wirelessman, Dale Clemons, in Marconi Company uniform, at the helm of the SS Congress *in 1914.*

WAKE OF THE WIRELESSMAN

by

B. J. CLEMONS

Published by The Glencannon Press
P.O. Box 341, Palo Alto, CA 94302

First Edition

Library of Congress Catalog Card Number: 95-80728

ISBN 0-9637586-6-7

The illustration on the back cover is through the courtesy of Jim Kreuzer.

Unless otherwise credited, all photos and illustrations are from the author's collection.

Dedication

To those who lived this story.

"If to one man we seamen owe a debt unpayable, Marconi holds the bond."

David W. Bone
1919

Acknowledgements

Many kind people made this book possible through their patience and enthusiasm. William L. Olesen, Curator Emeritus of the Los Angeles Maritime Museum gave me the courage to tackle this subject, then cheerfully dispelled the haze by answering questions and, through a lively correspondence which lasted a decade, made the work pleasurable. George King III, an active steam engineer aboard the *SS Sabino*, at Mystic Seaport, Connecticut, provided valuable information on steam engines and boilers.

My understanding of wireless telegraphy was greatly enhanced through the good graces of Jim Kruezer, of the New Wireless Pioneers in Elma, New York. A book purveyor and historian, he placed in my hands rare technical books about radio operation during the period 1914-17 which were essential to my understanding of wireless telegraph operation at sea. Bruce Kelly of the Antique Wireless Association (A.W.A.) Electronic Communication Museum in Bloomfield, New York, was kind enough to critique and fine-tune an early draft of the manuscript. Robert W. Merriam, curator of the New England Wireless and Steam Museum of East Greenwich, Rhode Island, graciously critiqued a final draft and unearthed the ship *Vigo*'s call letters.

Information about, and photographs of, the *Vigo* came from the Mariner's Museum of Newport News, Virginia; the National Maritime Museum, London, England; the Los Angeles Maritime Museum, San Pedro, California and the National Archives and Records Service, Washington, D.C. I'm grateful to each of these organizations for their information and the many fine photographs they supplied.

An interview with Lester O. "Frank" Marsteller, Dale's classmate at radio school, marked the beginning of my research. Correspondence with Dale's sister, Athlene Clemons Martin, filled in the blanks of family life and events in Storm Lake, Iowa.

The history of Dodge's radio school and Dale Clemons' days as a student would be incomplete but for the help of G. Edward Hershman, President, Valparaiso Technical Institute and Daniel R. Gahl, Archivist at Valparaiso University, Valparaiso, Indiana.

Special thanks go to Dianne Chapman, who introduced me to the craft of creative writing in 1979. My friend, Babette Mason had the commitment to listen to each chapter. Her reactions resulted in improving the quality of the story, her red pen applied the grammatic finesse. Joy Crawford's faith encouraged several fresh starts over the years and her suggestions filled in several gaps in the text. Bill Struck of Wilson Camera in Phoenix, skillfully converted drawings of radio apparatus and steam engine components into usable photographs. Madelyn Salins was tireless in her proofreading.

Finally there are those who deserve thanks for efforts "above and beyond the call." Becky Kerestes deserves a medal for typing so many drafts of the manuscript, believing that each was "the last." My brother, Tom Clemons, and Ward Parker gave unselfishly of their time in reading and commenting on the manuscript. I'm deeply grateful to my niece, Pam Seth and her husband, Frank. Their encouragement, from beginning to end, was a boon to my morale. I am honored to have as my editor Captain Walter Jaffee and thank him for being a believer in this story and a master at his craft. Last, but not least, a special thanks to Irene Davis for cheerfully living with the clutter and never once doubting the outcome.

Contents

PREFACE

For a youngster who lived in Storm Lake, Iowa, a thousand miles inland, getting to sea seemed as likely for Dale Clemons as an albatross landing in a corn field.

Farming was the center of life. Folks had finally come to terms with the crank telephone jangling on the wall. They had newspapers. There were telegrams to send or dread receiving when someone died. What else was needed? Most adults didn't even try to understand the new fad "wireless." Its language was foreign and difficult, something called Morse code.

But ask any boy who read. A wireless operator who helped in sea rescue was a hero equal to Abraham Lincoln. Youngsters everywhere wanted to be wirelessmen, if only pretend. And it wasn't that difficult. Anyone could put together a radio set out of junk parts; popular magazines told how to join in the fun. Boys built radio sets, learned Morse code and filled the atmosphere with electronic chatter.

In the early years there was no control — the air waves were wide open, as free as the sky. Then tragedy struck. Amateur operators "hogging" the air interfered with rescue operations at sea. The *Titanic* disaster of 1912 forced government control of radio use. Forever after, by law, anyone was free to "listen" to radio but every transmitter and its operator had to be licensed. Radio frequencies were assigned. Every ship carrying fifty or more people was obliged to install radio equipment. For some the new law meant the end of a hobby. For others the Radio Law breathed life into a mighty, far-fetched, dream. For Dale Clemons that dream would become reality.

B.J. Clemons
Phoenix, Arizona

INTRODUCTION

A ship at sea is a world unto itself. Far from the bustle of human society, its excitement and pace, the crew's universe is encompassed in narrow corridors and small rooms, seeing and talking with the same few people about the same things day after day. There is one exception. Often found in the smallest room on the ship, a single person sits, surrounded by dials and gauges, squeals and beeps. That small room is the domain of the radio operator. On this tiny speck in the vastness of ocean and sky, he or she twists dials and taps out signals, like a wizard or magician, without visible wires, conjuring voices and world events from thin air, his or her voice circling the globe, ears tuned to the universe.

I've always had a special regard for, and more than a little curiosity about, radio operators. At sea, they are our only link with the outside world. Many is the time when the melancholy, bordering on depression, of a long sea passage has been turned into joy with the receipt of a simple scrap of paper from the radio operator — a message from a loved one far away. Then, the gloomy gray sky and ocean suddenly become blue and sunny and the radio operator is the most noble and wonderful person on earth. And of even grander stature, if such a thing is possible, is the radio operator who is also a ham. When shipmates with one, I've had the rare privilege of sitting in the radio shack, microphone in hand, talking to someone eight or ten thousand miles off through a phone patch, for a short while losing all sense of time and place.

Buoying morale is probably the smallest part of the radio operator's job. "Sparks" (as all radio operators are called because their early equipment emitted electric blue sparks) provides weather and navigation warnings, news of the outside world, communicates ship's business to and from shore, arranges pilots, berthing, cargo and the thousand-and-one other things that enable the ships to travel the oceans. But probably the most dramatic aspect of the radio operator's role is embodied in gripping scenes of disaster at sea, when the faithful operator stays at his post sending or receiving distress calls and trying to help save lives.

But how did it all start? Who was drawn to that life in its early, unsure beginnings? *Wake of the Wirelessman* offers us a glimpse. Author B.J. Clemons weaves a fascinating you-are-there tale of a true pioneer. Early in this century, telegraphy ashore was by wire, but to function at sea it had to be wire-less. The hero of this story, Dale Clemons, was a graduate of the first wireless school in the United States. In 1914 he went to work as an employee of the Marconi Wireless Company aboard merchant ships. And here we touch history and a giant in communication. Guglielmo Marconi patented the wireless radio in 1896 (receiving the Nobel Prize for his work in 1905). Dale Clemons was among the earliest people trained to make it work.

With the outbreak of World War I, Dale fulfilled a boyhood ambition — saving lives using the new invention. But for him, it was more than that. During this time he, and wireless radio, came of age. It was a difficult process on ships plagued with problems of both the nineteenth and twentieth centuries. How do you rig a sail so that it and your ship's engines will allow you to outrun a submarine? How do you dodge a torpedo? What do you do, halfway across the Atlantic, when the drinking water becomes contaminated? What do you do when three out of four of the ship's boilers fail? These and many other problems, including personal tragedy were faced on Dale's ship, the *Vigo*.

But *Wake of the Wirelessman* is much more than a factual recounting of a wirelessman's adventures. An indefatigable researcher and skillful storyteller, B.J. Clemons' work appeals not only to the intellect, but to the senses and emotions, as well. Readers feel, hear, see and almost literally smell life aboard ship as they ride with the wirelessman braving the war zone. World War I is brought into perspective — the surprising attitude of the Spanish toward the United States, the early use of convoys, the devastating menace of the submarine. And we learn some startling things about the effectiveness of wireless radio, as both tool and weapon.

The story reads with a special poignancy today (in 1995). We stand on the cusp of another historic transition, different, yet so similar, to that which brought the first need for radio operators aboard ship. Modern seafaring and modern electronics have conspired, via satellite and computer technology, to make the radio operator obsolete. Within a few years every officer on a ship will be able to pick up a telephone and talk anywhere in the world. And it all began with Guglielmo Marconi and adventuresome youngsters like Dale Clemons. The year was 1913. It started in Storm Lake, Iowa, a thousand miles inland . . .

Capt. Walter W. Jaffee

1

The Call of the Sea

The new hard rubber earphones fit snugly over Dale's ears, their dangling electrical cords snaking across the table to the receiver.

"What do you hear?" asked Mr. Neeley.

"A shrill whistle," Dale grimaced.

"Tune the coil."

Dale slowly turned the dial, then stopped. Wide-eyed, he whispered, "Morse code." His wonder turned to frustration as the steady stream of dots and dashes ran together in a discouraging jumble.

Smiling, Mr. Neeley said, "Nothing worthwhile comes easy, especially wireless."

For now, Dale was content to listen. Occasionally, late at night, he heard powerful land stations on the West Coast transmitting messages to ships at sea. He longed to know what they said.

Again the kindly old telegraph operator fed his curiosity. One night, at a prearranged hour, Dale sat listening. Across town Mr. Neeley transmitted the letter "A" from the loft of his barn. The rest of the alphabet followed, slowly enough for him to recognize each letter and practice writing them on a pad. Then, it was his turn to tap the telegraph key and from that moment there was no turning back.

By age sixteen Dale's fascination with wireless had bred a restless discontent. He rushed through chores and neglected homework for the chance to reach into the ether and connect with someone, somewhere — anyone like himself. Listening to the raspy sound of wireless crackling in his earphones, he liked to imagine himself aboard ship, surrounded by choppy waves.

When it was his turn to answer he tapped out his initials, "DRC" on the telegraph key, mimicking a ship's call letters. He was always anxious to know how far away his signal was heard, wanting to extend the reach of his ears as far as possible from little Storm Lake, Iowa.

Dale's domain was a small round cupola room perched high at the corner of a stately Victorian home. It had just enough space for him to sit at a little table overlooking the restless waters of Storm Lake.

There should have been plenty of space in the three-story house on Third Street. Dale Clemons' half-brother, Guy, had married and moved next door. But somehow it still wasn't quite enough room for a teenage boy to be happy living with two sisters. The older one, Lucille, liked to tattle on him.

"Mama, Dale didn't pump enough water."

"Not again," groaned Dale. That meant stopping what he was doing and going some distance to haul a bucket of water up three flights of stairs.

Drawing the water wasn't so bad. He liked mechanical things and knew to be patient priming the pump. The handle felt loose at first then grew heavy, slowed by the weight of rising water. On the count of three it began spewing out and

The Clemons' home at Storm Lake. "Dale's domain" was in the cupola over the porch.

soon filled the wood bucket hanging by its handle under the spout.

Watching the bucket fill, he recalled Guy's admonition. "Bide your time," he often said, "Get through high school, then I'll help you convince Papa of what you want to do. Meanwhile be glad for that precious piece of the world up there."

"Da-ul. Watch the time. Remember we eat at six."

"Gotta stop." Dale cut the transmission short and sent out a call to his best friend who lived across the alley. "O-T-T-O, answer." The response was too faint. Dale hurried downstairs, grabbed the fishing pole and tackle bag from underneath the back porch and squeezed through overgrown bushes into the alley, hollering, "Hey Otto, your battery is dead."

His friend appeared at an upstairs window, made a face and motioned for Dale to pipe down and wait. Soon the gate opened and he appeared, "Your earphones must be busted."

"Not mine. Could hear Kansas clear as a crow. Let's go fishin'."

"I can't. That's what I was trying to tell you. It's butchering day. I have to help make sausage."

"Come on. Clouds are building. Might not catch enough for dinner without help."

"Then you better tell your mom. I gotta go."

"Already know what she'd say," Dale muttered. He walked on toward the lake, kicking loose stones in his path. Once there he threw off his shoes, tossing them and the fishing gear into the round-bottomed boat. Then he untied the rope and shoved off into the normally choppy waters of Storm Lake. Whenever the weather looked bad, he was supposed to use the "safer" flat-bottomed boat but his mind was set on rowing fast to get across the lake. The green of a small, treed island where the big lunkers hid under submerged logs and ledges near the western shore beckoned. "Ought to be biting good there, and one will be plenty for everyone."

He pulled at the oars smoothly, not bothering to look over his shoulder. His direction came from keeping the boat-house lined up with the pointed roof of the cupola which jutted out like a turret on a castle. He fished often and was expected to provide a fish dinner once a week, the only home chore Dale liked. He hated driving cows to pasture on the way to school and having to bring them back at night for milking. Cows walked too slowly, shortening his time at the depot where he went to learn about electricity, his main interest in life. He earned money after school cleaning storage batteries, sweeping the Depot floor and emptying spittoons, banking five cents a day. At one time he made a lot more collecting empty bottles in alleys and along the railroad tracks. The bottles brought two cents each from an old one-legged soldier with an illegal liquor still in his barn, until Lucille found out and tattled. Then his mother, Ella, put her foot down. He'd disgraced the family position in town. Papa just preached the same old sermon, "If it's money you want, there's work waiting for you in my store."

Out fishing on lazy summer afternoons, he'd land the boat and sit on the island for awhile enjoying the shade and solitude, reading a book or just lying back and gazing at passing clouds which carried him away to strange places he read about. The clouds looked like sails bellied out in the wind. He thirsted to be aboard a full-rigged ship, fighting for headway, rounding Cape Horn. And he dreamed of seeing the mammoth machines, pictured in magazines, digging a ditch across Panama. *Oh to be there when two mighty oceans collide.*

His reverie was broken by a violent gust of wind. "Pull! Pull!" he said aloud. "Wind's getting worse. Holy cats! Sky's black. Tie up till it's over." It was all he could do to maneuver the boat between rocks near the island and get ashore. "Hurry. Sounds like a twister." He swung the rope around a stump and dove under a fallen tree. In a whistling roar, limbs came crashing down, followed by pelting rain, then hail so dense he lost sight of the boat. When the downpour lessened, lightning came. He knew better than to walk to the edge of the lake looking for the boat. When the storm finally ended, Dale was cold and wet and could hear his stomach growling. Sharp rocks hurt his bare feet. It was nighttime and too dark to find the boat. Deciding to wait until daylight, he made a warm nest of pine boughs and dozed off.

Dale awakened to silence, a night sky more beautiful than any in memory — just him and the stars reflected on the black glassy surface of the lake. It was like being suspended in space. He rolled over on his stomach to enjoy the flickering lights of the town, golden in color, their streaks dancing on the surface. Then he noticed something startling — a line of lanterns swinging, moving along the shoreline. *Oh, no. They're searching.*

"Hey! I'm here," he shouted and waved, then listened, cupping both ears with his hands. Not a sound. *Oh for a wireless set.* He sat down and watched. Bonfires flared up here and there for warmth. Then, against the faint orange reflection, he saw a silhouette, his boat. *I can make it if I rest often.* Weak from hunger and trembling with cold, Dale eased into the water telling himself, *Swimming will warm you up.* Although it was farther than it first appeared, he did rest often and managed to conserve enough energy to swim the distance to the boat. Then came the hard part — climbing inside without capsizing. He tried, but the boat tipped, again and again. He felt weaker. His legs moved as though made of lead. His arms were growing numb and, for the first time in his thirteen years of life, Dale Clemons felt panic. *Can't swim back. Can't hang on forever. You're gonna sink.* "No. No. NO!" On the third "NO" he reached inside himself and found the extra "push" he needed, vaulted himself up on stiff arms, then flung a leg over the side, counting on momentum to roll his body into the boat. It worked. He lay there breathing heavily, eyes closed, feeling a flood of relief. Suddenly, he remembered, *No fish. Boy, am I gonna get it.*

Fumbling for the oars, he positioned them in the oarlocks and began rowing like a steam engine piston, nonstop, sometimes losing his grip and falling back, but keeping the boat moving. He was still rowing hard when someone who waded out to meet the boat took hold of his arm. "Ease up, Nibs." It was Guy. Someone else flung a warm blanket over his back. Then he was lifted and carried ashore. "Papa!"

"Thank God you're safe."

Dale insisted he could walk beside his father. It looked like the whole town had gathered on the beach and yet everyone seemed strangely quiet as they moved back to make way for Waldo Clemons and his son. Turning toward the house, Dale thought *Here's where I get it.* Instead, his mother had hot cocoa waiting on the stove. There was a fire going in the parlor fireplace. His little sister Athie was arranging a comforter in the big stuffed chair while Lucille filled a pan with warm water for Dale's feet. Then the whole family gathered around to hear the story. The girls — wide eyed — told of seeing the twister funnel dip down. "It's a miracle," said Ella, stroking Dale's head gently. Waldo whispered, "All's well that ends well."

Within a few days life was back to normal but, as time passed, the family grew more and more concerned about Dale. He neglected his school work. Instead of conjugating verbs he "wasted time" reading about sailing ships navigating stormy seas. Summer school punishment made no difference. Dale flunked Latin and didn't care. Instead of studying grammar, he lay in the dark listening with ear phones to the music of Morse code — dit dah dit dit — his language. He yearned to join the wirelessmen he heard working aboard ship.

Ella Sanders Clemons seldom got down on her knees but she wanted to talk to Dale alone and sent him out to the garden to dig potatoes, then joined him.

Dale sat back on his haunches, grinning at the sight of his mother with her sleeves rolled up, wearing a worn-out dress rescued from the rag bag, run down shoes and grandma's old sun-bonnet. She looked natural and wonderfully warm, shorn of her usual dressed up exterior.

"Glad to see you, Mama. Something wrong?"

Ella didn't answer. She'd brought a bucket of water, scooped up a dipper full and offered it to him.

"You must be thirsty by now."

"I am." He drank half and tossed the rest on his face, then sat blinking for a moment, watching his mother. She settled down on the ground and joined in the search, plunging both hands into the loose black earth.

"Shared work is more fun. Ever wonder why?"

"Probably 'cause it goes faster."

Dale knew it was more than that. Shared work carried with it a pleasurable feeling of being connected. He watched his mother gather the uprooted potatoes and empty her pretty hands into the open gunny sack lying between them. Even the earth smelled sweeter with her nearby.

"Find small ones, Dale, enough for dinner." They placed the tenderest potatoes in her lap to be later gathered in her apron and carried to the kitchen.

"Do you miss Nebraska?" he asked.

"NO. Whatever made you ask?"

"'Cause you came out here."

"When I need to think things through, being close to the soil helps."

"Sounds like you're worried about something. Hope it's not me again."

"Yes. The plain fact is, your father and I are both worried. You're not giving your best to your school work. You need to buckle down and . . . Wait, let me say my mind, then you can speak." With a long sigh, she continued. "Dale, I understand you because of the ways we're alike. You're not cut out to be a farmer and I hated that life. Even so, I'd rather see you push a plow than waste your learning years, playing with wireless."

"Oh, Mama, why can't you see? If we're really alike, you'd know. Remember last summer up on the farm when we were out climbing hills, chasing cows. You saw treeless, bleak land. But to me it was the future — good high ground for radio towers. Today it's Morse code, but somebody just figured out how to transmit the human voice. That's what's ahead — singing and music of all kinds coming through the earphones, Mama. You should be excited."

"About pipe dreams? That's where we differ. And it worries us to have your mind wander like this. I think Guy's restlessness is leading you astray and that's a mistake. College is the door to your future."

Dale realized trying to convince her was futile. Watching her out of the corner of his eye, he thought, *Well, at least she cared enough to come down. No wonder she worries about grades. She was a school teacher herself, almost.* "Guy told me how you and Papa got together. Said Papa was in bad trouble. His first wife had just died and he got left with Guy who kept looking around for 'Mama.' He said you didn't come down here to get married. You moved in to keep house and teach school. He thinks you must have worked very hard to earn your teaching certificate but you gave all that up to be his mother and make a home for Papa — someone you'd just met."

"That's how love is. It changes everything. And that's my point, Dale. You're going to want to marry some day. Best be ready to support your own family."

"I will, Mama. I promise."

"Don't promise me. Be true to yourself."

He wanted to thank her but liked her answer too much to risk changing the meaning to something he might not want to hear. Silently he watched as his mother gathered up the potatoes in her apron.

Looking away, she said quietly, "That's enough. Start on the pole beans, Dale."

One summer, John Philip Sousa's band came to town.

"Everyone will be there. Shine your shoes, Dale."

Dale had been selected by Mr. Chaunci, the Buena Vista College bandmaster, to join several other envied Iowa amateurs to sit in for the playing of "Stars and Stripes Forever." This most rousing Sousa march would close the program. The music called for extra cymbals and snare drummers plus a large piccolo section. Dale practiced on a borrowed instrument, a smaller version of the flute he usually played. The shrunken size made fingering difficult and at age sixteen, his fingers were still growing. But he realized a lot of practice was needed because the snappy solo had to come out fast and loud without a mistake.

The whole family was excited. Ella put on calm airs and her Sunday best, worrying only about the feathers and fake fruit getting arranged and sewed on solid to the broad brim of Lucille's floppy straw hat. Disgusted by the sight of corsets being laced and high top shoes that took an hour to get

Dale practicing the flute before playing with the Sousa Band.

squeezed on and buttoned up, Dale went out into the barn and blew piccolo music to protesting cows whose mooing drowned out the sound of an occasional sour note.

Red, white and blue bunting encircled the bandstand which had been freshly repainted gleaming white for the special occasion. People came to Storm Lake from all over the county, attracted by the famous John Philip Sousa. The crowd was even bigger than the one that turned out for William Jennings Bryan. Of course, all he did was talk. Sousa's program guaranteed attention. All the benches filled up hours before the show was due to start. The Clemons family traditionally sat at a picnic table in the shade, but this time Dale was expected to reserve one near the bandstand. Luckily he remembered because, as the band members arrived, no tables were left and open spaces on the grass were nearly gone.

The waiting people were so crowded together they shut out the lake breeze. Ladies resorted to fanning themselves. Their parasols, nervously turning this way and that, were a hazard to anyone wearing a stiff-brimmed hat.

Dale sat head to head with two other piccolo players. Then there was a gasp followed by polite clapping. *He's here!* The famous bandmaster ascended the stairs like Moses up the mountain. Dale's mouth dropped open in surprise. He'd seen a newspaper picture of Sousa in uniform, but in person his appearance was stunning. He wore a tunic draped with gold braid that shimmered in the sun and contrasted sharply with the black uniforms of the band. By comparison, there was no mistaking the local musicians. Dale's own uniform consisted of knickers, a white shirt and a borrowed cap with "Buena Vista College" stitched across the front.

Finally the baton was raised and musicians snapped to attention. The sound made the hair on Dale's neck tingle. He'd never heard music played so loud. The horns surrounding him played with palpable strength while the percussion instruments boomed their pulse. In no time it seemed came the clarion call of brass and a nudge from the man seated next to him, "Stand. Deep breath. Go!"

Dale was carried along by those around him. Every note came out sharp and clear, as though flowing out of one instrument. He wished the piccolo's part would last forever, like the flag it heralded.

The piece ended in a roar from the crowd. The players stood motionless as if in a trance. People began moving forward, crowding the stairway. Impatient, Dale vaulted over the side railing to the ground below. Wanting to find his family, he stepped up on a stump to look around. Then he heard, "Yoo-hoo." It was his sister, Lucille, calling out as she ran toward him, her long skirts gathered up, the fruit on her hat brim bobbing precariously, "Oh, Dale, I'm so glad I found you. Introduce me to Mr. Sousa."

"Don't need to. Just go shake hands like everyone else."

Dale saw his parents still seated at their table and walked toward them, shaking his head, "What a band! But I'm glad it's over." His mother hugged him, "I'm so pleased, Dale. You definitely have your Uncle Doc's ear for music. I just wish he could have been here." Dale turned to his father who shook his hand and said, "Did yourself proud, Son." Athie flung her arms around his neck, "I'm proud you're my very own brother."

"Thanks, Sis."

"Come sit down so we can eat," said Ella.

"You go ahead. I got work to do."

Dale grabbed an apple and returned to the bandstand. It was his job to fold up the chairs and stow them below the platform. Just as he finished and was closing the storage door, Mr. Sousa left a crowd of admiring women and approached him. "Keep that up and you can join my tour when you get to be eighteen. How would you like to travel the United States?" Speechless, Dale blinked and gulped but no sound came out. The bearded man in the dazzling uniform smiled and tapped his shoulder, "Practice, my boy. That's the ticket."

The invitation replayed itself in his mind as he drew water from a nearby pump. *See the whole country?* He shook his head. *Can't be serious. But if he meant it, I'd have to say, No. No sir, that's not far enough for me.*

Crossing the park on his way home he saw Jenny, surrounded by admirers. She waved and walked toward Dale, her sleeves rolled up, her face freckled and red from the sun. She pushed a wisp of long auburn hair back from her brow where perspiration glistened. He noticed every move, the way her shoulder turned slightly back and forth as she said, "Hello. You were wonderful, Dale."

Flustered, he looked down and dug at the ground with his toe. "Helped seeing you in the front row, Jenny. Are you . . . with someone?"

"Hank thinks so," she giggled, "but don't mind him."

"That's all right." He saw the husky football player approaching. "Jenny, I gotta ask you right now. If I were to go away to sea, would you wait for me?"

"Wait?" she touched his arm. "Are you serious?"

"About going to sea, absolutely." He shuffled backward. "See you in class." Dale broke into a run, congratulating himself. *You did it. Played with Sousa's band and talked to Jenny.* He leaped over a row of bushes, feeling as light as a deer and stopped to look back. *By Gosh, I even cleared the hedge. Face it, Nibs. Guy was right. There's not a thing in this world you can't do if you set your mind to it.*

2

Listening is Not Enough

Something is wrong. Dale lay in the darkness, awakened by the chimes of the grandfather clock downstairs tolling the hour. The sound seemed strangely ominous. The uneasy feeling of something bad about to happen persisted through breakfast. Finishing his meal, Dale asked his father's permission to leave the table, placed his dirty dishes in the wash pan, said good-bye to his sisters and kissed his mother on the cheek. Soon he was cutting across the pasture toward summer school. He liked learning. It was school that he disliked.

Strolling behind three milk cows, he carried several library books slung over his shoulder fastened together with an old leather belt. Crossing the field of deep, sweet-smelling grass, he chewed on the end of a stem, enjoying its sweet, fresh taste. Suddenly he remembered, *I forgot to do my Latin lesson. That's it.* But he decided it was best to attend the class, rather than cut it. He'd have to admit to forgetting the homework, but that way his parents wouldn't find out.

Latin lessons were trivial compared to the news Otto had for him after class.

"Stop worrying, Ott. That Radio Law doesn't apply to you and me. If it did, Mr. Neeley at Western Union would have said so by this time." *Listening is not enou*gh. *It's sending that count*s.

True, a whole year had gone by since Congress passed the 1912 Act to Regulate Radio.

Dale's confidence grew with his argument. "It's just plain impossible," he tried to reassure his friend. "The only ones who have to pass a test and get licensed live near an ocean. The Government doesn't care what goes on in Iowa."

"Think what you want, Dale. My key's already in the trash can. And you better read the notice I just saw. They'll be after your hide starting Monday."

Seeing the words in print was frightening. He read the entire notice on the Post Office wall.

"That's not fair. I did nothing wrong." Angrily he kicked a tin can down the street all the way to the Depot, expecting his mentor Bert Neeley to be sympathetic. They had talked it over once before, back when the law was first considered. At that time, they agreed. Amateur operators were right to oppose any law which violated their freedom of the airwaves! And Bert rejoiced with Dale when their side of the argument was won in Congress. So what if the U.S. Navy didn't like it.

No laws governed radio communication until after the *Titanic* sank in 1912. The dramatic rescue operation made believers appreciate wireless all the more, but that disaster quickly changed minds about the need for regulation.

Dale wasn't surprised to see a disturbed look on the old man's face. Naturally he would resent the government intrusion on freedom of the airwaves. But Mr. Neeley had other thoughts. "Yes, yes," he'd not only seen the notice, he had copies. Handing one to Dale, he checked his name off a list.

"It happened again!"

"What?"

"Idle wireless chatter reached the Great Lakes and interfered with rescue operations, exactly like the Titanic. Some arrogant rag chewers said, 'Go to hell' and refused to relinquish the air."

"I'd never do that."

"Doesn't matter WHO. This time misuse cost lives."

Dale blinked, "Sounds like you're blaming me."

"I'm blaming your attitude. Wireless is no Goddamn plaything. It's time all you smart alecks got taught a lesson. If you tromp on the rights of others, you deserve to lose, damn it!" Neeley pounded his fist so hard on the desk, pennies jumped up and rolled off, scattering on the floor. Dale crawled under the counter and gathered them up. Without a word he handed over the coins, stuffed the notice in his pocket and left. His brother, Guy, would know what to do.

Guy Harvey Clemons at twenty-six was tall and slender like Waldo but had the handsomest face Dale had ever seen. His light brown wavy hair looked golden in the summer sun and even in winter, he looked tan, healthy and intelligent. His deep-set blue eyes showed the goodness of his soul and nearly always sparkled with good humor. They looked right at you and made you know he was sincere.

They hugged in greeting and Dale playfully punched his brother's chin.

"Let me wash up and we'll grab a sandwich at my house."

"Fine, if you got extra." Entering Guy's house, Dale set out plates and glasses while his brother sliced roast beef. "How's Audrey?"

"Feeling lots better. If it's a boy we're going to name him Roger."

"That's my middle name."

Guy grinned. Too embarrassed to say more, Dale took a big bite of roast beef sandwich.

"So, how's summer school?"

"Terrible. But that's not why I came." He told Guy the upsetting news about the new law governing wireless and said, "I know what Papa will say. Won't even let me listen any more but it's sending that counts, Guy. I have to get a license."

"You're right. He'd say, 'Give it up.'"

"I won't."

"Shouldn't have to." Guy walked to the window. "We're wasting time." He looked back at Dale. "Do it now."

"You don't mean . . ."

"Yes, I do mean go to that wireless school in Indiana. This law is bound to create demand. Show me the advertisement again."

Dale pulled out the torn page of a magazine he always carried with him.

ATTENTION ADVENTUROUS YOUNG MEN
(ages 18 and over)
Here is your chance to earn money in a new and growing field while traveling the seven seas.
Mr. George Dodge is waiting to open the door for you.
Dodge's School of Telegraphy proudly announces the addition of a new course in wireless telegraph (radio) communication.
Graduates of our special 8 month course in marine wireless become eligible for employment by the Marconi Wireless Telegraph Company of America and immediate placement on a ship.
INTERESTED?
Write to: Mr. George Dodge, Valparaiso, Indiana

"The next class is in September. There's time if we hurry."

"Quit high school? He'd never let me."

Dale's brother Guy was always supportive. Here he poses with his wife, Audrey.

"Hold your horses and help me think. The folks are going to need some first class convincing. I can say you need to be on your own and take on responsibility. Will you promise to come back and finish high school?"

"Guy, if I'm going, I'm not coming back 'till I've been to sea."

"That's the whole idea, Dale. Take time off. You can finish high school later. This chance may never come again."

"Wow." Visions of *Two Years Before the Mast* loomed before Dale's eyes. He gulped. "Think he'll let me?"

Guy nodded. "Yes. I believe he will. Papa likes to see people reach goals. As for Ella, when Waldo decides to do something she doesn't interfere."

"I don't know, Guy. They both think wireless is nothin' but a toy. My grades are bad, and . . ."

"Listen, Nibs." Guy leaned forward to look Dale straight in the face. "It doesn't matter what they think of it, wireless is your ticket to sea. Travel abroad is what this is all about. You can't get an education like it in any classroom."

"You sound like Uncle Doc."

"Good. That'll help."

"What should I say?"

"As little as possible. Let me argue, you just nod."

"I will, Guy. But I wonder. Why are you going out on a limb for me?"

He looked down. "Want the truth? Being a dentist didn't turn out like I expected. I'm best working with gold. I like to make delicate bridgework but I spend most of my time smelling stinking breath trying to save rotten teeth for people who don't give a hang until they lose them."

"It's you who should quit, Guy. Do something else."

"Can't. It's too late. Go while you can. And keep a journal for us both." His voice broke. Dale noticed and filled the uneasy silence.

"What does Uncle Doc always say? 'Follow the high road.'"

"Forget that pompous crap. I say this. 'To better know yourself, get off the beaten path.'"

"When should we approach Papa?"

"After church next Sunday. We're expected for dinner."

Extra leaves were placed in the dining room table to make room for the expanded Clemons family and a guest, Reverend Turnbull, from the Presbyterian Church. As the Reverend sat with his napkin tucked under his double chin, enjoying a second helping of mashed potatoes and gravy, Dale and Guy glanced at each other, wondering how to handle his unexpected presence. After dinner the men would be moving into the parlor. It would be impolite to deny the kind old Reverend his favorite overstuffed chair where he liked to sit for hours talking politics with their father.

Seated across from each other the brothers resigned themselves, with raised eyebrows, frowns and nods, to the realization that their meeting was off.

As Dale scooped up the last morsel of peach cobbler, he heard his father's voice, "Pity you have to leave so soon, Reverend."

"We'll do up some chicken for later," said Ella, motioning to Audrey who carried the big platter out to the kitchen.

The brothers slowly followed their departing guest who graciously shook hands and accepted a hefty parcel of home cooking, jars of jelly and bread and butter pickles. Then Lucille walked their guest down the broad front steps, chattering at length about that day's sermon which "almost brought tears to my eyes."

As if he'd known all along what his sons wanted, Waldo turned to them, put a hand on each of their shoulders and, with a smile said, "Now we can talk." Arranging their wicker chairs so they could face each other, they settled down on the front porch to enjoy the cool lake breeze.

Waldo held out a handful of licorice drops he'd scooped from a barrel at the store and brought home in his coat pocket. Then, loosening his belt with a sigh, he sat back. Just as Guy was clearing his throat to speak, their father surprised them both.

"I've seen the notice at the Post Office, Dale. I s'pose it was a shock to you."

Using his father's words as an opening, Guy, with fluent grace, set forth his best argument.

Waldo listened carefully, all the while rubbing the knuckles of his right hand against the stubble on his chin, nodding slowly. Then he asked, "When?"

"This month. Then by springtime he'll be at sea earning money. And after two years he will come back and finish high school. Right, Dale?"

"Yes. I promise."

"Leave school? Why can't you wait?"

Dale blinked and bit his lower lip but didn't answer. Waldo continued, "Bad business, quitting before you finish. It can become a habit. You could end up drifting through life."

"Not Dale. He's got a goal!" said Guy.

Waldo interrupted. "I want to hear his reason. Tell me, son, how do you justify dropping out mid-way through high school?"

"I want to round Cape Horn. The Panama Canal will soon be finished. Once it opens, ships won't go the long way around any more."

"Why would <u>you</u> want to?"

Dale sat staring at his father. *Don't you dream of going someplace besides Chicago? Wouldn't you love to explore a jungle island or stand on the Great Divide or look for the North Pole? I want to see the tip end of a continent and hear and feel the "Roaring Forties."* Instead he said, "To know what it's like."

"Well," Waldo slapped his knee, "I've decided to let you find out."

"Oh, thank you, Papa."

Waldo chuckled. "It's the only way I know to get this out of your system." He reached inside his coat pocket and withdrew a pad and pencil. "Let's see what you'll need." He began listing expenses, starting with train fare to Indiana then added in the tuition, a new suit and shoes, extra shirts, socks and underwear.

Dale pointed to the list and said, "Cross off the suit. Mine is fine. But wirelessmen do have to buy a uniform."

"Do they? All right. One uniform. You add the sum." He handed the pad and pencil to Dale.

Waldo agreed to provide everything Dale needed. He'd pay tuition for the eight month course at Dodge's Wireless Telegraph Institute and put up rail fare for the 600 mile journey. "Providing you meet my conditions."

One, Dale must repay every cent of the cost of becoming a wirelessman from his earnings at sea.

"Secondly, you must promise to graduate from high school and continue on to college."

His mind whirling, Dale found it hard to believe. The elusive dream so near to being lost was about to happen years sooner than he dared imagine. Wide-eyed, he nodded. "I can and I will do it all," he said firmly.

The father-son agreement was sealed with handshakes and warm hugs. At that moment, Audrey and Dale's sisters, who were listening from the other side of the open windows, came bursting out onto the porch to join in the celebration. Ella appeared, carrying a pitcher of fresh cool apple cider.

Their arrangement cleared the air and the peaceful effect even went beyond the house on Third Street. Waldo joked about no longer having to face neighbors who complained, "Every time Dale uses that noisemaker our Edison light globes blink." Another neighbor once demanded a dozen eggs claiming, "All that unnatural buzz-buzz racket late at night upsets my settin' hens so bad they won't stay on the nest." And not only the noise. The brilliant flashes of blue lightning visible for miles in the dark countryside were mysterious enough to get a farmer to hitch up his horse and drive a wagon all the way around Storm Lake just to ask, "What in tarnation iz zat?" Waldo could only shrug and sigh, "Darned if I know." But now he could joke about his boy being sent off "to disturb peace somewhere else."

And so it began. On July 30, 1913, Dale R. Clemons at age 17, signed the Registration book and officially enrolled in Dodge's Institute of Telegraphy in Valparaiso, Indiana — the only school of its kind in the western hemisphere.[1]

---

[1] Herschman, Edw. G. to author. "History of the School," Valparaiso, 1980.

3

Radio School

Quiet shaded streets and farm fields surrounded Valparaiso, Indiana, making Dale feel at home. He enjoyed the view, looking out his dormitory window across a rolling sea of green tree tops and sweet-smelling grass. Sometimes he felt a cool breeze that found its way down from Lake Michigan, thirty miles to the north.

The student body was greeted sternly with one rule. "Waste no time. You paid to come here. You came here to learn and learn you shall." George Dodge was not like other teachers. He'd been a telegrapher himself and loved the subjects methodically set before the fumbling newcomers. They were stepping stones to the students' becoming capable licensed radio operators. Like someone anticipating a feast, Dale eagerly looked over the "menu":

Basic Electricity, Batteries, Motor Generators
Basic Wireless Principles
Signal Detectors - Vacuum Tube and Non-vacuum Tube
Spark Transmitters
Arc Transmitters
Alternators for High Radio Frequencies
Antenna Systems
Basic Radiotelephone Techniques.[1]

Even the school's history was interesting. After the Civil War, the senior George Dodge founded a school for telegraph operators to meet the demand of the railroads. By 1874, rail lines were expanding in all directions out of Chicago, and Mr. Dodge's school quickly earned a respected name. Then, with the dawn of the 20th century and Marconi's wireless telegraph invention, the young Mr. Dodge demonstrated his vision by adding a department of Wireless Telegraphy Instruction in 1909. A Wireless building and boarding hall were erected in 1910.[2] That was the magnet that attracted amateur operators like Dale, who was the youngest in a group of 20 students ranging in age from 17 to 27.[3]

Young men like himself came from all over the United States. As they stood to introduce themselves, Dale counted twelve states represented in the fall class of 1913: Pennsylvania, Texas, Louisiana, Kansas, Ohio, Kentucky, Michigan, Illinois, Missouri, South Dakota, Indiana and, of course, Iowa.

There was never time for boredom to set in. After a morning of lecture or laboratory study, the student body moved into a large hall outfitted with separate stalls equipped with telegraph keys. There they donned earphones, ready to receive and practice sending complex messages in Morse code to assigned partners. Dale's partner was Frank Marsteller.

---

[1] Edw. G. Hershman to author, Valparaiso, 1980.

[2] Hershman.

[3] *Class of 1913.* (Valparaiso: Dodge's Institute of Telegraphy, 1913) Enrollment page.

The Morse code practice room at Dodge's Institute of Telegraphy. Photo taken when Dale was a student.

Speed and message accuracy were the goal. The main license requirement was the demonstrated ability to transmit Morse code at the rate of twenty words per minute. Accuracy was the difficult part, they were told. "Learn to think in Morse code." Some fell by the wayside, content to remain amateurs. Frank did fine until the instructor stood by with a stopwatch. Hearing him stumble, Dale would call out "toot-toot," a joking reminder of what some viewed a lesser alternative, working for the railroads. The jog helped Frank pass.

Dale wrote home, "We want each other to succeed." When anyone dropped out, Dale said it wasn't the fault of George Dodge, who was like no other teacher Dale had encountered. Mr. Dodge reduced abstract subject matter to the simplest of terms. He seemed to have an endless supply of examples and patience and was ever willing to explain until a student's blank stare brightened in a show of understanding. But whenever anyone settled back, confident in his ability, Mr. Dodge posed questions that boggled the mind and quickly brought an awareness of the vast arenas yet to conquer.

Try as they might to complete the difficult course, class size diminished over the succeeding weeks like the falling of autumn leaves. Some students, capable of the work, were forced to leave because they couldn't afford to continue. These were poor farm boys who shared Dale's dream of sea adventure. It was their misfortune to be called home to work in the fields during fall harvest. One fellow quit early when he found out that a wirelessman is responsible for diagnosing and making radio repairs while his ship is at sea. Some simply ran out of tuition money. Observing bright students forced to drop out, Dale recognized his own good fortune.

Late one night Dale noticed a light on in Mr. Dodge's office. Needing extra pocket money and train fare to Chicago, he stopped by to ask if his check from home had arrived. He found a tired teacher doing the added work of school owner. Hair tousled, dressed in pajamas, Mr. Dodge sat behind a desk peering through smudged glasses. With an empty milk glass at his elbow, he poured over bills and record books, trying to figure out how to meet expenses and still provide room and board for a young man who couldn't afford another month's tuition (not even at the reduced rate of $12 which Mr. Dodge had arranged).

Removing his glasses, Mr. Dodge seemed glad for the company. The look of concern in his eyes prompted Dale to inquire, "Something wrong?"

"We're about to lose Elmer Hoskins. Same old story. Been called home. His folks can't see beyond this year's crops. If they'd let him be, Elmer might some day earn enough to hire farm help. Trouble is they don't really want him to break away. It's sad when boys give up trying."

He flipped to the back of the ledger. "Look here." His fingers moved down a list of names. "All of these fellows had to drop out. He'll be back. He won't. Sven — your classmate — is back for the third time in two years, trying to get through the course. He'll make it. He took a job. The boy works weekends washing dishes at the hotel. I'm just sitting here figuring out what corners to trim to keep Elmer enrolled another month. Sorry, Dale, what was it you wanted?"

"Oh, nothing," he backed away. "Just saw the light. Thought I'd stop by and say good night."

Autumn leaves were on the ground when the eagerly-awaited advanced work began. One at a time, each member of the class was assigned to sit in the school's big wireless operation room joined to an aerial. Dale preferred to take his turn late at night when the reach of radio was magically extended hundreds of miles by the raising of the ionosphere. Here he learned to listen to different frequencies by adjusting the tuner and "copying" messages. Seldom confused and never discouraged, he could copy code with his eyes closed. He became deft at placing sliders in positions on the receiving dial to mark the frequencies of now-familiar coastal stations, making them easier to find. Almost an insider, he felt complete, grown up and powerful, seated before a real wireless station. Here, too, he learned firsthand the tonal

Dale at his listening station at Dodge's School of Telegraphy. It was a position he would become familiar with in the years to come.

differences from one transmitter to the next and gained skill copying real wireless messages.

Once each hour for five minutes the air waves stilled.[4] All radio transmission ceased as radio operators worldwide joined in listening for distress calls. Nationality didn't matter. International Morse code symbols were understood by every wirelessman. By law, they would lay aside ship's business and tune their receivers to the designated 600 meter wave length (500 kc) reserved for distress calls.

One quiet night, during the silent period, the crackle of static was interrupted. Dale's partner, Frank, was first to hear the hourly silence broken by a heart stopping "··· --- ··· (SOS) ··· --- ··· (SOS)." He lifted one earphone for Dale to listen in. They heard SOS repeated several times followed by a latitude and longitude in the Atlantic Ocean, then the ship's name:

"*SS Volturno* afire caught in gale. She's buckling. Come fast." While Dale and Frank both copied, someone else ran to get Mr. Dodge. During the next few days a drama unfolded at sea as rescue ships from ten nations responded to the call. Six of them changed course and rushed to the aid of the stricken vessel. Unable to concentrate on anything but the *Volturno*, Mr. Dodge rigged a way to patch in earphones so that the whole class listened each night to the life and death struggle taking place far from land. For days it continued. Ship communication with shore was accomplished by an impromptu network of wireless stations on ships. Able to span great distances, they relayed vital information to one another and to and from the sinking ship. Throughout October 8, 9, and 10 the work went on. Finally it ended on October 11. In mid-afternoon, Elmer, the student from Louisiana, heard the outcome announced by a large Marconi coastal station. He rushed into the practice room at 3 PM, notes in hand and called out the news. "It's over. One hundred twenty-

---

[4] This was later changed to the current practice which is to observe the silent period for three minutes at fifteen and forty-five minutes after the hour.

four people died but five hundred twenty-five were rescued. The message says: `A small dog was the last to leave.'"[5]

When the applause and cheering and good-natured laughter quieted, Mr. Dodge walked to the end of the room to face his students. Deeply moved, he seemed speechless. Then, shaking his head, he pointed to them all in a sweeping gesture, slowly asking, "What will you remember? That a dog didn't drown? No. You witnessed the marvel of our age. Should anyone doubt that, remember this, 'Mr. Marconi's invention brought safety to sea travel for the first time in the history of seafaring.'" Notes were taken. But something else had transpired. This rare experience honored the low-paying job of a wirelessman with a dignity and value as great as life itself.

When Christmas came, Dale elected not to go home. He spent the holiday at Mr. Dodge's, celebrating Christmas with a gathering of students and teachers from the University. A package from home arrived with his first long trousers. Suddenly Dale became conscious of growing up.

After that, time flew.

By March, the class of twenty-one had dwindled to ten graduates. But Elmer was among them and so was Frank Marsteller. On the dreaded day of license testing Frank was tense and had trouble. Every time the government inspector came into view, he froze up. Finally the inspector snuck up on him as he pounded out code at the required speed. "You pass," he said to the startled student.

Mr. Dodge arranged employment for those who asked and then invited the departing class to join together one last time for a graduation dinner. Classmates parted with handshakes, sensing a hard-earned bond that time could never erode.

Dale found George Dodge wasn't someone easy to walk away from. He wanted to say, "You've changed my life." He

---

[5] Karl Baarslag, *SOS to the Rescue,* (New York: Oxford University Press, 1935; reprint, *Famous Sea Rescues,* New York: Grosset, Dunlap, circa 1940) pp. 164-171.

groped for something better as he packed his Gladstone bag and felt under the bed for dirty socks or anything else overlooked. But when the moment of parting arrived, Dale found himself still at a loss for words. It didn't matter. George Dodge was sensitive and wise and he put Dale at ease, just as he'd done the day they met, handing him a note as they parted. Clutching the piece of paper, Dale walked away from what had become a second home. Rounding the corner, he hid behind a tree, tore open the envelope, and read, "Whenever you've had enough of shipboard life let me know, Dale. I'd like to have you come back and teach Marine Wireless some day."

Dale boarded a westbound train and plopped into a seat by the window. Mind racing with excitement, he said to his steamed-over reflection, "Hey, you with the nose. You work for Marconi Wireless Telegraph Company of America. You'll be making thirty dollars a month."

Then, leaning back, he thought of home and his brother, Guy. Smiling, Dale recalled entering a dark theater and yelling, "Call for Dr. Guy Clemons," during a silent movie. The interruption was their father's idea, meant to help attract customers to Guy's new dental office. Waldo Clemons, owner of a general store, believed in advertising. He understood people and the buying and selling of goods.

"I don't understand it." Dale had confided in Mr. Dodge. "My father is all for progress yet he can't see any future for wireless."

"Surely, not now." Mr. Dodge answered. "Your father paid your tuition in full and wants you to go to sea."

"He wants me cured," said Dale, "I'm expected to choose a profession like dentistry — something everyone needs."

He remembered the advice Mr. Dodge gave them on graduation day. "Follow your own beacon but don't expect others to see it, let alone understand."

Staring at his reflection, Dale nodded. *It doesn't matter what people think.*

With confidence, Dale stepped off the train in Storm Lake. The teenager who left home wearing corduroy knickers buttoned at the knee and a boy's cap on his head came home dressed in a suit with long trousers and a felt brimmed hat.

The house on Third Street looked surprisingly smaller than Dale remembered. Even Storm Lake seemed pond-sized after a sweeping view of Lake Michigan. But the front steps assured him he belonged there; the worn place fit his shoe soles. To a delicious scent of baking bread, Dale opened the front door and announced, "I'm home."

Family came from every direction. His mother walked from the kitchen smiling, wiping her hands on an apron. Lucille and Athie ran down the front stairs in a thunderous race to see who could hug Dale first. Waldo, holding a newspaper, stepped out of the parlor into the hall, nodded and smiled.

The United States of America

NUMBER 4857

DEPARTMENT OF COMMERCE
BUREAU OF NAVIGATION

LICENSE
TO
RADIO OPERATOR, COMMERCIAL First GRADE

This is to certify that Dale Rodger Clemons
has been examined and passed, pursuant to the Radiotelegraphic Convention, in
(a) adjustment, operation and care of apparatus;
(b) transmitting and sound reading at a speed of not less than 20 words a minute, Continental Morse;
(c) use and care of storage battery or other auxiliary;
(d) knowledge of international regulations and Acts of Congress to regulate radio communication;
and is hereby licensed as required by law a Radio Operator, Commercial 1st grade for two years. The candidate's practical knowledge of adjustment was tested on a Marconi set of apparatus. His knowledge of other systems is shown below.

Excellent

WILLIAM C. REDFIELD, Secretary of Commerce.
E. T. CHAMBERLAIN, Commissioner of Navigation.

Examining Officer: [signature]
Radio Inspector
Oath of Secrecy executed.
Notary Public.
Place Chicago Ill. Date Jan 6 1914

1 First or Second. 2 Twenty or Twelve.

Dale Clemons' license as a wireless operator. Issued January 6, 1914 it gives him an "excellent" rating and certifies he can receive 20 words a minute.

"You all look so good to me. How's Guy and Audrey and the baby?"

The family settled into comfortable chairs. Hours went by as questions were fired back and forth to catch up on missed holidays, fill in details or tell stories omitted from letters. But Dale put off sharing the most important thing, waiting until he was alone with his parents. He produced a scroll tied round with a satin blue ribbon.

"Your Diploma!"

"Better than that, Mama." He unrolled the document, and held it out for Waldo and Ella to see. It was his radio license.

Dale grinned with pride, "I'm a professional."

4

The Dream Come True

A shortage of licensed men in the new profession worked to Dale's advantage. He was assigned to the West Coast Division of the Marconi Company where shipping trade was expected to increase with the opening of the Panama Canal. The manager of the company's marine office in San Francisco maintained a list of ships in need of radio operators. Dale merely had to select his ship from the list of names and destinations written in chalk on a huge blackboard. By talking to other wirelessmen he learned which ships were favored and which to avoid, a decision based both on destination and popularity of the master.

On that first morning, Dale eyed the list hungrily. He wanted a variety of experience but where to start? Finally, he settled on the *SS Santa Clara*, a 223-foot wood-hulled steamship.

This reconstruction of a shipboard radio shack housed in the Smithsonian Museum of American History depicts conditions as Dale found them in his first ships. Photo by Babette Mason.

Soon he stood in his first seagoing radio room (also called a radio shack).[1] Much had changed while Dale was in school. The sphere of radio became heavily populated. Now it was there in front of him, the real thing. Marine radio gear stood within his reach. Shiny black boxes with knobs and dials and fine brass fittings, ear phones with trailing black cords — a boy's wildest dream had come true. Here he was at age eighteen, hired to serve as the far reaching ears and voice of a ship.

Dale would have known where he was just from the smell. A unique mixture of pungent rosin, warm copper wire enlivened

---

[1] The first seagoing radio room was a lean-to (or shack) erected on the deck of a ship and served as Marconi's laboratory when only two other wireless stations existed, both ashore. Gleason L. Archer, *History of Radio to 1926*, New York: The American Historical Society, Inc., 1938.

by a prickly hint of sulphuric acid, greeted the newcomer. And he relished the smell and taste of electricity, the blue flashing spark gap of radio transmission singed the very air he breathed, adding ozone, a pleasing aroma, like the sea itself. He was overwhelmed at first and thankful for the chance to watch and learn the ropes from an experienced wirelessman.

The *Santa Clara* was a good choice. The ship was in the coastwise trade, never far from land, bringing lumber from Seattle to help rebuild San Francisco which was still recovering from the fire and earthquake a few years earlier. It was a two-way effort. On the return voyage to Puget Sound, broken concrete and splintered timbers were carried — rubble to serve as landfill on the Seattle waterfront.

Ashore for the first time in Everett, Washington, Dale became enthralled with the milling operation. After watching the giant trees fall he followed as they were pulled by mule teams to nearby streams and floated downriver to the mill, located conveniently near the harbor. There they were cut into lumber and stacked on the open deck of waiting freighters. Dale was so engrossed he didn't hear the *Santa Clara*'s horn announce departure. Suddenly becoming aware of the time, he ran to the dock but the ship was out of sight. The chagrined newcomer to seafaring life was forced to take the train to Portland. When the ship arrived, he was doubly embarrassed to find no one had missed the ship's junior radio operator.[2]

His next ship was the *SS Norwood*, a similar vessel also in the coastwise trade. On board, his job included relieving the senior operator for meals and at night. This left daylight hours free to learn his trade and talk to the crew. When not studying radio, he enjoyed listening to the sailors swap stories. The ship's officers were glad to pass the time while on watch or during meals. Dale learned how frequently ships met disaster in the

---

[2] The *Santa Clara* was wrecked a few months after Dale got off, at Coos Bay, Oregon on November 2, 1915 with a loss of 21 lives. Cdr. W. A. Mason, Wreck Chart of Calif., Oregon and Wash. Coasts, 1963.

rough coastal waters of the Pacific Northwest. He gained respect for the rugged Oregon Coast, especially the entrances to the Columbia River and Coos Bay where shifting, swirling cross-tides threatened to wreck every vessel and utmost skill was required to avoid disaster. He heard of ship hulls splintered by powerful surf after running aground on a soft and seemingly harmless sandbar.

There were many stories of ship loss. Menacing rock piles jutted out from shore. Lighthouses guided ships, but still accidents occurred. Landmarks could be misread. Dale was told a strange story of a well-seasoned ship master who took a heading from the only beacon in sight and ended up fast aground — fooled by a train headlight sweeping seaward as it rounded a corner. An old story teller scratched his beard and leaned back against the bulkhead to light a pipe, then explained, "A ship gone aground is done for. If the seas are up, breakers rip off hatch covers. She'll either roll over and sink — if the water's deep enough — or just lay there, pushed farther aground by the incoming surf, and get pounded to pieces."

He pointed the pipe stem for emphasis, "The sea always wins. Only question is how soon."

Sad evidence of ship loss lingered along the coast. Off Oregon and Washington, rusting iron ribs of old wrecks could be seen in several places jutting from exposed sandbars.

Dale confided in a letter to Guy, "The joke's on me for picking coastal runs as the safest place to be."[3]

Experience, the leveling effect of time, put the horror stories into perspective, and shipboard radio work took on a comfortable routine.

Not all newcomers were as fortunate as Dale. Many were decked by seasickness. Still it took time for him to acquire "sea legs" — the ability to walk on a heaving deck without tumbling around like a sack of potatoes. In fact, steady footing came sooner than mastery of the wirelessman's work. The job of ship's radio operator was difficult, requiring him to hear faint wireless

---

3 Dale Clemons to Guy Clemons, Aug. 21, 1914.

signals above the noise of the ship's engines and other distractions.

Distress calls were a rarity. Even so, most of Dale's on-duty time went quickly. He was learning. Handling a backlog of shipping business messages and passenger communications, he developed a "fast fist."[4]

"Please repeat," the message common among students, took on new meaning aboard ship. Ship noise and static and other stations could disrupt message transmission. Dale learned to sort out sound and, like a hunting dog pointing, focus on one wireless signal. In addition to a "fast fist," he learned to "copy behind" (hold incoming words in mind while writing others on the pad). Best were those rare moments when he worked another brass-pounder blessed with speed equal to his own.[5] Then the sparks of blue lightning literally flew.

Because the signal distance of a small shipboard radio station was limited to several hundred miles, wirelessmen worked together receiving and relaying — moving messages from one location to another. Finally a day came when Dale lost sight of himself as a beginner and sensed being part of a mighty brotherhood — a wireless connection of ships generating power enough, together, to span the width of a vast ocean. The words being transmitted might be as mundane as a 'bon voyage" greeting or the captain's request for berthing instructions or as important as a call for rescue at sea. Dale's dream was becoming true.

After four months, he advanced from small lumber-carrying freighters to the newest and fastest passenger liner in service on the West Coast. Flagship of the Pacific Coast Steamship Company, the 8,000-ton 400-foot *SS Congress* had five decks

---

[4] "Fist" refers to the way a wirelessman handles the key. Radio operators often recognize their compatriots simply by the speed and timing of the dits and dahs in their transmissions. Like a written signature, his "fist" gives the operator a unique identity.

[6] Early telegraph keys aboard ship were made of brass due to that alloy's ability to conduct electricity. Because of this wirelessmen were called "brass-pounders."

The SS Congress *was Dale's first experience on a ship carrying more than a few passengers. She was operated by the Pacific Coast Company.*

and a hull of steel. Her power plant was the latest design — a 7,800 horsepower triple-expansion oil-fired engine that turned two propellers.[6]

Now, to the familiar list of coastal stops such as Vancouver, Eureka and Portland, were added interesting ports of call to the south of San Francisco: Monterey, San Luis Obispo, San Pedro, San Diego, others in Mexico and beyond. The beauty of the Pacific increased as the *Congress* moved south toward the Equator. Stops to off-load and receive cargo were chances to explore foreign countries such as Guatemala, Honduras, Nicaragua and Costa Rica where lumber and cotton were delivered in exchange for coffee, chicle, sugar cane, cacao, gold, silver, lead, tin, rubber, bananas, mahogany, rosewood, cedar, balsa and other commodities.

Going to sea was an education. He began to appreciate how fortunate the United States was to be almost totally self-sustaining in food production, importing only coffee, sugar and tea. It was shocking to see grinding poverty in Central America. Walking through impoverished villages put his own good fortune in perspective.

Working on the luxurious *SS Congress*, Dale also acquired social polish. Assigned to dine at the captain's table, he

---

[6] Olesen, William, curator emeritus, Los Angeles Maritime Museum.

The officers of the SS Congress assembled for a group photograph. Dale Clemons is second from the right.

soon outgrew his shy country-boy awkwardness and learned to enjoy conversing with well-educated, intelligent men and women.

Dramatic rescue calls from other ships were infrequent but radio aided ship navigation, gathered weather reports, conducted ship's business and served passengers. The ship's noon position at sea was announced daily for publication ashore, and in turn, passengers were provided with news from land. Part of the wireless operator's job was to prepare a daily newspaper and reproduce copies using an Edison Rotary Mimeograph. News dispatches were collected by the Marconi Company press service from major capitals of the world and transmitted by powerful shore stations built to serve merchant ships. The shipboard newspaper even included baseball scores and closing stock market quotations.[7]

---

[7] *The Yearbook of Wireless Telegraphy — 1914.* London: Marconi Press, Ltd., 1915.

The call of adventure was still strong when Dale decided to leave the *Congress* for a smaller ship, one more likely to slip through the narrow channel now opened through the mudslides which had closed the Panama Canal. As the *Congress* entered San Francisco Bay on Dale's last voyage aboard, he told his watch partner, Ned Gage, of his plans. "I was eighteen when I started, charged up with a sense of progress and the prospect of involvement."

"Still feel that way?" asked the junior operator.

"Yes. Don't you?"

Ned shrugged. "I did, at first."

They felt the powerful engines of the liner vibrate and heard the water surging at her stern. Dale signed off the radio log for the voyage, then removed his license from the rack on the bulkhead. He noticed Ned doing the same thing.

"Changing ships?"

"It's over for me."

"Don't leave, Ned. Give the job a chance. Coastal runs are just a warm-up for the real stuff."

"Dale, I'm a fisherman. Next time you're in port look me up. I'll be on the *Rachel Gage*, fishing for salmon."

Dale packed his bags, thinking about Ned. But he understood, remembering what it was like for a newcomer.

The work is not what you expect. You're treated like a dumbbell. You feel lost and out of place.

A marine wirelessman was made to feel like an intruder. He was not a seaman and had no knowledge of shipboard life. The crew couldn't fathom the usefulness of radio. Before wireless, able-bodied seamen handled all signal work using flags and lights, sometimes firing cannon in darkness or fog to announce their ship's presence. The wirelessman appeared lazy. His hands never got black with coat dust and tar. They resented his comfort, working and sleeping hidden away in a warm dry cabin while they did the hard work of running the ship, exposed to the worst weather. They were jealous of this high-minded landlubber who dressed and acted like a ship's officer. And they complained.

"He talks to the Old Man. He signs the crew list like us, but goes ashore like a passenger." It was true. Each time the ship reached port, the radio operator was free to go ashore and stay away while someone else tended to re-coaling and loading cargo and passengers. Most seamen didn't understand radio, let alone realize it was illegal to broadcast from a ship station while in port.[8]

"He don't belong here. Don't even know sea talk," Dale overheard on his first ship.

The senior operator warned him, "If you value the shape of your nose, give the crew a wide berth."

Dale was even more surprised to discover some ship masters resented radio. They cursed the new law which required radio be installed just because fifty or more human beings happened to be aboard a ship.[9] They resented the owners being able to stay in contact while the ship was at sea, peering over their shoulders from thousands of miles away. To such masters radio was an intrusion on their cherished traditions.

They don't realize there's nothing easy about our job, Dale learned. Plenty of practice was needed for a wirelessman to learn how to work the radio transmitter on a rolling, lurching ship. Steam engines pounded, bulkheads throbbed and rattled. He had to learn to ignore constant noise while trying to copy and send Morse code messages with speed and accuracy.

Late one night during September of 1914 while still aboard the *Congress* and copying press dispatches, Dale received startling news: "·-- ·- ·-·" WAR! World War I had exploded in Europe. The effect was immediate. Shipping business increased and with it the demand for wireless operators. Dale ignored those who weren't willing to accept wirelessmen and plotted the continuation of his two-year adventure and the fulfillment of his promise to his father.

---

[8] David W. Bone, *Merchantman at Arms*, (London: Chatto & Windus, 1919) pp. 120-124.

[9] H. W. Hancock, *Wireless at Sea, the First Fifty Years,* (London: The Marconi International Marine Communications Company, Ltd. 1950) p. 76.

Off the *Congress* and ashore in San Francisco, Dale climbed Telegraph Hill for a panoramic view of the storied seaport. Under cloudless skies the Bay looked as blue as a shimmering sapphire and unexpectedly calm. The brassy blare of ships' horns echoed across the harbor. Tugboats whistled to announce their presence among the grand gathering of merchant ships. Here and there square-rigged windjammers and graceful schooners with clipper bows loomed out of *Two Years Before the Mast.* But shipping was changing. Most of the seagoing vessels were modern steam-powered ships with black smoke billowing from their tall stacks as they steamed to and from the Embarcadero, carrying passengers and cargo. Ferry boats crossed the Bay. Dale wished for a telescope as he peered through a rolled up magazine, trying to see which ships had radio equipment, evident by the shiny antenna wires stretched taut between their masts.

Searching for new experience — and a look at the Panama Canal — Dale chose the oldest ship on the list, the *Pennsylvania.* An iron-hulled vessel powered by sails and steam, she promised a taste of the good old days when sea travel went hand-in-hand with hardship. He wrote home with pride, "The 'Pennsy,' my ship, had a hand in making history." Her maiden voyage was from Philadelphia to Liverpool in 1873. Powered by the first compound steam engines to be built in the United States, she, with her sisters, *Indiana* and *Illinois,* formed the American Line. Retired from Atlantic service, the *Pennsylvania* was brought by the Pacific Mail Steamship Company for use in their coastal runs from San Francisco, with freight and mail, south to Panama.[10]

Aboard the *Pennsylvania* he encountered an odd but fascinating mix of steam and sail power. She was built during a time of transition when boilers were not yet trustworthy enough to dispense with sails. The boy who loved sea lore savored the aroma of hemp and oakum caulking so often read about. And he memorized the sight of canvas filling with westerly wind and

---

[10] E.L. Cornwell, ed., *The Illustrated History of Ships*, (New York: Crescent Books, 1979) p. 281.

found hypnotic pleasure in being lulled asleep by the creak of spars and rigging.

At long last Dale arrived at the Canal Zone only to learn that events had once again conspired against him. The *Pennsylvania* was scheduled to return to San Francisco. Disappointed, Dale hiked inland where he saw the mud slides and watched the dredging operations and promised himself, *some day.*

The *Pennsylvania* proved to be much too slow to suit Dale. She couldn't get out of harm's way. Returning from the voyage to Central America in 1915, Dale was checking over a list of vessels, looking for a new berth, when trouble struck. First a burst of heavy wind rocked the ship. This was followed with high seas, then a twenty-foot rogue wave overwhelmed the vessel. The radio cabin roof was smashed. Part of a mast came crashing down, narrowly missing the chair where he sat. Dazed, he found himself soaking wet and enmeshed in debris that included one end of the radio antenna wires. With the wires down there was no communication with the outside world. He had to raise the antenna, and quickly, to signal an SOS if necessary. He needed help. His partner, felled by seasickness, stayed in his bunk while Dale struggled alone. It was as if he was in a bad dream, trapped and trying to free himself, hands numb from the cold, trembling with fear. Was the ship sinking? Finally he managed to climb over broken wood and tangled wires to search for help. He found some deckhands huddled under cover. None of them was willing to venture on deck in the storm, let alone climb the mast to restore the antenna.

Help came in the form of a young Mexican pantryman who volunteered to scramble aloft. He insisted, in broken English, that he knew how from climbing palm trees to gather coconuts. Sure enough, up the slippery surface he went, barefooted, clinging to the swaying mast. Fortunately the antenna rig wasn't destroyed and could be raised. While Dale heaved on the halyard, the boy grabbed the rising support arm and managed to secure the downed antenna end to the mast well enough for it to stay in place. Then together they went to work in the radio

This photo of Dale Clemons in dress white uniform was taken during his Pacific years while on board the SS Pennsylvania.

room. While the boy cleared away debris Dale checked his equipment. He signalled "-·-· --·-" (CQ), a general call, and waited. A crisp acknowledgment came through like music from heaven. The wirelessman signalled "- - -" (TTT), the preamble to a safety warning, then reported the latitude and longitude of the storm.

As suddenly as it began, the storm lifted. Winds died, the sea calmed and the sky began to clear. At nightfall, Dale continued working in an almost roofless radio room under a canopy of night sky bright with stars, with only a few scratches to show for his close brush with death.

Still awake with exhilaration after his watch, he wrote an account of the accident to his brother, Guy. "Don't tell the folks about it. Just say I've only had coastal runs thus far. Been waiting till I feel proficient. I'm ready now."

His next ship was the *SS Colusa*, a sturdy passenger-carrying freighter that was broad in the beam and shaped like a bulldog. Everything about her was definitely British. Built in 1913 in Glasgow, Scotland, this new 408-foot, 5,700-ton freighter[11] had a British commander whose orders were spoken in a polite low tone. The crew's response was swift. After the harrowing

[11] Olesen.

experience on the *Pennsylvania* it seemed especially gratifying to hear the radio cabin respectfully referred to as "the Marconi Room." But to Dale, the ship's route was the attraction. The *SS Colusa* was bound from San Francisco for Australia to pick up a cargo of nitrates destined for New York City. This assured Dale passage through the Panama Canal and/or a possible rounding of Cape Horn.

The long awaited deep water passage turned into a nightmare. The assistant operator couldn't tolerate the work and got drunk to escape. This left Dale, the Senior Operator, to man the radio in mid-Pacific without benefit of relief. Static increased to an unbearable level near the Equator. He had to listen for the faint bleep of wireless amidst a barrage of screeching rock-crusher grinding static battering his ears. In fear of missing part of a message, Dale breathed shallowly and avoided swallowing while copying.

Finally arriving in Australia, Dale wrote to his mentor, George Dodge, from Sydney on July 24, 1915.

> The wharf was half a block from the main street where we first docked at Port Pirie, South Australia. The whole population was out to see the Yankee ship.
>
> Getting good experience. Have some ideas on how to improve your course. Suggest more emphasis on repairs and improvising.
>
> The other operator I replaced had been using the radio full power for six months. He burned out the transformer. Had to rebuild it myself. Have built one tuner and a complete receiver since I've been out here. Made everything except the variable condenser. Bought that from Marconi Co. Even before we moved out of range, the manager of the Polsen station at Los Angeles asked to BUY my tuner. He thought I'd sell. Polsen is our competition. They're trying to get this steamer. I heard that the owner was thinking about taking off the Marconi equipment and installing Poulsen. That got me going. I overhauled everything, aiming for greater distance. I'm working a 3 kw 240 cy syn set with a 103 tuner.[12]

---

[12] Dale Clemons to George Dodge, July 24, 1915.

The SS Colusa *was Dale's favorite ship and the one that would fulfill two of his life's dreams — traversing the Panama Canal and going "'round the Horn." Photo courtesy of the Los Angeles Maritime Museum.*

Bound for Boston, the *Colusa* left New Zealand on a northeast heading with a twenty-eight day passage to Panama expected. The canal routing would reduce the traditional crossing from Pacific to Atlantic by 12,000 miles. That sounded good to Dale. He wanted as little to do with the Equator as possible.

But he had to cross it once more. In a letter to his brother, Guy, he explained the difficulties of long-distance wireless work:

> . . . we have a thick woolen blanket which we twist about our head. When we are working long distance as we must do, the signals are sometimes so faint that the rustle of water many feet below our cabin makes them unreadable, this even with the doors closed. So we get huge blankets and twist them around our brain box. It would look strange to see us getting faint press, sitting there with the blanket over phones and head, our jaw hanging limp, every

> door and window wedged trying to get these messages through. Add to this that the mouth begins to water but you dare not close it for the roar of the muscles performing their duties would perhaps drown out the signals.[13]

There were diversions along the way. In the same letter Dale wrote of an island they passed:

> I must refer to the one island we passed. This is Pitcairn Island and I took two shots at it with my camera but it was hazy weather. This island has a history. Many years ago, about 1790 there was a mutiny aboard *HMS Bounty* there at the time. The boatswain and chief officer scuttled the ship, that is after having disposed of the rest of the crew and stealing twenty Samoan wives each; and made their home there. They live there yet, these offspring, and are said to be very religious. The women wear mother hubbard dresses only, the men are togged in trousers. They don't care to have visitors and have a regular little nation of their own. The population is 85 men and 110 women in 1910. They have the old ship's bell yet and they surely can ring it too. They are nearly all named Adams after the Boatswain of long ago. The island is under the English flag.[14]

Delayed by storms, the ship arrived in Panama after thirty-five days. Prolonged exposure to heavy static had taken a toll. Dale arrived at the Canal Zone exhausted, unstable on his feet and barely able to hear past the ringing in his ears. But physical discomfort was soon forgotten.

Dale posted himself at the rail to watch the *Colusa* pass from the Pacific to the Atlantic. The vessel entered the first of three sets of locks to be gradually lifted above sea level by the power of water filling a narrow cement chamber 1,000 feet long. Bounded at each end by massive steel gates, the locks raised the ship gradually to a height of eighty-five feet above sea level. After transiting the interior of Panama the ship was lowered gently back to sea level twelve hours after it entered the first lock.

---

[13] Dale Clemons to Guy Clemons, October 13, 1915.

[14] The book *Mutiny on the Bounty,* by Nordhoff and Hall, was written in 1932.

The power of the still new marvel, electricity, was impressive. The ship was towed by "electric mules."[15] The massive gates were opened and closed by electric motors which assured gate closure so snug that not a drop of water leaked. The chamber filled with water drawn from man-made lakes where the power of falling water was harnessed to generate electricity enough to run the entire system. No horses were needed, no coal or oil was burned. Water and electricity were harnessed in a powerful tandem. An operator stood in a tower controlling passage of the largest ships in the world by pushing electric powered buttons.

Hardly noticing the Atlantic Ocean coming into view, Dale stood looking back over his shoulder, awed by the engineering marvel of the age. Its simplicity was stunning. As he turned away, he suddenly realized he had found his life's calling. He would become an electrical engineer. He would finish high school and begin college with a purpose. He had a reason to complete his education.

Impatience set in. *Forget high school. I'm going direct to Buena Vista College!* He embarked on a letter writing campaign to get himself accepted. A stormy eight day trek from Panama to Baltimore helped strengthen Dale's resolve to leave the sea. He lost interest in the dream of rounding Cape Horn.

But that choice was not his to make. Nature took Dale in tow. Barely two days after the *Colusa* cleared the man-made "ditch," mud slides closed the Panama Canal for the next seven months.[16] Dale had signed on for the full voyage. Although the ship was going to Baltimore, New York and Boston, he was required to return with it to the port at which he signed on, San Francisco. And the voyage of 38,000 miles which began in June 1915, didn't end until late December.

---

[15] Many of those hired to build the canal came from the mining industry where mules were used for hard larbor. The term carried over to the electric locomotives used to pull ships through the locks.

[16] David McCullough, *The Path Between the Seas,* (New York: Simon & Schuster, 1977) p. 613.

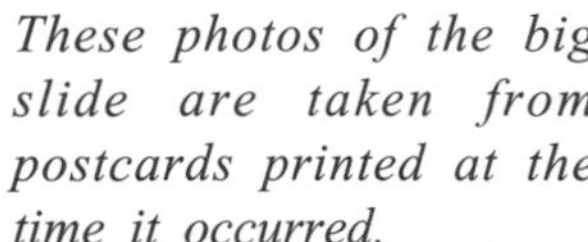

These photos of the big slide are taken from postcards printed at the time it occurred.

The return around South America was tedious. Dale filled in his spare time by studying basic engineering courses.

To combat loneliness, he bought a parrot:

> Bought a fine Panama parrot in Brazil. All his feathers were out and looked so homely that the fellows all laughed at me and took pretty red and yellow ones. But I had studied birds a little and while the others screamed, died etc, mine speaks a few words, feathered out and when I play the flute he raises his voice in song. He is now beautiful and tame. Sits on my shoulder and plays with my ear while I shave or dress. Always wakes me in the morning by whistling very softly then laughs hearty and loud just like a human. Often we would be talking in the room and perhaps laugh then Polly joined and laughed too, making it very comical. Expect to bring

him home if he lives and I think he will. He is certainly a beauty. Never screams.[17]

Off Cape Horn, as the powerful ship struggled for headway he jotted bored notes:

Thanksgiving Day 1915: Cape Horn

Lonesome down here. Freezing cold. Ship rolling hard. Been looking at the same rock pile for three days. Nothing to do. No radio traffic.[18]

To overcome boredom, he transmitted the entire turkey-and-fixings Thanksgiving menu out in a general call to anyone who would listen. He got an answer. It came as a string of cuss words from another brass-pounder whose ship was also stalled in the Roaring Forties. Low on rations he'd just dined on hardtack and beans.

The leg up the West Coast of South America was equally uninteresting. He missed peaceful Iowa. Where being at sea once held a fascination and charm for him, now the job was too confining, something to be got through. Finally the day came when California, and the end of the voyage, were near.

From Dale Clemon's personal diary.

December 22, 1915. We were a hundred miles off the coast of California, when the steward called me out on deck. "Come see this," says he. So I scanned the horizon, then the sky and saw nothing but the blue Pacific with some whitecaps and a smear of clouds. "What?" I asked. He said, "Land. Can't you smell it?" Before long I could smell clover, that and the perfume of greenery came out to greet us weary wanderers. Now I'm shutting down and going ashore. I could eat grass but I thirst for milk.[19]

---

17 Dale Clemons to Mr. & Mrs. Waldo Clemons, December 22, 1915.

18 Dale Clemons, diary, November, 1915.

19 Clemons, diary.

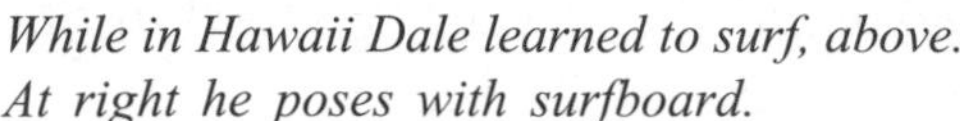

While in Hawaii Dale learned to surf, above. At right he poses with surfboard.

Dale walked away from the Marine Office in San Francisco with a fat pay check and enough mail to last all afternoon. Lying on a grassy slope in Golden Gate park, he looked up at trees as though seeing them for the first time. Branches moved lazily in the gentle breeze overhead. Dale finished drinking his second bottle of cold fresh milk, having read every letter twice. His sister Lucille had married and moved to St. Louis. And as promised, Jenny was waiting for him.

During the voyage, as a special gift of appreciation for his father, Dale bought him a Panama hat. As promised, he had managed to repay the cost of radio school from his salary of $1.00 a day.

There was one more voyage, a working vacation to Hawaii. Dale signed aboard the Matson liner *Lurline* as wirelessman. In Honolulu he soaked up sun and was cooled by gentle trade winds. Lying on smooth sand he watched palm fronds shimmer overhead, then went to luaus to watch the graceful hula dancers. On Waikiki beach he learned to surf and dreamed of swimming with Jenny in the warm quiet water of Storm Lake at midnight. All too soon

He played tourist in Waikiki and here captured the essence of a luau on camera.

the week on the island of Oahu ended and Dale returned to San Francisco. There he boarded a train for home.

During his two years at sea Dale Clemons visited every major port on the east and west coast of the Americas and traveled as far as Australia. Making ten voyages, he worked on eight ships, in some cases for as long as nine months and others for as little as five days. The ships were: *Santa Clara, Norwood, Congress, President, Pennsylvania, City of Topeka, Colusa,* and *Lurline.*[20]

[20] Dale Clemons, back of radio license, 1914-1916.

5

COLLISION COURSE

Tanned by the tropical sun, Dale stepped off the train dressed in his summer white officer's uniform. Jenny was waiting. She ran toward him and they came together in a long embrace.

Being away made Dale appreciate the calm of Iowa and its sweet-smelling corn fields. Swimming with Jenny in the cool waters of Storm Lake made being home seem even more of a pleasure. All too soon the joys of summer gave way to the serious business of school.

Shortly before the beginning of the new school year, Dale was called to the dean's office at Buena Vista College. His application had been rejected.

"You lack required credits."

"But I have a letter of acceptance."

The dean frowned, "We acted in haste as a favor to your father. We hadn't seen your record. Dale, you barely passed high school grammar and failed Latin."

"I didn't care about those subjects then. But I do now, Sir. Let me finish high school and double up on college courses. I can pass. Please, Sir, don't hold me back."

"You'd have to really apply yourself. According to your record . . ."

Dale interrupted, "I was just a kid, then. Now I know what I want — to become an engineer. All I need is a chance to prove what I can do."

With obvious reluctance, he was accepted as a "special student" after receiving the dean's stern warning, "Don't make us regret this." With a new sense of purpose, Dale became a fixture in the library.

The school term was well underway when Dale finally awoke to what was obvious to most people in town. Otto, loyal as ever, brought him up with local happenings. When asked, "Where's Jenny been lately?" he muttered a cryptic, "You better learn to drive a car." But Waldo's shiny new Model T Ford was no match for the bright yellow, high-powered racer often parked outside Jenny's house.

Late one afternoon he stood on the library steps waiting for Jenny. He heard her laughter before she came into sight, waving to several boy friends and some new admirers. *Be reasonable,* he told himself. *She can't sit home all the time, waiting.* When she turned, smiling, and ran toward him, the sight of her made him forget everything else. He crossed the steps diagonally in long strides to sweep her into his arms. She kissed his ear and giggled.

"Be careful. You'll squash your sandwich."

Dale peered inside the brown sack she carried. "Smells delicious," he said, sitting on the steps to eat.

Between bites he made a feeble joke. "Latin is all Greek to me." She didn't laugh. So he said, "Wish you were taking classes, too, so we could suffer together."

"School bores me. So does practically everything in this town."

"When I'm an engineer, we can go any place you like and I mean far from Iowa."

"When will that be?"

"Depends on how hard I work."

She frowned.

"I've got an idea, Jenny. Let's really get engaged, announcement and everything. Then you can see your friends and have fun while I'm studying. What do you say?"

"I don't know, Dale. Ask me again tomorrow."

When the library closed at nine, Dale found himself too impatient to wait. Walking to Jenny's house, he crossed the lawn and saw the yellow car parked at the curb. Inside the darkened side-porch where the swing hung suspended from the ceiling he saw the silhouette of two people.

"Jenny, is that you?"

He heard two voices. The man stayed back in the shadows while Jenny came down the front steps looking flustered.

"What are you doing, Jenny?"

The argument began. "You're no fun anymore. You spend too much time with books."

"I have to Jenny. Be patient."

"You didn't say anything about college or spending all your time with books. I waited. But you don't listen, Dale. I'm tired of knitting and canning corn and . . . and . . . always doing what you want." She turned and went back up the stairs.

"Jenny, come back. Please."

Dale sat down on the curb and waited, determined to sit there all night, if necessary, for a chance to have it out with the owner of the yellow car or talk some sense into Jenny.

But eventually her rejection sank in. It hit him hard, too hard to go home. He spent the rest of the night wandering through the streets. Dogs barked as he passed and occasionally someone called from a window, "Are you all right, Dale?"

Toward dawn he found himself telling his story to a red-headed woman he met standing in the door of a second-rate hotel on the edge of town. "How could she do this unless . . . unless, she never really cared about me? I don't know which is worse, her lying or not caring. Which do you think happened?"

Gradually he came to terms with himself and devoted all his time to school work. And the wireless. He erected a ship-sized antenna rig on top of the house. His Amateur Radio Station, official call sign 9VW, was licensed for 750 W transformer input. The antenna was an inverted "L" sixty feet in height and 118 feet in horizontal length. The radio station was authorized for 175 meter wave length.

But, once again, fate changed the course of his life. On February 1, 1917, Germany announced the beginning of unrestricted submarine warfare. Merchant ships, including those of neutral nations, found entering the war zone would be sunk on sight. In the first month, 143 ships were sunk. On March 3, came the news that neutral American merchant ships would be armed. Then, on March 19, three unarmed American vessels were sunk: *SS City of Memphis, SS Illinois*, and *SS Vigilancia.*[1]

On April 6, Dale sat in the back row of English class, hunched down, working a slide rule, his mind on calculus. He only half-listened as Helen Bigelow, his former debating partner, stood on the platform gesturing stiffly while reading an essay on women's suffrage. He agreed, and thought about what he might say in response. *Women should be allowed to vote in elections — that is everyone but my dizzy sister Lucille. She'd vote for the most handsome candidate and stands convinced that sweet smellin' hair slickem axle grease is a sure sign of polish.* He laughed out loud at his own joke. Helen stopped, index finger poised in the air. Everyone turned around and Dale slipped the slide rule into his pocket and slumped lower in his seat.

---

[1] Francis March, *History of the World War,* (Philadelphia: United Publishers of US and Canada, 1919) pp. 731-734.

AMATEUR APPLICANT'S DESCRIPTION OF APPARATUS

DEPARTMENT OF COMMERCE
BUREAU OF NAVIGATION
RADIO SERVICE

I. GENERAL DESCRIPTION OF STATION.

Name of applicant: D. R. Clemons. Age: 20

Place of birth: Alta, Iowa.

Storm Lake, Iowa. Buena Vista.

II. POWER SUPPLY.

III. ANTENNA.

IV. GENERAL INFORMATION.

October 17, 1916.

INSTRUCTIONS TO RADIO INSPECTORS.

SKETCH OF ANTENNA.

Provisional.
LICENSE FOR ....GENERAL........ AMATEUR RADIO STATION

DEPARTMENT OF COMMERCE
BUREAU OF NAVIGATION
RADIO SERVICE

Pursuant to the act to regulate radio communication, approved August 13, 1912, ... D. R. Clemons ...., a citizen of the State of .... Iowa ...., having applied therefor, is hereby granted by the Secretary of Commerce, for a period of ...two... years, on and subject to the restrictions and conditions hereinafter stated and revocable for cause by him, this License to use or operate the apparatus for radio communication (identified in the Schedule hereinafter) for the purpose of transmitting private radiograms or signals, notwithstanding the effect thereof extends beyond the jurisdiction of the State or Territory in which the said station is located: Provided, That no interference other than may result under the restrictions contained in this License shall be caused with the radio communication of stations of the Government of the United States or licensed stations.

2. The use or operation of apparatus for radio communication pursuant to this License shall be subject also to the articles and regulations established by the International Radiotelegraphic Convention, ratified by the Senate of the United States and caused to be made public by the President, and shall be subject also to such regulations as may be established from time to time by authority of subsequent acts and treaties of the United States.

3. The apparatus shall at all times while in use and operation be in charge of a person or persons licensed for that purpose by the Secretary of Commerce, and the operator of the apparatus shall not wilfully or maliciously interfere with any other radio communication.

4. The station shall give absolute priority to signals or radiograms relating to ships in distress; shall cease all sending on hearing a distress signal; and shall refrain from sending until all the signals and radiograms relating thereto are completed.

5. The station shall use the minimum amount of energy necessary to carry out any communication desired, and the transformer input shall not exceed ~~one-half~~ one kilowatt.*

6. The station shall not use a transmitting wave length exceeding 200 meters.

7. The station shall not use a transmitter during the first 15 minutes of each hour, local standard time, whenever the Secretary of Commerce by notice in writing shall require it to observe a division of the time, pursuant to the Twelfth Regulation of the act of August 13, 1912.

8. The President of the United States in time of war or public peril or disaster is authorized by law to close the station and cause the removal therefrom of all radio apparatus, or may authorize the use or control of the station or apparatus by any department of the Government upon just compensation to the owners.

9. The Secretary of Commerce and Collectors of Customs or other officers of the Government authorized by him may at all reasonable times enter upon the station for the purpose of inspecting and may inspect any apparatus for radio communication of such station and the operation and operators of such apparatus.

10. The apparatus shall not be altered or modified in respect of any of the particulars mentioned in the following Schedule except with the approval of a radio inspector, or other duly authorized officer of the Government.

*Strike out "one" if the station be within 5 nautical miles of a naval or military station; otherwise strike out "one-half."

Top to bottom: Front of Dale's application for his amateur station, back of same document showing antenna design, and the approved license.

At that moment the door burst open. There stood Eric Long, the senior most likely to graduate with honors. It was unusual that he would interrupt sophomore elocution. Eric apologized for the intrusion, "But this can't wait," he said excitedly, "We're at war!"

There was a gasp, then stunned silence. The professor asked, "How do you know?"

"The *Des Moines Register*. Happened last night." His voice raised, Eric added, "President Wilson has finally come to his senses."

The students jumped up cheering and clapping, then began throwing papers in the air. The professor tried to restore order, rapping the desk with a wooden pointer, but it was futile. Students brushed by him and began writing slogans on the blackboard, "DOWN WITH THE KAISER!" "GERMANY STINKS!"

The flag was uprooted from its stand and carried around the room with everyone falling in behind, except Dale, who sat quietly sharpening a pencil with his pocket knife. As his classmates began parading out the door, he helped the professor erase the blackboard, then silently gathered his things and left.

At the telegraph office Dale took out the pencil and printed a message, forming bold black letters.

> To: The Marconi Wireless Telegraph Company of America
> New York.
> Message: Request reinstatement STOP and assignment to the
> war zone. STOP
> Dale R. Clemons, Storm Lake, Iowa.

Dale sat in the small outer room in Guy's dental office, thumbing through an old copy of *Harper's Magazine*. Restlessly, he glanced at the pictures, then tossed it aside and rested his head against the wall. The door opened and Guy came out.

"What are you doing out here, so quiet?"

"Got time to clean my teeth?"

"Why? It's only been a month."

"'Cause I'm going. Just sent a wire to New York asking for a ship."

"Oh, my God!" Guy closed the door behind him. "You can't go to war, Dale. You hate guns. You can't even watch a squirrel die."

"I'm not joining the Army."

"The War Zone ain't the Pacific, Dale. I wish you'd talked to me first." He paused, then asked "Have you told Papa?"

"Not yet. Waiting for Marconi to answer."

Guy took the percolator off a gas burner, blew into a cup and filled it. Handing it to Dale he asked, "What made you decide?"

"Apple blossoms, I guess." Dale looked out the window. "Woke up smelling spring in the air. Hard to explain."

"Try."

"I was one of the few who made it to sea. A lot of my classmates at Dodge's were poor farm boys who had to go home for spring planting and such. I have to do this."

"Don't break your promise, Nibs. Papa gambled that you'd finish school. Don't drop out again."

Dale looked up. Guy read the determination in his eyes. "Well, we never know what life will dish up. Talk to Papa. Speak your heart, then see how you feel."

The railroad telegraph office smelled, as always, of stale cigar smoke and burnt coffee. Dale had learned Morse code here in exchange for cleaning batteries and sweeping up the floor. Mr. Neeley died while Dale was away at sea. And the new Station Master looked too young to be wearing the same green eye shade, the same ink-stained apron. Even the old pencil stub stashed behind one ear seemed to belong to Mr. Neeley and no one else.

The telegraph sounder chattered a satisfying sense of urgency. Dale sat down on a bench, waiting for the answer to his wire. Each time the clicking resumed he couldn't help but "read" the message telling of train delay and arrival times. As his mind turned to other things, he leaned back and closed his eyes.

The station master cleared his throat. Dale opened his eyes to see the message in the man's extended hand. He was relieved by its simplicity: "COME AT ONCE."

He thanked the telegrapher and whispered, "Mum's the word about this, all right?"

"Yes, Sir."

At dinner, Dale sat, eating slowly, listening to the grandfather clock ticking.

"You seem quiet tonight, son. Feeling all right?"

"Fine." He glanced at his mother and sister, "Can we talk alone after dinner?"

"Right now," Waldo answered, pushing away from the table and leading the way down the dark hall to the parlor.

"What's on your mind, son?"

"This." Dale unfolded the sweat-dampened telegram. Waldo read it quickly and shook his head, undisturbed, "Tell them to get someone else. You're enrolled in college."

"Papa," Dale cleared his throat, "it's not that simple."

"Horse feathers. You don't work for them anymore."

"But there's a shortage of wireless operators."

"Dale, we've been over this before. You're through with that life."

"Radio is my life."

"If you mean that monstrosity on the roof, it will never earn you a living. You're not going to amount to anything unless you finish college."

Dale bristled, "How can you ignore what's happening?"

"Calm down, son. I know how you feel. You'll get over Jenny."

"This has nothing to do with Jenny."

"No? But you're still pining for her."

Dale looked down, gritting his teeth.

"You're better off without her. She would have made you miserable. Jenny acts selfish. Genuine love is generous."

"This is not about Jenny. Can't you understand?"

"I'm trying." Waldo handed back the telegram.

Dale drew in a deep breath, "American merchant ships need wirelessmen and that's what I am."

"Poppycock." Waldo sighed, then placed both hands on Dale's shoulders and spoke quietly, "Please, son, if you want to save lives, study medicine."

"It's too late for talk."

"And I'd like to know why?"

"Because I volunteered. THIS is the answer."

"Oh." Waldo's arms dropped limply to his sides. "So, all you want from your old man is train fare. That it?"

"No, sir. I want your permission."

"You don't need that. You're of age."

Dale felt like a child who'd been dismissed. "You still think of radio as a waste of time."

"You're wrong, son. I'm just afraid you put too much faith in it."

"I guess we never will agree."

The talk continued. They argued about the war. Dale's sudden change of mind was unsettling. Waldo believed, "That war in Europe is no concern of ours." As for the plight of merchant ships, "Why rush away to help strangers? You're needed right here."

Dale stopped listening. Their differences stifled the feelings of affection, gratitude and respect he held for his father. In the end, they parted uncomfortably, leaving important things unsaid. It was a parting Dale would regret.

A puff of black smoke rose above the flat Iowa horizon. The approaching train was still too far away to be seen or heard.

"Plenty of time," Dale said, smiling to Athie as he slid his travel-worn Gladstone bag onto a bench.

The air was still enough to hear the crunch of coal crystals under their feet. Main Street was almost deserted. The only activity was a horse munching from a feed-bag as it waited, hitched to a buckboard, while a farmer and a clerk from the feed store loaded sacks of flour, rolls of barbed wire and the staples of spring planting.

Hand-in-hand, Dale and Athie walked to the train depot's blackened window, hazed over by an accumulation of soot and smoke from passing locomotives. Just then the telegraph sounder sprang to life.

"Remember that, Athie?"

"How many times was I sent here to drag you home?"

"Too often," he said, hugging her, lifting her feet briefly off the ground. Then they laughed and made faces, talking to each other's reflection in the window.

They heard the train coming.

Athie grabbed her brother's hand. "I'll miss you."

"Goes both ways, kiddo." He reached for his bag. "Not much time." They drew close and hugged. "Take care of Mom and Dad. Don't let'em work too hard. And you write to me, young lady."

"Just come back, Dale."

"I will. I'm too ornery to get hurt. I'll send a New York address first thing." The noise of the approaching train grew louder, drowning out her words.

Dale sat gazing out a window, hardly noticing the train jolt as it began moving forward. Absently clutching a brown sack lunch in his lap, he watched houses and back yards give way to an expanse of freshly plowed fields, wondering if he'd ever return to Storm Lake.

"Why must you go?" His mother's words lingered like a sore seed of doubt. She said, "I hope you're not letting anything send you away."

Dale tried to clear his mind by focusing on the telegraph wires dipping up and down between posts, watching them gather speed.

Within a few hours he found himself walking through the vast cavern of Union Station in Chicago. It echoed with the steady deep-voiced drone of destinations and gate numbers being announced. Mobs of travelers crisscrossed the terrazzo floor and tobacco smoke hung in the air of the lofty lobby where pale blue-grey streaks of light jabbed down through the building's tall windows.

Pausing at a newspaper stand, Dale saw huge black letters announcing "FRENCH TAKE CHEMIN DES DAME."

"Wherever that is."

Everything was unfamiliar. Dale felt at a loss. Was he doing the right thing? If only he could talk to someone. Then he remembered George Dodge. Almost without thinking, he found himself aboard the train for Valparaiso, Indiana.

Then he was in the familiar office, warmly shaking hands and talking with his former teacher who listened and provided the reassurance and the confidence Dale sought.

"Yessiree. You did the right thing. Wirelessmen are as scarce as hen's teeth. And when the war's over, come back here and work for me."

"Thanks, Mr. Dodge," Dale said with a sigh of relief. "Thank you very much."

"Don't thank me, son. It's you doing us all a real favor. But one thing you could do."

"What's that?"

"Stay for dinner. Catch the next train. You've got time. They're having a pot luck supper over at the college."

A smiling woman welcomed them, ladling food on their plates as the aromas of beef stew, strawberry cobbler and fresh bread permeated the air.

"Help yourself to seconds," she said, then beamed, "you're just in time to hear my daughter, Pauline."

That was the whole idea. Free food was sure to attract an audience. Not many people cared to hear music students pound the piano. "They need practice playin' in public." Mr. Dodge explained between swallows of coffee.

Placing the empty dishes into a tub, Dale was about to leave when the server touched his arm and said, "Don't leave yet. Here she is."

Pauline, who, unknown to Dale, would soon become a beacon in his life.

He heard the music before he saw Pauline. Heavenly music seemed to flow out of her graceful hands and soothe his soul. He lost all sense of time as he watched her on the piano bench, alternately striking chords and caressing the keys, lost in the beauty of the harmony she brought forth. He was still sitting, lost in a haze, when he heard Pauline's mother speak and realized they were both standing in front of him. Pauline smiled and he looked into her large dark brown eyes — expressive eyes that radiated warmth. As he rose, they were introduced and he faintly heard her gentle voice in his pounding ears. They shook hands and a bond was formed — or so it seemed to him in that brief instant when neither spoke. Then the spell was broken. An older man moved in, drew her close to his side and whisked her away.

Oddly, the disappointment didn't last. Something had happened. George Dodge, sensing this, slapped him on the back. "Glad you came, Dale."

Then at the train station, he repeated, "My offer is still good. After the war, come back and teach."

GRAND HOTEL
Rooms $1.00 - 1.50 and up
Broadway and Thirty First Street
NEW YORK, NEW YORK

Dear Folks: May 2, 1917

Had a very good trip so far as trips by rail are known. Could see the countryside all along, trees in bloom, everything very green. Arrived here this morning.

The company kept me waiting for three hours. Walking there I'd turned down many offers from ship captains walking the street searching for brass pounders. The Marine Office Manager finally just said, "Go get yourself a room and come back tomorrow." Tonight they called me and gave me a freighter. *Vigo* or *Viga*, didn't catch the name for sure. Don't know her destination or sailing date. I board tomorrow. Would feel easier if I knew what kind of ship she is.

Will write from the other side. Do not be alarmed about no mail. Expect delays, but I don't think there's any danger.

Best love to all

Dale

6

The Assignment

Dale Clemons awoke the next morning wondering about his ship. As he shaved, other questions ran through his mind. *Large or small? Was she fast? Freighter or passenger? What was her destination? What was the captain like? What about her radio?*

The razor slipped. Dale grunted and applied a pinch of toilet paper to the cut. When he finished shaving he held a styptic pencil on the nick until the bleeding stopped. "Sparks" he addressed his reflection in the mirror, "you don't have to accept." That point decided, he proceeded to hone the straight razor in smooth strokes back and forth on a whetstone. "*Vigo*." He pronounced the word aloud. "Strange name. I hope it's American. I won't sign on a foreign ship unless it's British." He packed his travel bag and walked to the window, opening it wide to draw in the sea air.

Street sounds rolled in with the fresh air. Leaning out, he saw the entire street crowded with people walking briskly past. The odd thing was all the horse-drawn wagons in the street were at a standstill, blocked by some unseen obstacle. A line of trolley cars stalled on their tracks clanged at each other. He went out and within minutes was breathing pungent street smells of horse manure tinged with the aromas of fresh coffee and cooking food, accented here and there with the scent of printer's ink drying on morning newspapers. Caught up in the exhilarating mood of New York City, he moved ahead, keeping pace with elbow-brushing, eyes-directed-ahead, never-speaking, going-about-their-business Manhattanites.

Thinking of breakfast, Dale located a small cafe he found when the *Colusa* was in New York. Here on a side street, The Red Hen served a hearty breakfast topped off with a generous slice of apple pie fresh from the oven. As always, he ended the meal with cool milk, savoring the feel on his palate. Then he felt ready, almost eager, to be aboard ship again.

Turning toward the East River, Dale soon found himself easing through a milling crowd of men gathered outside the Marconi Marine Office. Like himself, most were in uniform. A few older men wore business suits. They were ship masters trying to hire wireless operators. When offered a job, Dale shook his head. "Already have a ship."

Entering the crowded waiting room, he overheard something that sparked his interest. Once a week, Germany was allowing one ship bound for England to pass unharmed, provided it was painted with zebra stripes and flew a checkered flag.[1] "She's out there now waiting to sail. Can't miss her, she's painted all over with red and white stripes."

"What's her name?" asked Dale, but got no answer.

Pressing forward, he elbowed his way to the counter where phones jangled continuously. Suddenly impatient, he called out,

---

[1] Hartley Howe, *The Compact History of the United States Navy,* (New York: Hawthorne Books, 1967) p 199.

"I'm next!" The bleary eyed Marine Manager glared, asking hoarsely, "Who are you?"

"Clemons, Dale, transferred from the West Coast."

A search produced a card and a smile.

"Oh yes. Yours is the *SS Vigo*."

"So I've been told. What is she?"

"A freighter. Lying off Staten Island. Take the ferry to Stapleton." That was it.

Boarding the ferryboat, Dale stood at the rail enjoying the sweeping view of New York Harbor. He'd never seen waters so crowded. All the berths were full. Dozens of ships lay at anchor, deeply laden with cargo and ready to go. Tugs crisscrossed the bay, some pulling barges, others nudging steamships through tight places. Ferryboats slid past each other, their whistles blasting notes of friendly recognition. Shrill staccato toots of small boat whistles were drowned out by long deep-throated blasts announcing ship departures. The sustained cacophony echoed from Brooklyn to New Jersey and back. The stirring sights and sounds brought back the same rush of emotion Dale felt when he'd first glimpsed San Francisco. But there were differences. Each merchant ship had a cannon-size gun mounted prominently on her bow.[2]

The ride to Staten Island ended too quickly. Standing on the dock waiting for a water taxi, he saw only one ship anchored in the narrows off Stapleton. She didn't look like a freighter nor any merchant vessel Dale had ever seen. The *SS Vigo* was a steamer with sails rigged fore and aft like a schooner. She looked more like a yacht than a freighter. "Beautiful lines," he said aloud, admiringly. Her masts and funnel raked backward. Combined with a protruding clipper bow and graceful overhanging

[2] On March 12, 1917, President Wilson directed the Secretary of the Navy to furnish guns and naval gunners to American merchant ships. The first gun was set in place two days later. Josephus Daniels, *Our Navy at War,* (New York: George H. Doran Company, 1922) p. 26.

The Vigo *as she appeared under the French flag in 1915. Courtesy The Mariners Museum, Newport News, Virginia.*

counter-stern, the overall impression was one of speed. Still, something was missing. "There's no bowsprit."

Just then the water taxi, an open steam launch, chugged alongside the dock. Dale waited for half a dozen seamen to get off, then stepped down inside the bobbing boat with practiced ease, nodded to the pilot and said, "*SS Vigo* for me." As the boat pulled away, he slid the Gladstone bag under a bench and braced himself, enjoying the pleasurable sensation of cool sea air filling his lungs.

As they neared the *Vigo* more unusual features came into view. While most ships in the harbor had black hulls, the *Vigo*'s was dark grey. She was a three-island vessel with a well deck fore and aft of the midships house. Instead of one gun, she had an additional cannon mounted on the stern. Strangely, there were no bulwarks along her cargo decks. Then Dale saw the ship's radio antenna, a well-designed flat top rig strung taut between the masts looking new and glistening golden bronze in the bright sun. Tracing the lead-in wire with his eye, he located the radio cabin amidships just in front of the funnel. As the launch drew closer he noticed a peculiar feature. The cargo decks were rounded highest in the center then sloped downward toward the ship's

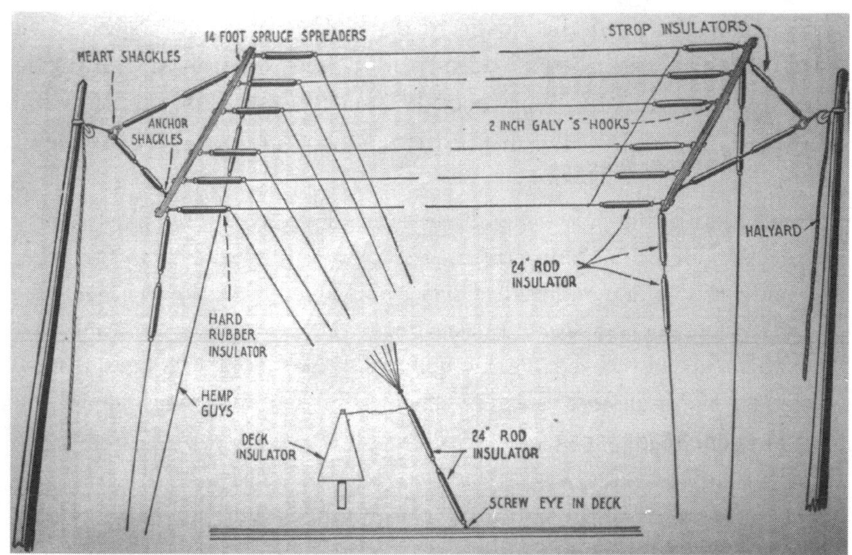

This drawing, taken from Practical Wireless Telegraph *published in 1917 by the Marconi Wireless Telegraph Company of America, depicts the recommended layout for the "Standard Marconi Aerial" that Dale had on the* Vigo.

sides where they joined flush with the hull. Baffled, Dale stepped forward to ask the launch's skipper, "What can you tell me about this ship?"

The old man looked Dale up and down and shifted a chaw of tobacco in his mouth before answering. Shaking his head, he said, "Can't seem to hold a crew."

The launch slowed and sidled toward the forward well where a Jacob's ladder hung down to the water. Several rough looking seamen jumped over the rail into the launch before it came to a stop. Surprised, Dale looked at the boat's skipper, then leaped quickly across the gap and grabbed the Jacob's ladder. Standing there, he got a close look at her hull. Fresh paint concealed iron, pitted with age. He shuddered. After the Pennsy ordeal, Dale had vowed never to go out on an old ship again. He climbed up the ladder and over a rail made of flimsy pipe, noting there was nothing to keep waves from swamping the cargo decks in rough seas.

Standing on the deserted deck, Dale looked again at the radio antenna and noticed with relief a new funnel, an unmistakable sign that the ship was recently overhauled. His attention was drawn to a commotion coming from a passageway directly ahead.

> I saw a roly-poly kid dash out of an alley way and run along the deck, dodging a shower of dishes, crocks, pots and pans that a hurlyburly loud mouthed, heavy swearing chief steward was heaving at him. Then the steward dashed after the culprit, waving a meat cleaver as he chased the kid forward, and from the sounds that issued out of the fore peak, one concluded the kid was being chopped into gory pieces.[3]

"Hey!" Dale shouted, "Someone's getting killed down here." A crew member appeared on the bridge shaking his head. Although he wore a leather cap with no insignia, Dale instinctively knew the man smiling down at him was a ship's officer and a good man. Judging from the scraggly greying beard he would be about forty-five years old and he seemed at home aboard the *Vigo*. "No one's getting killed. That's just Carr lettin' off steam." As the man descended the ladder, Dale saw that his rumpled uniform was the color of coal dust.

"Don't worry," he added with a chuckle. "Our crazy cook only chases Tom. Ain't never caught up with him yet." The *Vigo*'s chief engineer introduced himself as John Reynolds, was pleased to meet the radio operator and volunteered to answer questions about the "steam schooner without a bowsprit."

"Everyone wonders about this ol' girl. French-built, she started out carryin' small cargo. Then got converted to a cable layer, that's when her bow piece went, needed space to install a cable sheave. She's still got circular cargo holds built for cable storage. Can't figure why her decks are rounded, probably easier to haul cable aboard."

"That explains it, no damage to the cable insulation."

---

3 Dale Clemons, "Armed Merchantman," 1940.

"Yeah," he looked Dale in the eyes, nodding. "Glad you're here Mr. Clemons," he extended a soot-blackened hand so tough it felt gloved.

Chief Engineer J. J. Reynolds, posing at one of the guns.

"You'll find Captain Ryan up in the chart room and coffee in there where I'm headed. Welcome aboard." He disappeared.

"Thanks." Dale walked to the ladder on the port side and climbed to the bridge. The *Vigo*'s 300 foot length came into view. *Sure is a beauty,* thought Dale. Pausing on the quarterdeck, he was pleased to see two lifeboats secured in davits only a few steps away from the radio cabin. He faced forward and went up the final ladder to the bridge. The sight of the mast with a gaff and boom — fore and aft sails bent in readiness — and at each side black-tarred shrouds (rope ladders) for climbing aloft stirred deep feelings. Stepping inside a deserted wheelhouse, Dale gave in to the urge to step up on the helmsman's box. Looking down at the binnacle compass card, he took hold of the ship's wheel. Worn wooden spokes fit perfectly in each hand. He looked for the one spoke with a brass cap at the tip. Eyes closed, he could feel that cold metal indicator, put there to show the helmsman the center and help him steer straight.

"Who's there?" A voice cut in from behind the chartroom door. Dale jumped down just as the door swung open.

Capt. Ryan didn't smile. He appeared irritated at the interruption. After looking Dale up and down, he grunted, and motioned for him to sit on a stool with the chart table between them. Dale was surprised to find the master of the old ship a young man in his mid-thirties. And yet his captain's cap looked mashed by decades of wear. The once rigid stiffening had been battered out of it and the gold stitching at the front had lost its sheen. That, and old work clothes, gave Capt. Ryan an unpretentious look the wirelessman liked immediately.

Without speaking, the captain shoved some paper-work aside and opened the Marconi Company folder containing Dale's papers. He turned the pages slowly, sometimes glancing at Dale, a wary eye peering out from under a shaggy brow the color of sand, then closed the folder. "Good record."

Filling a pipe, he lit it and crushed the charred match head between two fingers before dropping it in a can near his foot. Pushing his cap back, he rubbed a reddened imprint on his forehead, exhaled resolutely, then began explaining the pending voyage.

"Our destination is Genoa, Italy. We've been cleared to sail but my crew isn't complete. Our Navy gunners arrive tomorrow." Dale learned that the radio was newly installed. Then the captain added, "I s'pose you know you're the third wirelessman they sent out here?"

"No. What happened to the others?"

"Nothing much. They refused to work alone."

"Alone?" Dale stood up, "No one told me anything about working alone. I'm sorry, Sir, I can't do that."

"Why not?"

Dale looked at the captain, "A person has to sleep."

"But you have worked alone before."

"We weren't at war."

The captain smiled, "Take it easy, you're not alone in that. This trip, we're all greenhorns."

Collecting his papers, Dale stood to leave. The captain leaned back against the bulkhead and asked, "So what will you do? Ask for another ship?"

"Won't have to. I passed up half a dozen offers on the street."

"I'm sure you did. We're all desperate." The captain looked at Dale, "I'm still waitin' for the right man to show up."

Dale hesitated. "When I arrived some of your crew were in a hurry to get off, like they'd seen a ghost."

"Oh, that. One of them found the old figurehead stowed below. Superstitious nonsense. Didn't take much to convince the others. Loss of her figurehead took away the ship's protection from evil spirits."

"It's just a wooden carving."

"You have to understand seamen. They worship God but cling to superstition. Almost no schooling. Few can read but they know seafaring. And they're loyal. Without a ship they'd be sleeping in alleys dead drunk, going hungry, getting thrown in jail. Aboard ship, they work hard. That's all I ask. A man's beliefs are not my business unless they cause trouble. I don't argue. I let 'em go." He looked directly at Dale. "I don't want men who get spooked easily."

Dale flushed and nodded. Capt. Ryan stood up, came around the table and opened the door.

"Go have some coffee. Think it over."

"One thing I need to know now. What's the cargo?"

"See for yourself." Ryan spread out the pile of papers he was working on. "We're hauling everything from calf livers to horseshoe nails. Machinery, sugar, cotton, chemicals, lubricating oil. That's the bulk of it."[4]

"Chemicals? What chemicals?"

"A whole list. Caustic soda, dye stuffs, Benzol mainly."

"Explosives?" Dale backed off.

The captain frowned, "For our guns, Lad. What did you expect?"

"I don't know. Guess I didn't think."

---

4 Cargo Manifest, *SS Vigo*, Voyage #1, Washington, D.C.: National Archives and Record Service Judicial and Fiscal Branch, May 7, 1917.

"At least you're honest enough to say so." He relit his pipe and crushed the match, again showing no sign of pain, then continued. "Here's how I see it. Every hold crammed with cork wouldn't keep us afloat if we get hit. But that is NOT going to happen! I got a plan to get us through — with the help of wireless."

"Wireless? What plan?" Dale slid back onto the stool.

The captain smiled like someone who'd just hooked a fish. "That, I can't talk about unless you sign on. Oh, did I mention you get a war bonus?"

"No, how much?"

"Double wages."

In the end it wasn't wages but curiosity that got the best of him. With the confidence of youth showing in his signature, Dale R. Clemons, the twenty-one-year-old wirelessman, signed his name with a flourish on line number thirty-four of the Ship's Articles and in so doing committed to serving as the only radio operator for one voyage of the *SS Vigo*. Captain Will Ryan verified the date, May 3, 1917 and rubber stamped the words "SIGNED AFTER CLEARANCE."[5] Then the shipmaster escorted Dale to the radio cabin and said, "A Navy officer from the yard will drop by and tell you what you need to know."

"Navy? You're joking."

"No, I'm not. We'll have a talk after you see him. I'm going ashore. Have to replace those men who jumped ship," said the captain calmly as he unlocked the radio cabin. Then he turned and handed Dale the key.

"Treat this like gold."

---

[5] Crew List. National Archives.

7

Radio Silence

Stepping inside the radio cabin, Dale was greeted by the tantalizing smell of fresh varnish and rosin. The radio was brand new. Clearly, it had never been used.

The skylight let in a pale glow that revealed an array of dials and brass fittings on a black, panel-type, two kilowatt transmitter which stood six feet tall. Dale removed his cap, black tunic and white celluloid collar. He undid the top buttons on his shirt and rolled up both sleeves, all the while looking over the controls of a radio far more powerful than he expected to find on a freighter.

Easing into the swivel chair, he opened the equipment manuals and began reviewing the diagrams that showed the circuitry of the apparatus. He could afford no mistakes. There was enough power in the equipment to electrocute himself. He would soon be holding at bay a 110 volt DC-powered, snarling wildcat generator of 380 volts of (500 cycle) alternating current,

The type of Marconi receiver Dale used. Credit Practical Wireless Telegraphy, *Marconi Wireless Telegraph Company of America, 1917.*

tamed inside an insulating tank which transforms the power into electromagnetic waves released at will by the wirelessman. In quick short bursts (dots) or longer spurts (dashes) all this energy would obey his finger tips as he lightly depressed and released the telegraph key to interrupt the flow of current being transmitted up through the antenna, an array of wires 130 feet long strung taut between masts eighty-five feet in the air, sending invisible radio waves outward in all directions, moving at the speed of light. And with the flip of a lever, his antenna wires became a net, plucking messages from thin air where they were funneled through a receiving tuner and heard in the earphones as code for him to decipher into words.[1]

With mouth-watering anticipation Dale closed the book, reached down to his left and started the generator. Its innards began to whir, creating a low sound that quickly rose in pitch. Soon the air was tinged with the scent of hot copper and electricity, a unique smell that he enjoyed. Putting on the headset, he adjusted the earphones. He switched the transmitter control to the 300 meter band and a low power reading. Then he placed a hand on the aerial change-over switch and thrust it down sharply. The brass couplings engaged with a "chink." With his right arm resting comfortably on the table, his first two fingers contacted the telegraph key lightly, then flew into action. "-·-· --·-" (CQ). First he sent the general call which asked anyone listening to

---

[1] Elmer Bucher, *Practical Wireless Telegraphy,* New York: Marconi Wireless Telegraph Co. of America, New York Wireless Press, 1917.

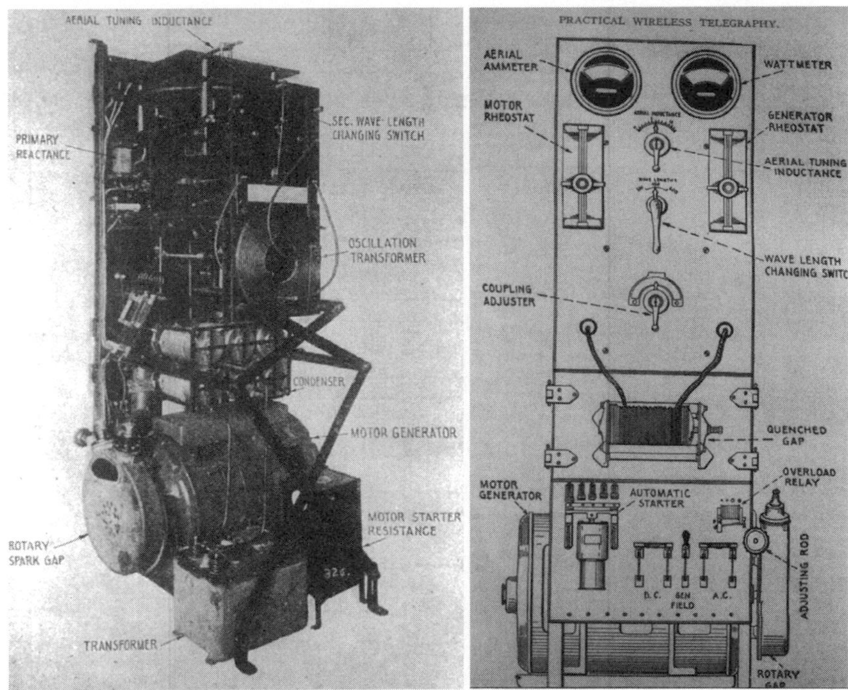

The photo, left, shows the rear view of the type of Marconi transmitter used by Dale aboard the Vigo, *the drawing, right, the front view. Credit* Practical Wireless Telegraphy, *Marconi Wireless Telegraph Company of America, 1917.*

respond. He could hear his spark gap transmitter giving off a sizzling "szz szz" sound with each impulse as it threw out flashes of blue light. His nose hair began tingling with the pungent scent of the ozone by-product.

He preceded his message with the ship's registered call letters KMC[2] then sent "trnsmtest." Dale threw the aerial switch up and awaited a response, adjusting the receiver dial. It came promptly, a clear high-pitched whistling note which could only be produced by a Poulsen arc of the type used by the US Navy. "KMC sgnl strng QRT," then nothing — no signature, no location. *That's no help.* His fingers itched to respond in the tradi-

[2] "Ships Recently Equipped with Marine Wireless," *The Wireless Age,* Feb. 1917.

tional polite parlance, "Need distance check ol' man, where are you?" but QRT meant "stop sending." Puzzled, he was distracted by a commotion in the passageway outside his room.

He opened the door. Someone was standing empty-handed outside the second mate's cabin while the messboy struggled with three pieces of luggage, insisting, "But, this is your cabin, sir, Mister Merrick."

"A broom closet? Let me see that corner cabin."

"You can't go in there. Captain Ryan wants the second mate here, Mr. Merrick."

"We'll see about that. Where is he?"

"Ashore." Dale opened the door wider and answered. "He just left."

"Who are you?"

"Clemons. I work the radio."

"God, not while I'm trying to sleep."

"If I make too much noise, just knock on the wall and let me know it's your bedtime and I'll shut down."

"That won't be necessary. When will the captain be back?"

Tom sniffed and rubbed his nose with the heel of his hand. "Not 'til tomorrow."

"Drat! Take me to the first mate." Away they went.

Dale watched them disappear. *So, that's our navigator. What's he doing here?* Dale speculated, then answered his own question, *Probably just graduated from some sea academy. More likely, flunked out*, he thought disdainfully.

Dale went down to the engine room for a look at the ship's main generator. Somehow electric lighting, refrigerated food storage and an uncommon abundance of fresh drinking water seemed out of place on an old ship. The chief engineer explained that luxuries expected on a modern passenger liner had been added during the freighter's conversion to a cable layer. Electric lighting was needed for cable laying work to continue at night.

"When did that end?"

"Not sure. It was over when Captain Ryan took command in 1915. She'd just been moved from LeHavre to New York. We've been making short runs, here to Halifax, carrying barbed wire, until she got sold. She's only been American-owned for a month. Still not used to the new name *Vigo*."

"What does it mean?"

"I have no idea. Been too busy to wonder."

There was no doubt about her business now. Every square inch of available covered space in the two deck steamer was crammed with cargo in bales, boxes, barrels, crates and sacks.

Climbing to the main deck, they walked along the passageway leading to the galley. The engineer explained, "There's a fancy officer's saloon up on the quarterdeck but we don't use it, except for meetings. Ryan likes things done simple so we eat close to the galley at that table." He added a warning in a low voice, "Stay out of Carr's way. He's blind as a bat."

Tasty beef stew and beans flavored with molasses were heaped on a metal platter and served by Tom, the messboy. The same youngster whose life earlier seemed in danger now stood working quietly beside his attacker. Dale whispered, "That's him, the fellow I saw chasin' the kid."

John chuckled. "Forget it. 'Scraps' will never hurt Tom. Can't get along without him."

On returning to his cabin Dale stopped short. The door to the radio shack was standing wide open. He was greeted by a scowling officer of the US Navy who pointed to the door key and said, "Never leave this room unlocked!"

"Yes sir," Dale answered, wondering if he was expected to salute. The officer sat down at the radio table and opened a briefcase, then began removing books and papers.

Easing himself onto the edge of the bunk, Dale listened as the officer expressed the Navy's gratitude to the many Marconi operators who had volunteered their services. Then he explained the strict control Capt. Ryan hinted at earlier.

"The US Navy has taken over all radio operation.[3] Quite frankly, Mr. Clemons, if we had enough radio operators of our

---

[3] *Annual Reports of the Navy Department for the Fiscal Year 1917*, (Washington, D.C.: GPO, 1918) p. 64.

own you wouldn't be permitted here. But we don't and we need your experience." Then came the disheartening news.

"Radio silence is the cardinal rule. No transmission is permitted unless your ship is in danger of sinking."

The Navy man went on. Radio silence applied even when the wirelessman heard an SOS call. "Your captain is under strict orders to keep moving."

"And let men drown?"

"Navy ships are conducting all rescue operations now. It's no longer your concern."

"Wait a minute. Why do you think I volunteered?"

"Forget what you used to do. The fact is, you're more valuable than ever. Wireless is the only advantage we have."

How could that be? he wondered. His thoughts were still on radio silence.

"What do you know about the radio direction finder?"

"Just what I learned in school. I understand the principle. Know there are several designs, none of 'em accurate."

"That used to be true. What I'm about to say is highly secret and must remain so.

"Engineers of the British Marconi Company have developed a system of pinpointing the position of a ship by receiving its radio signal.[4] As for range, their new direction finder pretty well blankets the war zone. But the Germans don't know about it. Their submarine commanders use wireless, freely communicating with headquarters, thus giving away their exact location. Your job, Mr. Clemons, is to listen. The intelligence information on enemy location is transmitted every night during the regular midnight press broadcast. You'll be told locations of sinkings followed by what we're calling enemy sightings. Mark the locations on a map for your captain."

"Does he know about this?"

---

[4] Paul Schubert, *The Electric Word*, (New York: The McMillan Co., 1928) p. 139.

"He knows to expect reliable radio reports of enemy location."

> The captain and I will maintain a chart here in the wireless cabin, on which we will show by colored pins the positions of enemy craft and sinkings as these are reported. Already there are two pins up off Newfoundland and one in the south Atlantic, the latter for the raider *Seeadler*, even before we are at sea.[5]

He flipped to a page of the manual and handed it to Dale. "Memorize the new SOS procedure. Include what happened — use abbreviations for torpedo, gunfire, mine explosion. Also, identify your attacker such as U-boat or surface raider."

"Who will respond?"

"Good question. Depends where you are. The nearest shore station will acknowledge and dispatch a destroyer, British most likely, could be French or Italian. No matter. We all use English in our messages."

He closed the book. "Now comes the most important change. When in the war zone, you'll receive fresh reports of enemy locations. We have boats, disguised as fishing trawlers, patrolling the region watching for submarines and warning merchant ships of their presence. They use a special code word coined for this exact purpose, "ALLO."[6] You'll then hear a sighting location: a town name, cape or the nearest point of land. Alert your captain so he can alter course."

"What if we sight a submarine?"

"Maintain radio silence!" the officer answered firmly. "The penalty for breaking radio silence is a fine of $25,000 plus a jail sentence and permanent revocation of your operator's license."

Dale gulped. "Sir, I have to test this transmitter on full power."

---

5 Dale Clemons, "Armed Merchantman," 1940.

6 David Bone, *Merchantmen At Arms*, (London: Chatto & Windus, 1919) p. 117.

"Use a dummy antenna. No signals, not even in port. We don't know how good the German direction finder is but we're using ours to shut down amateur stations. We have to, some are in enemy hands."

He handed the book and some papers to Dale for study. "Any questions?"

"How can one man handle this job?"

"Set up a work schedule. Sleep when you can."

As the officer packed his briefcase he lapsed into casual conversation. "Ever wonder what shape we would be in without Marconi? I s'pose you know he barely missed being aboard the *Lusitania* when she was torpedoed."

"No!"

"Scuttlebutt has it the Germans were aiming to kill him. Now he's out there again, headed back to his homeland to join in the fighting."

"We're going to Italy."

"I know." The Navy officer snapped his briefcase shut and stood to leave, hand extended, "Good luck to you, Mr. Clemons."

Outside, the sun was getting low on the horizon. Dusk and dawn were Dale's favorite times for exercise, a good excuse to be on deck. He put on old rubber-soled shoes and began running around the quarter deck for exercise. Then he descended the ladder and walked toward the stern for a look around the ship. There he noticed an auxiliary steering wheel on the poop deck and beyond that a canvas-covered gun. Its platform was oak — eight inches thick braced with steel supports. He stepped up beside the cannon barrel. It jutted out ten feet extending beyond the taffrail. Below was a sturdy cradle built into the hull which still contained the play-out wheel — remnants of the *Vigo's* former cable-laying life. Seeing that connection brought him closer to the old vessel, first christened *Portena*, then renamed *Contre Amiral Caubet*, and now about to start over under the U.S. flag as the *Vigo.*[7] He was beginning to like the sound of it for its brevity.

---

[7] John L. Lochead to B.J. Clemons, The Mariners Museum, Newport News, Virginia, January 5, 1971.

8

THE ARMED GUARD

Five battleships — the *Texas, Arkansas, Wyoming, Nevada* and the flagship *New York* — were contributing men to the gunnery crew of the *Vigo.*[1] Dale Clemons, John Reynolds, chief engineer, and Philip Merrick, second mate, were on the bridge deck sipping their morning coffee when they heard about it.

"Where will they bunk?" asked the chief.

"Says here, 'eight in the fo'c'sle, eight in the stern.' The deckhands have already complained to the chief mate about being too crowded in the fo'c'sle," said the second mate.

"What did Brennan do?" asked Dale.

"Told 'em to shut up."

---

[1] Naval Orders, Memos and Reports, Washington D.C., National Archives Records Service, Navy and Old Army Branch, Military Archives Division, 1917.

"Well they can't bunk aft," said the chief. "Only ones who can sleep with that propeller racket is my coal heavers and oilers from the engine room."

A shrill whistle blast drew their attention. A Navy tugboat pulling a barge slowed to a stop along the *Vigo*'s port side. The barge was piled high with wooden boxes. Several Navy sailors were on board. Barely glancing at the ship, they scrambled aboard like a football team taking to the field, then began transferring boxes.

The tug moved forward bringing the barge alongside the foredeck where more cargo was transferred to an open space near the bow gun.

> Chest after chest of 3 inch rifle ammunition came aboard — some of it solid and the rest shells of the explosive type. Six chests are lashed to the sides of each gun platform. Deck magazines fore and aft are full, and as much again went below decks in the stern. Then there were four cases containing Bennet-Mercere machine guns, each with an extra barrel and a hundred ammunition clips . . . A case of Colt's automatic pistols and four cases of Krag-Jorgensen rifles are also stored in the salon just below me. . . [2]

Dale stepped aside as the Navy chief set the box of automatics down. He was short and stocky with reddish hair and a thick red neck that ballooned out as he barked orders. Calling out last names he gave instructions for the stringing of telephone wires to connect each gun position to the bridge. From time to time, he glanced at Dale, looking more and more agitated. Finally he asked, "Who's in charge here?"

Dale answered, "Mr. Brennan, the first mate."

"Don't stand there, get him up here."

---

[2] Dale Clemons, "Armed Merchantman," 1940.

Unsure of the proper protocol, Dale did as he was told, then returned to the radio cabin to test the transmitter. While taking readings on dials he heard a voice ask, "How's the war going, Sparks?"

Dale looked around. There was no one there.

"I'm up here," said the voice. Bent over the skylight was a smiling sailor with his hat brim turned down. He looked like Dale's brother, Guy. "Can I borrow a screw driver? Lost mine. The damned thing flipped overboard."

"Sure. I have some extras. Be right up." Dale climbed the vertical ladder to the roof of the radio cabin and saw a sailor clad in dungarees sitting tailor fashion, trying to untangle a coil of telephone wire which was somehow wound around one foot. The more he tried to free himself the tighter it got. "Hold still," said Dale chuckling. He handed over the tool and undid the wire, deftly straightening it out. As he watched, the sailor finished seating eyelets then threaded the wire through openings to secure it in place.

"I'm Steve Christian, gunner's mate in charge of the after gun. Chris, for short."

"Dale Clemons."

They shook hands.

"Sorry for the interruption." said Chris.

Dale shook his head. "Glad for the chance to talk to someone."

Their backgrounds were similar. Steve Christian was from Kewanee, Wisconsin, where he grew up with a lake for a playground and a love of ships.

"What do you think of the *Vigo*?"

Chris shrugged. "My only regret is losing the coin toss that gave bow gun to Wyman. We're from rival ships, both gunner's mates."

Dale learned that both Chris and Chief Petty Officer Baxter came from the battleship *New York* where Baxter was turret captain. "That's what I don't get. How come they let you leave?"

"For experience with rapid-firing guns."

Part of the Vigo*'s Armed Guard crew at one of the guns. The one pointing at the camera is Chris.*

Chris finished securing the wires, then stood up and asked Dale, "How's it look?"

"First-rate."

They jumped down to the quarterdeck. Chris promised to return the screwdriver at voyage end, "with notches cut in the handle, one for every U-boat we sink."

Dale laughed and nodded, "That'll make some souvenir. I'll remind you about it."

About to return to the wireless shack, Dale saw a barge piled high with crates approaching the *Vigo*. From the main deck he heard Merrick exclaim, "Can't be more cargo, we're cleared to sail."

Nevertheless, additional crates did arrive. A heated argument ensued. The pilot of the tugboat insisted he had papers showing thirty-eight crates consigned to the *SS Vigo*. Brennan, the chief mate, agreed he was expecting Hudson auto chassis destined for the Italian front, but he insisted, "You're too late. There's no room. Not even on deck."

"Those are my orders. That's where I was told to put them. `Stow on deck.' Signed by Captain Will Ryan," said the tugmaster.

"Damn!" Brennan's face grew red as he walked, swearing, to the mast and gave orders to the deck hands. "All right, let's try to get these crates on the foredeck." The Navy gunnery chief appeared like a hornet guarding its nest, insisting on clear decks for his gunnery crews. Brennan got angrier. "You ain't got no say about cargo," he snarled, then hollered, "Lower away!" to his crew.

As the first crate was lowered onto the forepeak deck, Merrick elbowed in. "There must be some mistake."

"No mistake. We got papers for thirty-eight trucks," said Brennan producing consignment slips. "Thirty-eight. See?"

Merrick's eyes narrowed. "That says thirty-eight chassis. Each crate has two chassis. Chassis aren't trucks. They're just the wheels and the lower part."

Baxter added, "Still too many."

Brennan answered with a scowl, "Sixteen 'crates' it is." He walked across the open deck space. "Eight here," he pointed, using both hands to show placement. "And stow eight on the poop deck."[3]

The tug captain objected. "What about the other crates?"

Brennan answered, "Take 'em back unless you want help from us floating 'em across." And to the waiting deck hands he bellowed, "Stack 'em careful. I want her on an even keel and her head high."

By dusk all was peaceful aboard the *SS Vigo* — temporarily.

Returning to the ship early the next morning, Capt. Ryan noticed that she lay lower in the water than when he went ashore. But his attention was quickly diverted with other problems.

---

[3] Clemons.

During the night, fighting broke out between the armed guard and merchant crews. "Chips," the carpenter, had erected a canvas barrier down the middle of the crew quarters to segregate the Navy sailors from the ship's crew.[4] The trouble started when Baxter conducted inspection and found fault with the wooden bunks and straw-filled mattresses assigned to his crew. He insisted that the Armed Guard sleep Navy-style in hammocks. Since there was ample room, no one complained. Then, when all was quiet, someone sliced through a hammock rope with a knife and the stern quarters exploded.

Baxter promptly moved his men up on deck where hammocks were strung between cargo crates. The Navy gunners were to be quartered on deck, served meals on deck and have their own separate water supply.

Brennan reported the news to Capt. Ryan on his return. A meeting was hastily called in the officers' salon. "If Baxter gets his way, no merchant seaman can set foot across a line he calls Navy territory."

The captain listened quietly but said nothing until Brennan asked, "What should I do?"

"Arrange for food delivery."

"That's a mistake." said John, the chief engineer. "Baxter acts like we're the enemy."

The captain shook his head, "The CPO is just doing his job. Some of those gobs are raw recruits, never been to sea. They have to learn Navy discipline."

"Well, it won't last," said Chips, the oldest man aboard. He smiled a toothless, mischievous smile. "High seas is guaranteed to make cockroaches and bed bugs look plenty friendly."

John persisted. "Smells to me like snobbery. I ask you, what's wrong with us all drawing water from the same spout?"

---

[4] All ships' carpenters are nicknamed "Chips" for the byproduct of their work, just as all wirelessmen or radio operators are nicknamed "Sparks" for the same reason.

"Navy rationing," Ryan answered. "Each sailor is allowed two quarts a day. With our oversized tanks we'll be issuing two buckets per man. That would upset their rationing system." Without waiting for further discussion, Capt. Ryan pushed a wooden chest across the floor to Dale and announced, "Our radioman has just been appointed ship's doctor."

"What? I don't know a thing about medicine."

"Your record shows a doctor and a dentist in the family. That's close enough."

That evening Dale began looking over the collection of bandage materials and numbered bottles containing liquids and pills. A guidebook showed which medicine to dole out and how much for a particular complaint. Some of the pills were huge, "horse pills." Seeing this, he laughed.

> . . . the ship's medicine cabinet [is] complete with numbered vials of pills of all colors, big pills, little pills, saws, bandages, jugs of castor oil, cascara, steel wire and a hammer! As our ship's Hyppocrates, all I have to do is to find if the patient's sawdust aches, where it aches, if his tongue is coated, and if he hears bells ringing. Then I consult the prepared chart in the big book. If it indicates pill number 8 where the lines cross, I dish out pill number 13 if it doesn't cross, unless his knees are shaky, in which two of number 21 are forced on the victim. Then I sit back to observe whether or not the patient lives through the night. If he doesn't, I'm not to repeat the dose![5]

Then discouragement set in. Nothing was turning out as he expected. Now he was medical officer. And the long-awaited talk with Captain Ryan about "the new use of wireless" wasn't a talk at all. The captain gave him a cork board backing for his sea charts and an additional box of colored pins for marking enemy ship locations. His only comment was, "Keep me informed."

---

[5] Clemons.

Dale lay in his bunk trying to sleep, listening to the rhythmic slush of the propellers of passing ships. *What if we get hit? Be lucky to stay afloat fifteen minutes.* He sat up. Pulling on shoes and a sweater he went on deck. At the rail, he watched buoy lights blinking red and green. Further out a lonely lighthouse beacon silently swept the sea. Toward New York City an array of lights ran like watercolor paints into the rippling bay. Directly across from where he stood, streaks of bright white jabbed into the black waters as work continued on into the night at the Brooklyn Navy Yard. Then the reflections were blotted out by a passing freighter — alone — a formless shadow moving out to sea.

Looking toward the *Vigo*'s bow, he noticed an occasional red glow of a cigarette from the sailors grouped there. *Thank God they're here to guard this ship!* The tense feeling lifted and Dale returned to his room and opened his diary.

5 May 1917

We have a mixed crew of merchant seamen and Navy gunners. We lack experience in submarine warfare and we aren't sure who to trust amongst ourselves. The Navy Chief doesn't trust any of us. Our captain seems strong but acts too calm. Hope he's not easily overwhelmed.

D.R.C.

9

UNDERWAY

On May 6, 1917, lifeboats were assigned and a drill held during an otherwise long and boring Sunday when no one was permitted to go ashore. The ship's chronometers were set at noon, to provide accurate navigation across the Atlantic. Watch times and meal hours were posted. The separate water supply requested for the armed guard was drawn in barrels and lashed in position near the guns for the gunnery crew. The ship's guns were bore sighted.[1] The ship's sails and rigging were checked. All moving parts of the engine were oiled in readiness for weeks of constant use.

Well before dawn the next day the order to start fires in the boilers was given. Now, black smoke rolled out of the *Vigo*'s funnel while below, in the core of the ship, firemen, naked to the

---

[1] This is a process whereby each gun's accuracy is determined by sighting through the bore of the barrel to a target ashore.

waist, swung coal by the shovelful into blazing furnace mouths at the bottom of enormous boilers. Coal passers kept a steady supply of fuel moving from the bunkers on each side to the stokehold floor where it was piled within reach of the firemen so their shovels' swinging motion could continue nonstop.

The chief engineer, standing on an elevated platform, kept his eyes on the pressure gauges. When the level was high enough, he reported by speaking tube to the bridge, "Engine room ready." The engine room telegraph pointer was shifted from "Stop" to "Standby."

Topside, enjoying a brilliant sunrise and cool air, five deckhands and the chief mate stood by for the order to "heave away" on the anchor. Overlooking the scene, Capt. Ryan relaxed against the rail of the starboard wing of the bridge. As soon as the rapid ringing of the ship's bell forward indicated the anchor was aweigh, the pilot ordered "slow ahead." His order was transmitted on the engine order telegraph and the engine room telegraph pointer ordered "Ahead Slow." The ship began moving. The harbor pilot entered the wheelhouse, ready to guide the *Vigo* forward through the Narrows and around Sandy Hook, then safely out into the Atlantic.

Standing outside the radio cabin, Dale heard and felt the engines begin pounding. The railings rattled. The deck throbbed under foot. A whistle blast announced departure. Soon he felt the breeze on his face as the *Vigo* cleared her anchorage.

Suddenly, an explosion rocked the ship. Steam shot up through the engine room grating in a roaring, white column that rose high above the stack. Dale grabbed the medical chest from his cabin and rushed forward just as a fireman was carried on deck, writhing in pain. His upper body was a fiery red and huge blisters were already forming on his chest and neck. Loose skin hung from his face. As Dale knelt beside him, the fireman began thrashing around on deck, crying, babbling in Spanish. Dale shouted, "Hold him down!" His own hands shaking almost uncontrollably, he grabbed a hypodermic syringe and sucked up a dose of morphine. Gritting his teeth, Dale buried the needle in the man's arm, then yelled at those standing motionless, "For God's sake, move. Get him ashore."

The fireman was quickly loaded on the pilot boat. As it motored away, the *Vigo*'s deck crew lined the railings, solemnly watching, then milled about the deck, grumbling. The accident was "a bad omen." Someone said, "A voyage that begins bad ends bad."

"Stow that bilge!" shouted the chief mate, Mike Brennan.

Back in his cabin, with the ship anchored once more, Dale overheard John's pained explanation to Capt. Ryan, "A boiler gasket split. New. My guess is it got brittle sitting there unused for so long. We should replace them all but it would take time."

"Go ahead," said Capt. Ryan. "Put it right."

Dale suddenly felt uneasy. *I better check the transmitter one more time*, he thought. He flipped the switch on the generator and nothing happened. No response. The electricity turned on lights but not the radio transmitter. "This can't be happening."

He tried again. Still no response. Moving swiftly, Dale systematically eliminated possibilities until he isolated the problem. The rotating armature — heart of the motor generator — was faulty. A new one was needed before the ship could sail.

Reporting the problem to Capt. Ryan, Dale was surprised at how calmly he took the news.

"I should go ashore, telephone the Marconi Company and have a replacement delivered."

"Can't it be fixed?"

"It would take me an hour just to find out, sir."

"Go ashore. The chief has to fix that gasket. There's time."

Dale had no problem hailing a ride. Several small boats were hovering close to the *Vigo*, drawn by the explosion. Phone call completed, he was soon back aboard awaiting delivery of a new armature. To save time he tried to take the generator apart but eventually had to stop. The armature was too heavy to move by himself.

The repairman arrived but without a new armature. Dale was chagrined to see he only brought aboard a bundle of tools.

"Where's my armature?"

The workman brushed him aside and proceeded to lay out tools.

"What are you doing? I can repair the thing myself. I asked for a replacement." No answer. It was as though he was invisible. The repairman casually conducted every routine test in the book. "I've done that. Damn it, you're wasting time."

Finally convinced, the repairman resorted to hammering on the armature's axle. He was so engrossed in what he was doing, he didn't notice the ship was underway. Dale said nothing.

Suddenly the repairman looked up, "What's going on?"

Dale answered with a smile, "You're aboard an armed merchantman bound for the war zone."

The man gathered up his tools and dashed out on deck, demanding to see the captain. Ryan stepped to the port wing of the bridge and listened, amused by the frantic pleading. "Lower a boat! Please. Oh, please put me ashore. I got a wife and kids." Ryan let him go on for a time, then said, "We drop the pilot at Ambrose. You may return to port with him."

The *Vigo* dropped her pilot and the Marconi repairman and headed out into the Atlantic, immediately running headlong into a storm. Buffeted by wind and pounding into head seas, she fought her way eastward with Dale Clemons alone in his room trying to figure out what to do with a dead radio. Bad omen, indeed.

10

THE STORM

The *Vigo* sailed blacked out. At night, she was hidden from enemy lookouts, gloved in darkness. Portholes and pilot house windows were painted over; shutters remained closed; running lights were extinguished. The ship was also warned not to leave a floating trail for alert U-boat captains to find and follow. Ashes from the boilers were dumped overboard only at midnight, and garbage, which attracted flocks of sea gulls, was burned aboard ship.

The bad weather continued and the crew went to work adding extra lashings and rigging safety ropes along the decks.

Dale needed help repairing the radio. He knocked on Merrick's door but quickly realized it was a mistake. The second mate was pulling on boots and a sou'wester, preparing to go on watch. His reaction to the wirelessman's request for help was to castigate him for not posting a storm warning. "Oh," said Dale, "And what did your barometer show — sunshine?"

Dale was glad to find a taut rope already in place along the wind-swept quarterdeck as he ventured outside in search of help. Working his way hand over hand along the coarse line, he fought the wind and salt spray that seemed to blow through him, chilling him instantly. Fortunately in a short while he found Chris nearby checking lifeboat supplies. "What are you up to, Dale?"

"My radio generator quit," he shouted over the wind. "It's too heavy for one person to lift. Can you give me a hand?"

They made their way back to the interior of the midship house where Chris followed him to the radio cabin. "I've got stuff cleared away. What I need to do is raise the armature up then slide her out. Then, if you can hold it steady, I can check the wiring."

Working against the constant roll of the ship, they eased the armature out. Chris held one end of the shaft, while Dale wedged the other end, supported by a chair, into the corner of the room. Removing black insulation tape from the soldered wire ends of the windings, Dale saw many of them separated. "There's the problem. Lousy job of soldering. Someone sure was in a hurry. The wire contacts lasted just long enough to melt the insulation." He sat back on his haunches. "I'll have to re-solder all these joints."

"Go ahead," said Chris amicably.

As the ship's roll increased, the sailor steadied the heavy armature while Dale, sitting in a cramped position, painstakingly stripped wire ends bare with a knife, then began re-soldering the joints. Before long Chris asked, "Why aren't you swearing? I would be"

"Won't solve the problem. Besides, it's repairable."

For the next hour they worked on the armature. First Dale twisted the wire ends together with pliers. Then, with his soldering iron, he melted pungent flux onto the wire ends and solder off a coil to fuse the ends together. The heat and the smell were somehow comforting in the close confines of the cabin as the wind howled and the ship rolled. While they worked, they

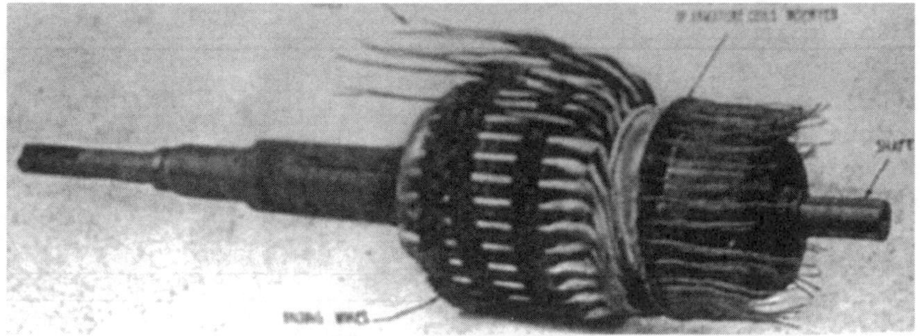

Motor armature for the generator with unsoldered ends. Photo from Practical Wireless Telegraphy*, The Marconi Wireless Telegraph Company of America, 1917.*

chatted casually. "How long will the sailors be housed on deck in this weather?" Dale asked.

Chris shrugged. He'd already erected a heavy duty canvas barrier around his gun. "Let her roll," he said, adding cheerfully, "I'll sleep under the gun platform."

> . . . we untaped, resoldered and inspected every one of the sixty joints, all the while sliding around and bracing ourselves as the heavy sea grew into big healthy swells as we drew further off shore. Finally we finished and on reassembling the job . . . [1]

. . . they replaced the armature and Dale put the equipment back together. "Cross your fingers," he said.

Dale flipped the switch. "There it is!" Dials lit and needles snapped to attention on the transmitter panel as the generator innards began whirring.

"My gosh. You really did somethin'."

"Not without your help. Thanks." They shook hands.

Seas were up when Chris opened the door and carefully made his way aft, dodging salt spray and gusting wind as he pulled himself hand over hand along the safety ropes to his gun

---

[1] Dale Clemons, "Armed Merchantman," 1940.

Details of the 2 KW 500 cycle motor generator. The armature is at the upper right. See diagram on page 79 for location in transmitter. Photo from Marine Wireless Telegraphy, *The Marconi Wireless Telegraph Company of America, 1917.*

position. Rain inundated the ship as it labored on, smacked by crests of waves crashing over the gun platforms. By nightfall, Armed Guard sailors off watch were allowed inside the foc's'le and after house. This left two men on watch huddled beside each gun.

> . . . we are working, rolling heavily, in the big seas that come boiling up astern as though intent on engulfing us. But somehow the old ship wallows, groans, heaves and rises on the crest and then settles back in the foam as these billows race on past us. Water is coming over everything outside — salt spray is blown flat and slithers along to strike us with crashing force from nearly every angle. Once in a while a thunderous cascade of water drops on the deck above me and smashes against the skylight in its race to leeward,

> leaving trickles of brine swishing into the cabin, wetting bedding, clothing and the floor.[2]

After supper, Dale watched Tom carry a steaming kettle of stew forward across the open well-deck for the armed guard. The messboy waited for a break in the swirling waters which rushed aboard each time the ship's bow dipped low. Then, as the ship's head rose, he made a run for it, only to be caught half way across the deck as a big comber crashed down on him. Undaunted, Tom returned to the galley for a fresh load of hot food and this time made it across the exposed deck, greeted by whoops and hollers from grateful sailors.

Just before midnight Dale went below for hot coffee. He heard disquieting news. "We just killed the galley fire." Dousing the galley fire signaled the worst was yet to come. Lukewarm leftover coffee was accepted with the knowledge that there would be neither coffee nor hot food until the storm passed.

Dale turned in, trying to sleep, but was awakened during the night by gale force winds howling through the rigging. The *Vigo* pitched and rolled and groaned, tossed up by enormous waves in slow motion. Somehow she'd find the crest before settling back, nose down into swirling seas. Jamming a lifejacket under his mattress, Dale wedged himself in his bunk, but the constant movement kept him awake. He heard pots and pans clanging in the galley, and, at one point, a loud crash as a stack of crockery hit the deck. The gunnery watch abandoned their posts and sought cover and warmth, content to lie atop the dry engine room grating. No one ventured on deck.

Waves capped with great masses of boiling white foam hurtled over the rails, threatening to swamp the vessel. Salt spray taking flight from building waves was blown flat in the powerful wind and came racing through the ship's superstructure like a screaming ghost while the decks came alive with swirling waters and truculent pools. No sooner did the ship throw off the froth

---

[2] Clemons.

and foam of one wave than another broke across her back, causing a shudder felt from stem to stern.

Occasionally the *Vigo* found a smooth glassy hollow in which to run safe in the valley between mountainous seas, then the vortex would erupt and smack down on the ship with savage force. Once again the *Vigo* quaked and struggled to regain the surface. On it went. Night merged into day. Caught in a timeless test of endurance, sea and sky and ship became one writhing grey entity. Those aboard were witness to overpowering forces in whose grip they hung suspended. There were no thoughts of when it would end, life was reduced to the next breath.

On the second night the storm unleashed its full fury. The sea hissed. The winds were so strong and loud no one slept.

Dale jotted worried notes in his diary, "She's laboring awfully hard . . . too heavily loaded." Brine trickled down the bulkheads in a steady stream, leaking through the seams of his skylight, and an inch of water sloshed around his feet. "What's keeping her afloat? She rolls crazy — too far, then lies on one side as if never to right herself again before finally remembering which side is up."

Brittle with age, the old freighter seemed close to snapping in half. Protesting sounds of steel under stress shrieked as the *Vigo* struggled to right herself. Dale gritted his teeth, listening to the tortured sound of metal grinding against metal, watching the six-foot-tall radio transmitter tilt, straining at its bulkhead mooring. He was afraid the huge panel would break loose and come crashing down on him. Finally he risked unbolting the top section so the entire unit could swing free of the ship's roll, hoping the generator's heavy base was sufficient to hold the transmitter upright.

While Dale focused on saving the ship's transmitter, the storm savagely plucked random trophies from her decks. Throttled by heavy waves, one, two, then three wooden crates were smashed open and half a dozen Hudson auto chassis rolled into the sea leaving twisted and broken railings in their wake. Then came another pirate wave, this one so enormous it fell as a wall of water swooping down higher than the ship's bridge, hammering her superstructure. A lifeboat on the port side vanished, leaving shattered wood remnants and frayed rope ends flailing wildly against empty davits. Only three life boats remained.

The storm's fury spent, the wind diminished, the violent seas diminished, and the *Vigo* settled back into a rocking, nodding motion. The blessed peace lulled Dale to sleep, head down, on his desk.

He was awakened by the sound of loud talking on the quarterdeck. Opening the cabin door, he saw a rim of white sky on the horizon — an end to the black overcast. It was their fourth day at sea.

The weary officers assessed ship damage. Peeling off rain gear, they made their way to the galley in search of hot coffee. The loss of a lifeboat and some broken railings seemed to be the worst of it. The crew was intact, their injuries minor.

Everyone had a story about the storm. The crew compared the past few days to "much worse" storms in their careers. The laughter was a pleasant release. Then Capt. Ryan arrived, his expression grim.

Ryan swung a bucket up onto the table, then scooped up a glass full of water. Oil globules rose slowly to the surface and formed a thick layer. It was a sample of their drinking water.

11

THIRST!

Bent railings and torn canvas could be repaired. Even the loss of a lifeboat was minor compared to the damage done to the *Vigo*'s drinking water. The problem was in number two hold where drums of benzol lay directly above the fresh water storage tank. The violent rolling during the storm ruptured some of the drums and leaking benzol gravitated into the fresh water tank.

"But I can't send a man down there," said Capt. Ryan. "If the drums shift again, he'll be crushed."

John Reynolds, chief engineer, examined a glass of the contaminated water. "Smells like kerosene." He swallowed a mouthful and grimaced. "Feels hot going down."

The young third assistant engineer, Wilhelm Granle, dipped a fingertip in the glass, tasted it and passed it along. "What's this oily stuff used for?"

"It's got something to do with dyeing cloth," said the captain. "Two hundred seventy-six drums, consigned to Fabrichi Coloranti in Milan. 'Coloranti,' that means coloring or dyeing."

Spreading out a cutaway diagram of the ship, he considered other water storage locations, looking for a substitute source of drinking water. The ballast tanks contained sea water. Their best hope, the fresh water tanks used for the ship's boilers, were unusable because a chemical descaling compound had been added.

The real shocker came when the captain unrolled the chart showing their position. Set back by the storm, the *Vigo* had progressed only 500 of the 2,115 miles of open Atlantic between New York and Fayal, their recoaling stop in the Azores. The officers gasped in dismay. Capt. Ryan continued, his voice calm. "We'll break out our sails and with luck be there in a week. As for drinkable liquids, I've looked at the stores list. We can issue lime juice, condensed milk, even draw juices from canned fruit for as long as the supply lasts. As for this," he raised the glass of water to the light, "let stand, the stuff rises. Each man can skim it off the top." Bending a spoon he scooped away the oily surface layer. "We'll just have to drink less."

> . . . this morning at breakfast . . . my glass of drinking water had on it about one eighth inch of heavy gassy oil after it had settled out. A lot of this oil is in the water, all churned up with it and it is steadily becoming worse. I couldn't drink it at all . . .[1]

They all knew that conserving fresh water was the rule at sea. Sailors bathed and washed their clothes in salt water, even cooking with it when necessary. Now, the *Vigo*'s contaminated water supply would be rationed to prevent everyone from consuming too much benzol. The captain reminded them they'd all been in situations where water rations were reduced during long voyages. He related an instance when a crew survived for weeks on one cup of drinking water a day because an old square-rigger

---

[1] Dale Clemons, "Armed Merchantman," 1940.

ORIGINAL—(For United States Customs Use Only).

SHIPPER'S EXPORT DECLARATION
OF MERCHANDISE SHIPPED TO FOREIGN COUNTRIES OR NONCONTIGUOUS TERRITORIES OF THE U. S.

Merchandise shipped by HERMAN & HERMAN, INC.
Address: No. 6 Street CHURCH City NEWYORK State NEWYORK
From 139 CEDAR STREET Via
For shipment on the S/S VIGO
From NEW YORK To port of GENOA Country of ITALY

Marks and Numbers	Number and kind of packages	Articles	Quantity	Value: U. S. Products	Foreign Products
D 2008 1-UP MILAN		30 DRUMS BENZOL	20342	$2310.00	73
		CONSIGNED TO: FABRICHE COLORANTI BONELLI MILAN, ITALY			

Waybill or Manifest No. Date Declaration C. H. No.

I, the undersigned, solemnly and truly declare that the above statement is a complete, just, and true account of all merchandise shipped by the party named; on board the vessel, car, or vehicle; and to the place or country named above; and that the description and quantity of each article is truly stated, and that the values thereof are the actual costs or values at the time and place of shipment for exportation.

Sworn and subscribed to before me at NEW YORK, N.Y. on APRIL 7 1917

Deputy Collector or Notary Public.

Signature: HERMAN & HERMAN, Inc.

This page of the Shipper's Export Declaration shows the benzol and its consignee. From GSA Judicial & Fiscal Branch, National Archives and Record Service, Washington, D.C.

sailed, accidently leaving her fresh water supply in casks stacked on the dock. "They didn't turn back and neither will we."

"Captain," said the second mate, "We can't last on this stuff for a week. We have to signal for help."

"We're on radio silence."

"But this is an emergency."

"Sit down, Mr. Merrick. Put your mind on what we can do to keep going."

Granle proposed scraping frost from the refrigerator coils. "It builds up fast." And there was condensate to be caught, drip by drip, in buckets wherever it formed. The word "condensate" gave Dale an idea. He remembered watching the Civil War veteran at Storm Lake brew whisky in a still. Explaining how it operated he said, "Maybe I can solder together some cooking kettles and tubing and distill fresh water from sea water."

The captain smiled. "It's been done before. Try it. I just hope you can wring out enough for morning coffee."

The chief engineer shook his head, "You're forgetting our firemen. They're stuck down in that heat. You know they're legally entitled to an extra ration of oatmeal and one extra quart of water per day. But, what they need to survive, we haven't got."

"Oh, yes, we do," said Brennan, the first mate. "The armed guard has a private stock. Remember? It's sitting in barrels beside each gun reserved for the Navy men."

The captain nodded. "I'll ask Baxter to share."

"Ask? He'll refuse."

Capt. Ryan smiled. "Not likely. Don't forget, he demanded a separate lifeboat for his crew. Well, that's the one that's gone. He's got a reason to bend. Oh, and we'll need armed guards on the quarterdeck. The water kegs in our lifeboats must not be tapped."

By noon the Armed Guard's water supply had been lowered through an open skylight into the engine room, for the exclusive use of the boiler room crew.

The water cutback was serious and the crew grumbled and worried. To Dale complaining was a waste of energy and time. He immediately went to work.

> I picked out two copper kettles from the galley one of which may be turned up side down over the other. I cut the bottom out of a smaller third one and inverted this inside the upper kettle, then soldered the gadget together.[2]

When he finished, the still — which resembled a squat hour glass with tubing snaking around it — was producing pure water, one drop at a time.

That done, Dale, along with the crew, began working on methods of collecting rainwater. Combing the ship, he gathered up empty bottles, then went to find something to use as a catchment.

Long and narrow, the sail locker housed extra wood spars and an entire suit of spare sails. He found canvas patch material in a bin beneath blocks of all sizes, swinging from overhead hooks. He saw a weathered bow-board carved with the ship's original name *Portena*. Against one bulkhead were barrels of line of

---

[2] Clemons.

every size, covered and neatly coiled like serpents ready to rise to some mystic cue. The entire locker creaked as though alive. In the dim light he saw a piece of canvas in a corner. Pulling it away, he gasped, stumbled backwards over a coil of line and fell. He stared at the suddenly unshrouded figure before him. The ship's old figurehead, a mermaid with large blue eyes and long flowing hair flanked at the waist by cherubic dolphins, stared back at him. Once a thing of beauty, now she was dirty and weather worn. "My God!" he said, with a shudder, hurriedly covering it up like someone who'd disturbed a grave.

Carrying a piece of canvas and some rope that Chips found for him, Dale climbed on top of the radio cabin to install his rain trap. He secured a triangular piece of canvas in place like a hammock, with a sag in the center. Glancing seaward, off the port bow, he saw a dim shadow. Vague at first, it emerged from a cloud bank, then took on shape and form as square sails rose tier by tier and a ship climbed the hill of the horizon. Word went quickly around and soon everyone was on deck. The square-rigged windjammer moved swiftly over the ocean, heeled to one side, cutting through the waves, heading for the *Vigo*.

> Because the [German] raider *Seeadler* is supposed to be a sailing ship we weren't taking any chances. She was rusty, had been at sea a long time. Long trailing growths of weed and moss dragged from the water as she rose and fell in the swell. Men looking over the bulwarks were wild looking. . .[3]

The Armed Guard went on alert. Navy men holding rifles lined the bow rails while others took up stations by their guns and swung the barrels toward the approaching vessel. On the bridge, binoculars were focused on the intruder. Baxter barked a warning. "What's she doing coming so close? Could be a surface raider."

---

3 Clemons.

In a strange, hostile silence the two old vessels, both survivors of a bygone era, passed each other, their crews lining the rails eyeing one another with suspicion. No one waved. No one shouted: "Where you bound? Where you from?" Or a simple "Hello" to brothers far from land. The Armed Guard on the *Vigo* waited tensely, looking for a sudden alteration of course, a change of flags, barriers falling away to expose concealed gun mounts. The graceful Cape Horner glided past, trailing brown seaweed.

"Been a long time out," said Capt. Ryan, "No chop at her stern. Pure sail." Half under his breath he exclaimed in awe, "Look at her fly."

They all watched until she disappeared over the horizon.

Time passed slowly. Each day took a toll on the health of the men. Try as they might to clear the water, they consumed more of the sickening benzol. Their food began tasting of it. They blamed the cook. At mealtimes they poked at full plates of benzol flavored hot food. Thirst forced them to continue drinking the foul liquid. When they did, it often came back up in a gassy rush.

Dale stayed at his radio, listening, jotting down news and weather reports, noting time signals at noon, and the all-important enemy ship location reports which came through at midnight.[4] Most of his time seemed to be spent waiting. Out of a growing sense of loneliness he began confiding his thoughts and fears in a sea diary.

> **May 13** Helps if we don't think or talk about water. Hard to stop. Water gets to be the only thing on your mind. My radio rig is a dandy. Pulls in everything from Newfoundland to Brazil. Still have far to go. We're all feeling sick. Merrick burst in here tonight and tried to get me to break radio silence. I said torpedoed is what we'd get.

---

[4] *Traffic, Rules & Regulations 1917*, (New York: Marconi Wireless Telegraph Co. of America, Wireless Press Inc. 1917) pp. 118-9.

He examined the battery stock of distilled water. A radio operator needed distilled water for his emergency batteries. Merrick saw the jugs and cursed Dale for not sharing. Dale remembered the taste of water drawn from a rusting pump spout in the park, the woodiness of an icicle pulled from a tree branch, the abundance of being able to scoop up a handful of clear, pure water from the lake while fishing. No more! The moment Merrick left, Dale gave in to temptation. He swung a half full jug to his mouth and gulped down tasteless distilled water, gulp after gulp, until he had to stop, gasping for breath. With no regrets, he wiped his mouth, savoring the cool feel in his stomach.

Revived, he realized the distilled water must be moved out of everyone's reach, including his own. The mate, Brennan agreed, suggesting, "Try the Old Man's room. He's in there now."

Dale carried two jugs to the captain's cabin. He knocked, heard "Enter," opened the door and explained his errand. The cabin was dark. It took a moment to see Capt. Ryan slouched in the center of a leather couch with a bottle of brandy at his feet. Motioning toward a door, the captain said, "There's space behind the bathtub." Setting the jugs there, Dale looked at the stateroom's interior. It was magnificently paneled with richly-grained dark wood. A massive poster bed of similar wood blended with finely-made cabinets and chests. Elegantly-carved fish and other nautical decoration on the furniture and elegant brass fittings equaled those aboard luxury liners. *All of this finery for a freighter? What was the Portena built to carry?*

His curiosity aroused, he turned, eager to ask the captain about the *Vigo*'s earlier life, but stopped short. Capt. Ryan seemed frozen in the same position. He gazed at the framed picture of a woman and was mumbling something.

"Sir, are you all right?" Dale asked.

Ryan removed his battered cap and ran a thumb over the worn symbol on the front. "This," he said, "belonged to my uncle. I'm not sure it fits me."

"What do you mean, Sir?"

The captain looked up. His eyes were red. He answered slowly and with effort, "I am responsible for crew safety and I am failing. How in the name of the seven mad gods of the seven wild seas can I handle what's ahead?"

Stunned, Dale sat motionless.

"Sir, I remember what you told me. You said, `What's needed is for each of us to take what comes and give our best'." An awkward silence followed. Dale got up and quietly left.

He walked away wondering, *What should I do? Keep quiet or tell someone our captain may be verging on a nervous breakdown? But if I'm wrong . . .* He knew he had to find out more about the captain. At that moment the ship's physical condition was less important than the wisdom of her master.

Dale remembered the torpedoed *Lusitania*. The listing ship righted herself and, misled by this change, an optimistic captain ordered all lifeboat loading stopped moments before the vessel's death plunge.

Books about the old days of sailing ships were rife with wrong decisions: greedy sea captains driving their ships to destruction in quest of speed, or leaving too much sail aloft in a storm and dismasting a ship. The result was always the same. Stranded sailors faced dying slowly from starvation or more quickly from thirst.

Dale turned to the chief engineer, the captain's closest friend. John Reynolds understood the concern but he knew what lay behind the captain's gloom. "The picture you saw was his wife, Molly. She died a year ago in childbirth and his son never drew breath. Poor Will. I'll never forget it, either. We left Portland, Maine in the summer of 1916. Molly looked radiant. Round though she was, she still came down to the dock and stood at the end of the quay waving. A week later when we returned it was to visit her grave. He's not really over the shock. There's nothing for us to do. Left alone, he'll get back on his feet."

Dale was still worried. "How long have you known him?"

"Over twenty years. As the saying goes, Will Ryan 'came up through the hawsepipe,' the hard way. He started out as cabin boy on his uncle's ship. When his hands could hold a shovel, Will graduated to coalpasser in my engine room. Never was a landsman like his brothers. They carry on the family business dockside in Brooklyn, moving and storing cargo. Not young Ryan, he waited for the day he was tall enough to pass for the right age and joined the Navy. Suited him right well for eight years. Then he got restless again. Felt he had no say in his life. Wrote to me about it, saying he was tired of taking orders from old men he didn't agree with. And so he came back to merchant ships — eyes on the bridge. First mate was rank high enough until he met Molly. She gave him the gumption to get Master's papers.

"He wanted a home in Maine and soon gave up tramping in deep water and long voyages. I told him about this ship. She'd just been brought over from France and was scheduled to work the route of a New England coaster hauling barbed wire from New York to Halifax. That gave him port time with Molly until that terrible day. He boarded up the house, and this ship became his home. He seldom went ashore. Work got him through the worst. But the war pulled him out of the doldrums. The minute he heard that his ship had been sold and that the new American owners changed her name to *Vigo* and that she would be crossing to Europe, he rose up and said, `Not without me!' and that's a good thing, Dale. Believe me."

Back in the radio shack, the midnight press shifted Dale's focus away from the ship and toward their destination:

May 15 Midnight Press.

Washington D.C. The government will send an Army to France. Congress passes Selective Service Law. Men ages 20-30 to register with draft board June 5th.

London. German submarine sunk by an aeroplane. April shipping loss total greatest yet - 800,000 tons, average rate 100 ships a week.

France. General Petain replaces Neville as C-in-C.

Moscow. Lenin arrives in Petrograd from Switzerland. Workers and soldiers want peace conference.

Rome. Tenth battle of Isonzo begun valiantly.

Berlin. British defeated at Gaza.[5]

In addition to the press coverage, Dale copied the grim news of sinkings reported by the powerful Navy station at Arlington,[6] noting with relief that the positions given lay far beyond the *Vigo*. Two black pins, one in the English channel, another at the entrance to the Strait of Gibraltar memorialized a terrible loss measured in tonnage.

The effects of benzol poisoning became increasingly evident as more of the chemical trickled into the water tank. The crew tried filtering but to no avail. They tried cover-up flavoring. They tried eating and drinking at separate times but found they were eating less and less. Finally, the captain ordered his men put on straight lime juice. He recognized the early symptoms resembling the ancient mariner's malady — scurvy.

Red blotches began erupting on arms, body and legs. Gums began to bleed, teeth became loose. Then came painfully swollen knee joints. Dale walked less and regretted having moved the distilled water. For solace he turned to an old seed catalogue Athie hid in his travel bag as a joke. Now it brought a measure of relief. The pictures literally made his mouth water — delicious tomatoes cut in half, dripping with juice his body craved. He imagined taking bites out of a whole onion, eating bright red radishes, cool, wet cucumbers, corn on the cob bursting with sweet flavor. But the best were melon pictures — he chose cantaloupe for flavor and watermelon for unfailing thirst-quenching, mouth-overflowing, stomach-cooling pleasure.

---

[5] *The Great War 1914-1918*, Chronology of newsworthy events of the First World War, (1917) pp 18-20, 53.

[6] When the United States entered World War I the Navy took over all radio operation in the United States, including Marconi Stations. The midnight press became known as "The Navy Press." Josephus Daniels, *Our Navy at War, 1922*, (New York: George H. Doran Company) p. 254.

The Vigo *in the Atlantic with all sails set. Taken from the bow looking aft.*

> May 16. Boat inspection and drill today. Captain Ryan was mad as hell when it was found that each of the breakers in the life boats was nearly empty. He read the riot act to us individually and collectively, threatened to shoot any man found tampering with life boat equipment, saying he'd watch them himself hereafter, would shoot first and ask questions later. He said he'd never been in church since he was baptized so it wouldn't bother his conscience a bit to plug any man found messing around trying to steal water.[7]

The corrosive effect of empty time on long voyages was something Dale learned to avoid. Unable to transmit, he spent most of his time tuning the receiver, listening. As always the dits and dahs of Morse code carried him off the ship and to the far reaches of the world. At any time he might hear coastal stations

---

7 Clemons.

broadcasting from both sides of the North Atlantic, or tune in to weather reports from the Marconi station in England or eavesdrop on a keyed conversation between two operators on ships in the South Atlantic.

One night Dale doused the light above his desk and opened the shuttered porthole hoping to find the sky dashed with stars and a shaft of moonlight livening a calm sea. Donning the headphones, he flipped switches and listened, hoping for sound. Turning the receiver dial blindly he heard a crisp signal then a response. Two Englishmen were working and he recognized one of the transmitters. No other had a sound like that. Excitedly he listened. The sender's fist was familiar. *I should know. Spent half a night relaying for that Aussie.* He remembered the ship's call letters, C-5. Dale broke radio silence.

"-·-· ·····" (C5).

The fellow answered. "Who's this?"

Dale responded, giving his old call letters WIN then asked, "Is that you, Archie?"

The answer was brief. "-·" (N) [no]; a pause then the group "--·- ·-· ··-," (QRU) [I have nothing for you]. Dale shrugged and signed off, "R CL 73" [OK I'm closing my station. Best regards].

OK. No relay work. I can go to sleep.

His deep slumber ended abruptly. A siren screeched. Feet pounded on deck. A shrill call, "Submarine dead ahead!"

"My God. I broke the silence. I caused this!" He felt and heard the *Vigo*'s bow gun firing as he frantically turned on the generator and prepared to signal for help.

> I tested my radio with one or two V's on the dummy antenna and left the generator running. Unreeled my long cords and stepped out on deck. I could see Chris . . . whirling the gun around to train off our starboard bow. He was yelling like a wild man as he spun the wheel, finally planting a squashing kick on the pointer's seat when the latter appeared too slow in getting himself on his controls. The crews poured pell-mell onto the platforms and the ammunition

> chest covers flew open with a bang as the first shell shot up to loading position. The forward gunners were already setting sights, calling out the numbers. As I looked a bolt of red fire stabbed out, a thumping crash followed and before the shell had screeched far on its way, another shell clinked into the chamber and the block thumped shut ready for the next shot. A big plume of white spray shot up . . . we could see dozens of seabirds fly up.[8]

The firing stopped. He heard laughter. Their target was the carcass of a dead whale. Tension relieved, the sailors laughed and turned to hooting and hollering catcalls at an embarrassed lookout in the crow's nest.

But Dale took the incident as grim warning. He must not lose control again.

One blessed night something woke him up. He lay there for a moment listening. It was raining! Grabbing an empty bucket, he climbed the ladder to his cabin roof. The canvas sling was nearly full of cold, heavenly water. He drank like a horse, then scooped water until his bucket was full. The *Vigo*'s officers and crew were all on deck, mouths open, faces to the sky, trying to catch rain water in their upturned hats. Then they all went looking for patches on deck where pure water had collected, like delighted children on an Easter egg hunt.

Dale rushed back to his cabin, retrieved the empty bottles he'd gathered and began filling them. He drank again and again until the gnawing fire in his belly diminished and finally disappeared. Then he brushed his teeth with baking soda and rinsed his mouth. He felt clean and refreshed for the first time since the storm.

The next morning he went to breakfast. All the crew were there, too, clamoring for food, their appetites revived, their spirits high. After breakfast, he went out on deck. For the first time since the voyage began, he felt at one with the sleek steam-

---

[8] Clemons.

powered schooner slicing through the Atlantic chop under sail. He stayed on deck for a time soaking up the healing rays of warm sunlight. But his comfort was short-lived. When he returned to the radio room he found the door ajar. He'd left it unlocked, and paid a dear price. His supply of pure rain water was gone. All that remained were empty bottles.

Mr. Merrick was the first person to appear at Dale's door. Dale angrily asked if he'd seen anyone entering the radio cabin. The prime suspect laughed and called Dale a hoarder. "Got just what you deserved!"

Midnight became the one bright spot. It was the hour when Tony came on duty in the boiler room. As Dale finished copying the press, he heard Tony through a nearby ventilator. First, the furnace doors clanged open. Then, as the ashes were removed, each door clanged shut and tools clattered to the floor. Finally, Tony stood bare-chested facing the open ventilator, bathing in a rush of cooling fresh air. Once revived, the stoker burst into song, singing in a fine Italian tenor. Every night, hope was renewed, for no matter how bad the news or how severe the benzol ordeal, Tony sang.

> And Tony, may God bless him! Down there in the fireroom sliding around on the grimy steel plates, heaving coal and trimming his many fires, he clangs his tools and up into the wild night comes his burst of song — and at a time like this too! Why can't we all be like that?[9]

On May 20 the *Vigo* finally arrived at the Azores two weeks out from New York. It was three o'clock in the morning, The *Vigo*'s rusty anchor plunged and settled on the bottom at Horta, the main port of Fayal, island crossroads of the Atlantic shipping trade. The rattle and vibration of the chain paying out filled the silence when the engines stopped. Then a deathly stillness settled over the ship.

---

9 Clemons.

In the first light of dawn, the crew gathered on deck, watching the water barge approach, pushed by a tugboat. Those with strength enough jumped or dove overboard and swam to meet it. Dale watched at the rail as armed guard sailors and merchant seamen slid side-by-side forward to the open well. By the double handfuls they funneled water into their parched gullets. Dale's knees were so swollen his pants wouldn't fit over his legs. He watched the shimmering pool arrive, then lowered his bucket on a rope.

The end of the benzol nightmare came later that morning. The men gathered around number two hold as volunteers worked their way down through steel drums. They found the water tank was undamaged. The tank lids were loose and had never been tightened. In frustration, some of the sailors began throwing out blame.

"Stow that. It's behind us," said Capt. Ryan firmly. "Our chief engineer wants to read something from the Bible."

John stood on a hatch cover, cleared his throat and with a booming voice read from Psalm 107.

> "They wandered in the wilderness in a solitary way [4]
>
> "Hungry, thirsty their soul fainted in them
> Then they cried unto the Lord and He delivered them
> out of their distresses. [6]
>
> "They that go down to the sea in ships,
> that do business in great waters [23]:
> these see the works of the Lord
> and His wonders of the deep. [24]

12

The Disguise

Brilliant sunshine sparkled on the blue waters as the *Vigo* crew lined the rail. After fourteen days of struggle at sea, the crew stared longingly at the shore. Nearby, several anchored ships flew the flags of friendly nations. Ashore they saw the town of Horta, clean white buildings with red tile roofs clustered in a protective valley surrounded by rich green hills. Looming in the background was Caldeira, a semi-active volcano whose pale lavender slopes rose to a sharply pointed summit wreathed in a cloud of its own making. In the stillness of early morning, sounds carried out to the ship: a dog barking, the dull clang of a cowbell, the ringing of church bells pealing in the steeple at the center of town, calling the faithful to Mass.

But captain's orders were "no shore leave." There was no explanation. And no questions were asked. Both the merchant seamen and Navy sailors knew to obey in silence. Complaining

One of the Azores volcanos from a postcard Dale purchased while ashore.

wasn't worth the risk of being confined to ship at their next port of call — Gibraltar.

"You're late," said Mr. Merrick, punching Dale on the shoulder. "The officers' meeting started ten minutes ago."

Captain Ryan's face looked tense and gravely serious. He said that the *Vigo* would be leading a convoy of merchant ships through the Strait of Gibraltar. Baxter, the Navy chief, was the only person in the officers' saloon who seemed to know of this beforehand. He smiled as the captain said. "We were chosen because we're the most heavily armed ship in the group."

"Kee-rrist," Brennan erupted, "We'll be sitting ducks!"

"Not if we zig-zag. Those are our orders from the British Admiralty office in charge of ship movement."

"No naval escort?" asked Merrick, fumbling nervously with a pencil.

"We'll see patrol boats along the coasts all the way to Italy but we're on our own."

How long had the captain known? Dale wondered. *Is this what troubled him?*

"Wireless reports," the words brought him back, "will guide us through. We'll know to avoid enemy locations." The captain nodded at Dale, whose heart leapt at the sudden recognition.

The discussion continued. "Whoever picked the *Vigo* must have been looking at a photograph."

"She's overloaded."

"Too old."

"Too slow."

"A ripe target."

Ryan let the spouting go on until each man had his say. Then he unrolled a crude sketch of the ship and set forth a bold plan. They would disguise the *Vigo*. "She looks fast and was twice mistaken for a surface raider. Ships turned away and ran over the horizon. That's because the *Vigo* looks mean. I aim to add to the illusion."

"We'll mount logs on the forward cargo decks and paint them to look like heavy guns. Empty crates will be set up and painted to look like gun housings. A half-drum mounted above the wheelhouse will make it look like we have a huge search light waiting to sweep the sea and expose the enemy to our devastating gunfire. When we're through, she'll look like a Navy gunboat. As a final touch, we'll paint out the "*Vigo*" on the bow and stern and replace it with 'S P 11' for submarine patrol. I chose eleven because it's easy to paint. Two swipes and it's done."

"Are you crazy?" Baxter bristled. "That would be impersonating a Navy ship. I'll arrest anyone who tries."

"All right then, I'll make it 'S F 11.' That's not quite Navy but close enough. And I'll do the job myself." The captain turned to Dale, handed him a large official-looking envelope, and said, "I want you to go ashore and deliver this to our consulate. You'll find further instructions inside."

After a short ride in the agent's launch, Dale walked painfully toward the consulate. His knees were still swollen. In the town square he sat on a bench, resting, then opened the envelope. He read the contents and laughed. The dispatch was part of Capt. Ryan's illusion. He wanted Baxter to think that

The town of Horta, Fayal, Azores taken from a postcard Dale purchased while ashore.

higher authority was involved. Inside were some blank papers and a hastily scrawled note. "Sparks, throw this away and enjoy the day ashore."

The only known remedy for stiff knees was exercise. The warm sunshine and the feel of soft earth under foot had a healing effect that gave Dale energy. He walked all morning, first moving slowly through narrow winding cobblestone streets then out into open fields where he found a dirt path neatly bordered by rock walls which marked off small plots of land. Stopping to rest, he leaned against a wall. Up the ridge he saw windmills with arms made of canvas triangles, arranged in a circle. Each mill had a cone-shaped roof, and the whole unit could be turned on its stationary base to swing into the changing wind. It seemed strange to be in a place where people still relied on wind power. He knew that this small island in the Azores chain was the hub of a great electric communications network linking North America and Europe by submarine telegraph cables. Yet nothing of technical progress was visible on the surface.

He was drawn inland, fascinated by the changing hues and sweet smells of the green fields and wildflower speckled hillsides, soothed by the bleat of goats and the laughter of children chorusing a celebration of life. His sore joints were loosening up now, warmed by sun and exercise.

> . . . finally wound up in the back country. The roadways are a series of walled-in paths rising in a series of terraces back into the hills. Lava, which abounds here, is used to pile up these walls to shoulder height. Numerous small fields, really big gardens, are thus enclosed everywhere, and much maize and beans grow abundantly. These walls are broken into small houses . . .[1]

Carrying his uniform jacket slung over his shoulder, Dale paused to gaze back at the sea stretching off into the distance. He turned to see an old man watching him. The farmer was using a sickle in the field but laid it down and stood waiting. Then he crossed the wall and motioned for Dale to follow him. Together, they entered a tiny rock dwelling that had a dirt floor and grass growing on its roof.

The old man said, "*Sienta, Sienta.*" Dale sat at a crude hand-hewn wood table. It was as though he was an expected guest. Fresh goat's milk and a generous serving of tangy, pale-colored cheese were set before him. The cool sweet milk seemed to have curative power. Again and again the bowl was filled from an earthen crock as fast as Dale drank it dry. The cheese was soft and easily chewed with still wobbly teeth. Dale exclaimed between bites, "I didn't know I was hungry. How did you?"

The old man simply smiled and offered more milk. "No more, thank you." He noticed the old man's bare feet, eyes dimmed by time and the misshapen joints of the hands that fed him.

"What's your name?" Dale asked in English, then quickly tried Spanish. "*Como se llama?*"

---

[1] Dale Clemons, "Armed Merchantman," 1940.

Brightening instantly, the farmer responded, "Miguel." Gentleness shone in watery eyes. Wanting to give something, Dale thought of his gold watch fob but decided that would insult heartfelt generosity. They sat conversing for a time, then he rose to leave and said that he expected to return. Part way down the path, he turned back and waved, "I'll bring you a pair of shoes from Italy."

On the last day before departure, a delegation of deckhands approached Captain Ryan. Their spokesman said they were there to set things straight. They weren't really complaining about the *Vigo*, "But we know her trouble. She's a hard luck ship. Things just go wrong and will 'lessen we fix it."

"Fix what?"

"Her trouble. The trouble is this ship ain't got no mascot."

"You're right. That's exactly what we need." The captain heartily agreed. He thanked the men and appointed a committee of two off-duty Navy sailors, the second mate, a deckhand, a fireman who spoke Portuguese and the wireless operator because he'd been ashore once and might know where to look.

The committee lowered a boat and rowed ashore, talking over their task. "Where do you find a mascot?"

Dale answered "Don't ask me. This island isn't anything like Mexico where you find parrots on sale in every port."

"Maybe we should wait 'til Gibraltar and get a monkey," said one of the deckhands. That idea was hooted down. "We need help now."

They arrived in town with hopes of buying a goat, a pig, even a horse if necessary, but found no one willing to part with an animal.

> There didn't seem to be a living thing loose ashore until we had walked inland a mile or so. Saw a black tom cat and gave chase. Chris got it by the tail, finally releasing the furry ball of feline indignation as it stormed squalling into a house with all of us in hot pursuit. A woman of great weight and determination rushed at us

out of the open door, brandishing a wooden club. She saw us, shrieked, turned and fled back into the house, proceeding thereafter to slam doors and shutters violently as we stood in open mouthed surprise, as she screamed volubly in high pitched and, I suppose, appropriate Portuguese. Farther on we encountered a pretty little kid, or goat, lumbering along the road upon his tiny tip-toes. Merrick made a dash and again held only the stubby tail. The poor thing bleated and cried, bolted for a hole in the fence which was filled with a thorny shrub. Merrick piled amongst the thorns and was wiped off, as 'twere. By then we were being followed by a group of country folk, good minute men all, armed with rakes and pitchforks, so we detoured trying to look innocent. Whenever we sidled up to anything alive the farmers raised a fine hullabaloo. Hours later we arrived at the quay empty handed, tired and completely disgusted, about sunset. Then just on the point of shoving off, Chris nudged me, grinned and pointed up to the edge of the quay. There sat a mongrel black and white dog; hair scraggly, sides sunken, tail wagging, very forlorn looking, studying us. Chris kneeled down slowly, snapped his fingers; "Here Mutt," he called as friendly as he could. We had our mascot in three short bounds. He whined, rubbed his head against our legs and looked up understandingly into our sour faces. Look around! No one was looking. So off we went to the ship yelling at the top of our voices. By the time we brought the boat near the ship the

Mutt, lower left, poses at one of the Vigo*'s guns with Chief Engineer John Reynolds.*

> whole company including Captain Ryan, was at the ladder to form a reception committee. Our prized doggy was hoisted aboard where he ran around, dodging, barking and otherwise giving evidence of liking his new home. Everyone was grinning kidlike and happy; lots of arm-in-arm talk, back slapping and good feeling all around came to us with Mutt. One of the gobs was appointed to make up a fine chased leather harness to be cut from a blacksmith's apron. Two of the crew gave Mutt a good purifying with soap and many rinses of water. So here he is tonight, lying on my carpet, stretched out full length, glistening, clean and happy in his new shiny harness much studded with polished brass and dreaming of whatever it is dogs dream about.[2]

While Mutt dozed, Chris and Dale discussed the captain's strategy.

"I don't understand the need for zigzagging," said Dale. "Seems like it will just slow us down."

"But to the submarine captain it's like peeking through a key hole," Chris said. "He can't take aim and be sure of a hit when our broadside keeps narrowing. And if we keep changing course, that's what happens. Besides, those torpedoes cost a thousand dollars. If those Krauts miss they have to answer to the Kaiser personally."

"Yeah, sure. From the numbers I'm getting they don't miss much."

"Don't complain. They ain't seen the likes of us."

"Chris, how come we haven't got enough destroyers?"

"The Krauts changed the rules too fast. Blame Britain for blockading Germany. What did they expect? With all the destroyers on blockade duty, the U-boats sneak under them and raise hell in the open ocean. Those Germans don't quit. I'm from Wisconsin and believe me, they're stubborn. And that's why we're here, Dale."

"What do you mean?"

---

[2] Clemons.

"They remember the last war. Shucks, our Navy plowed through the whole Spanish fleet like slicing butter with a hot knife. They want this war won before we get our shoes laced up."

One of the Armed Guard interrupted, "Take a look at this." The ship's transformation was complete.

"Holy Moses," said Chris. "She looks real."

Baxter had held back at first but finally joined in, unable to resist adding extra touches. He put the authentic taper on the wooden gun barrels and supervised placement of the search light, all the while complaining, "He expects too much. Now the Captain wants US to teach YOUR crew how to fire OUR guns. Benzol musta boiled his brain."

> May 24. At noon today a launch came alongside and took off about fifty sacks of white flour and in its place, left about two hundred loaves of black soggy warbread such as the people ashore use. Seems to be made of corn meal, peas, beans and is evidently made without yeast since it splashes like mud if dropped! With lots of salt and much chewing it can be swallowed eventually. The crew wonder why the exchange. . . . Someone must have fallen under the spell of one dark eyed young lady ashore, known as the coal dealer's daughter. She is an eyeful! We suspect Handsome Merrick of effecting the one sided exchange.[3]

Despite the grumbling and misgivings, the announcement that the *Vigo* was to lead the convoy gave the crew a sense of pride. Even before sailing from Horta, the deckhands painted the replacement lifeboat and refurbished the old ones until they all looked like new. Canvas covers were replaced, frayed rope was spliced, and the mast shrouds were dressed with black tar from deadeyes to truck. Chips was in his element, cheerfully filling cracks and seams in the weatherworn deck with hemp and tar.

The final touch was added by the captain himself. Ryan waited until the ship was at sea and by the first light of dawn

---

[3] Clemons.

painted “S F 11” on the bow. To do so he had to hang over the rail in a bosun’s chair, taking an occasional dunking in the process. He completed the job by smearing white paint in a sweeping bow wave below the name, creating the illusion of great speed. The *Vigo* was ready to brave the war zone.

13

NARROW STRAITS

From Dale's diary:

Azores to Gibraltar
1110 nautical miles
Day 1 25 May. Underway 6 AM GMT

. . . three submarines operating in the funnel-like approach to Gibraltar, apparently hinging on Cadiz, Spain, or its vicinity, and the opposite African Cape Spartel. A fourth submarine appeared off St. Michael, a neighboring island only a hundred miles from us a few days ago and is believed to be in this immediate vicinity.

Heard two SOS signals from torpedoed craft . . . Off Irish coast and far away. It shakes me up a bit to hear them and not do something about it.

Underway, Mutt established his place on the bridge, standing with his head thrust between the railings, his ears whipping in the brisk sea breeze. One by one, merchant ships flying the colors of Great Britain, Norway and Denmark, fell in line behind the *Vigo*. It was a stirring spectacle. Knowing that he'd soon be tied to the radio receiver, probably around the clock, Dale took advantage of the first few hours to acquaint himself with what was to come. He examined the chart of the eastern half of the Atlantic. A pencil line drawn through Fayal marked the meridian at 29° west. He added another mark at Gibraltar, just inside the Mediterranean Sea at longitude 5.2° west. Somewhere between the two pencil lines they would cross a deadly boundary and never know a peaceful moment again until they sailed for home.

Studying his sighting reports of submarines Dale noticed a rare sighting off the Azores with several red pins, representing attacks on merchant ships, clustered near the entrance to the Strait of Gibraltar.

He discovered they were no longer in range of either Cape Cod's South Wellsfleet station (call sign WCC) or NAA, the U.S. Navy station at Arlington, but it didn't matter. Ships crossing the Atlantic were usually within range of a high-powered land station, able to receive routine warnings and the time signals vital to accurate navigation and they were close enough to Europe to rely on signals from Poldhu, England (call sign MPD), the high-powered trans-Atlantic British Marconi station on the 2,800 meter wavelength.

The wirelessman's day was dictated by a listening schedule that began at dawn and ended at midnight.[1] Dale noted the following times he was required to be on duty:

> Sinking locations: Dawn and dusk.
> Storm warnings: 8 AM 4 PM 8 PM
> Icebergs and fields: 6 PM (April through August sightings expected north of latitude 43° and occasionally around latitude 39°, as far south as the Azores).

---

[1] *Traffic Rules & Regulations, 1917*, (New York: Marconi Wireless Telegraph Company of America, Wireless Press, Inc., 1917) pp 74-76, 118-9.

Time signals: 12 noon and 10 PM
The midnight press: 11:30 PM

The wireless telegraph made precise time-keeping possible and greatly increased navigation accuracy. The ship's chronometer was wound once a day. Thanks to wireless, it was possible to check chronometer accuracy at noon GMT [Greenwich Mean Time]. Wireless time signals were broadcast to ships as a series of dits, one each second, in a countdown to the hour which was announced as a sustained dah.[2] Any discrepancy between the ship's chronometer and the wireless time signal was noted and taken into account when determining longitude. An error of one second in time meant a corresponding error of several miles in position.

So critical was time to accurate navigation that Capt. Ryan, like most ship masters, personally attended to the daily winding and setting of the chronometer. Earlier in the voyage, to insure accuracy, Dale ran telephone lines from the radio room to the captain's cabin and the bridge so that time signals were received directly.

The *Vigo* was now close enough to Europe to pick up time signals from Poldhu and from the powerful Eiffel Tower station in Paris. Soon she would be close enough to the war zone for Dale to receive SOS calls directly and at some point he would start receiving ALLO, the secret warning sent by friendly fishing trawlers to report submarine sightings.

When, in those waters, dare a wirelessman sleep? Dale didn't want to look that far ahead. He had his schedule to follow and intended to sleep while he could, spending what little free time there was on deck.

Chief Baxter ordered gun practice daily and sometimes more frequently. At a meeting in the officers' saloon, someone suggested they were wasting ammunition that might be needed

---

[2] A. H. Verrill, *Harper's Wireless Book*, (New York: Harper & Brothers Publishers, 1913) p. 175.

The aft Armed Guard crew preparing for gunnery practice. Chris is the farthest back.

later. Baxter blustered, "We're here on a training mission. When I say we have gun drill, we have gun drill."

Capt. Ryan took the opportunity to again urge the training of auxiliary gunners selected from the civilian crew.

Baxter reacted like he'd been shot. The veins in his red neck bulging, he exploded, "NO! Not today. Not tomorrow. Never!"

On this issue the ship's officers sided with the Navy chief. Brennan and Merrick wanted no part of the Navy's job and said so. Dale avoided the gunnery subject but suggested two sailors be assigned to him to learn radio operation. Baxter angrily refused.

The captain didn't argue. "All right," he said, ending the discussion. Exhaling a deep breath, he stood. "Write this down. We begin a zigzag course at the 15° West meridian, Monday, May twenty-eighth. Given fair weather I expect to drop anchor at Gibraltar May thirtieth." Looking pointedly at the Navy chief, he said, "I want everyone not on duty to WATCH gun practice and assist as lookouts. That's black gang, deckhands and stewards — everyone."

Dale was gaining increasing respect for Captain Ryan's determination. Having transformed his ship to look like a navy

In a relaxed moment, Chris, left, and Dale, right, pretend to spar over the after gun.

ship, he was now intent on bringing her crew together. It wasn't an easy task. The animosity between merchant and Navy crews was almost tradition. Now, seeing the Armed Guard of the United States Navy actively practicing defending their ship defused the situation and bolstered confidence.

At gun practice Dale stood among seamen and assistant engineers near the stern gun. Looking down from the elevated gun platform, Chris motioned for them to move closer.

"These guns came off the *Newark,* a retired cruiser. She was a kind of cousin to us 'cause she was the last ship built by the Navy powered by sail and steam. But don't let that bother you none," he said with pride. "Our guns are the newest design . . . Bofors rapid-firing fifty caliber, three-inch shells and a twelve foot barrel."[3]

---

[3] Richard T. Speer, Histories Branch, US Navy Department, Washington, DC to author, 23 March 1981.

Chris continued, pointing out the working mechanism — a telescopic gun-sight on top, elevating gear, deflection wheel, gun-training gear, breech block and firing device with a recoil cylinder underneath — all used in the firing of a thirteen pound shell. He ended saying, "Now stand back."

The order to fire came from the bridge. Using binoculars, Baxter called the shots, speaking into a telephone. "Bearing three degrees. Range two. Deflection zero." The gunnery crew, composed of the gun pointer, trainer, sighter, plugman and two loaders, received the information and made adjustments.

"Number one gun ready."

"Number two gun ready."

"Fire!"

A whiplash crack. The spent shell casing slid out in a puff of smoke. The plugman stepped in and another shell was pushed into the breech. Clang. Close. Lock. "Fire." Then they switched to unarmed shell casings and continued.

Chris, using a stop watch, worked to smooth out the movement of tangled arms and confused movements. "Too slow. We need to fire six shots in sixty seconds. It takes teamwork."

On it went. Close breach. Lock. "Fire."

"Still too slow." Chris stepped in, explaining again as he walked through the required motions, then stepped back saying, "Try again."

Finally, they were ready for a full dress rehearsal. Moving back to the well deck, the crew waited for the warning siren to sound. A series of short horn-blasts alerted them to prepare for battle. They raced forward. Chris flipped off the gun cover in one smooth motion and within seconds firing began. It was an impressive improvement that brought cheers from the onlookers.

May 27 Midnight Speed 7.5 knots
Sea miles today: 214
588 miles logged
522 miles to Gbrltr.

May 28 6 AM We crossed 15°W meridian
zig zagging has begun.[4]

Dale finished his evening jog, stopping at the rail to gaze back at the line of freighters following close behind.

> It is a weird sight to see the big black shadowy ships strung out astern in a long line, each one turning off obliquely to starboard and then to port, making the change every five and fifteen minutes. Even without lights there is a pale fluorescence which glimmers faintly now and then at the bows of each ship as the turbulence builds up and falls away. A submarine wouldn't have much trouble viewing us in profile tonight, particularly since the Britisher at the tail end of the convoy chokes his fires regularly and sends up a plume of smoke that trails a good two miles over the water.[5]

The Armed Guard of the Vigo *preparing for gunnery practice at the forward gun.*

Ryan roared about the telltale smoke, but it was no use.

Close enough to see each other but out of touch, any contact between ships in the convoy to be made the old-fashioned way — by hoisting coded flags, of no use in darkness. No flares. No light must show. To Dale the whole notion of under-sea-boats seemed to belong in his old book about life "Twenty thousand leagues" down, a fanciful creation to be dismissed like the sometimes farfetched mariner's

---

4 Dale Clemons, diary.
5 Dale Clemons, "Armed Merchantman," 1940.

yarns of ghost ship sightings and sea monsters that seemed to grow bigger with every telling.

> One thing bothers me a lot: Its the terrific pounding of our French engines. A submarine could hear us through her pickup ten miles away, if not half way across the Atlantic. Visited the engine room awhile today and helped oil just for the experience. The condenser cooling water which one usually sees pouring in a big stream from the ship's side, on this ship, is pumped by a big two-stage pump directly connected with the high pressure cylinder cross-head. There is positively no air cushion provided in the design, and the hydraulic shock is awful when the engine delivers a downstroke. The entire ship quivers from the shock delivered eighty times a minute day and night; it never ceases. Our engineers are constantly watching a big cast bronze manifold leading from the sea to the pumps and to the condensers, having taken up the steel floorplates to permit this. They seem worried about the seam where the molds joined in casting, saying it is weak and thinned down too much at this point.[6]

At midnight Tony came on duty in the boiler room. Dale listened to his magnificent rendition of "O Sole Mio" as it burst forth in fine operatic style. To show his appreciation Dale sent down a package of cigarettes. On his next break Tony came up to visit. They spent an hour talking about Italy. Tony was going home to visit his family. He'd moved away but was worried about his parents. The war in Italy was being waged in the north and might endanger their farm. For generations his family grew olives in a hillside orchard. He wanted them to move south to safety. In appreciation for the cigarettes Tony gave Dale a small carved box he'd made of olive wood. As he left he promised to show Dale the beauty of his homeland, Italy.

Tony's concern for his people made Dale homesick. He noticed the date, May 29. *Tomorrow is Memorial Day,* he thought.

---

6 Clemons.

It was a holiday almost as good as the Fourth of July because it brought together everyone he cared about to share good food, baseball and cool drinks. *Oh for a letter from home. Maybe in Gibraltar.*

May 29 Zig zag speed 6.5 knots
180 sea miles a day. Distance to Gbr 335 miles
Europe traffic heavy.[7]

The *Vigo* had traveled 3,000 miles from New York and Dale had gained a new friend — Marconi's trans-Atlantic station Poldhu at Cornwall, England. It was easy to recognize not just by the call letters but by the tonal quality of the transmitter — a smooth, low-pitched sound with signals emitted by the sender at a sedate pace befitting the station's renowned stature. It was there in 1901 that Marconi's experimental letter "S" was transmitted across the Atlantic, demonstrating the potential of wireless radio.[8] Dale had studied so much about radio he could almost picture the original Marconi transmitter, a cluster of masts erected on a bleak rocky outreach, defying the ravages of nature like a lighthouse dedicated to mariner safety. And here he was, not very many years after it started, able to choose at will from numerous powerful transmitters on land beaming messages from every country in Europe, turned rivals by the war and reduced to deception. Telefunken, Marconi's rival, built Nauen (call sign POZ), the government station in Berlin now being used for propaganda. Daily, Paris contradicted Berlin's version of who was winning the war. He found himself hanging on every utterance from Poldhu. Surely they would tell the truth.

When not tuned in to scheduled broadcasts, Dale scanned the dial listening to marine wireless traffic. The airwaves were increasingly cluttered. Even so, he was able to single out individual transmitters. Each set had its own tonal quality and the

---

[7] Clemons, diary.

[8] H. E. Hancock, *Wireless at Sea*. (London: Marconi International Marine Communication Co. Ltd., 1950) p.32.

sender added his personal touch to the key — his "fist" — making the station as recognizable as a familiar voice in a crowd of people talking. Cape Race, Newfoundland (call sign VCE) suggested fog and had a bleak icy quality. FFU, the station at France's westernmost point, sounded like a bleating sheep. On the other hand, Monsanto, Portugal came in with a cheery, sunny, musical sound. And in sharp contrast, a German Telefunken quenched gap transmitter emitted a shrill signal.[9] These features helped Dale focus his search for valuable information. Before long he made an important discovery. He reported to the captain by telephone, "Sir, submarines may be getting help locating our ships."

"What makes you think that?"

"Just now I heard someone report a location. No preamble, just a location."

"So what?"

"A marine Telefunken acknowledged. That means it's a German."

"Sounds like you're on to something. Keep me posted."

May 30 6 AM. Crossed 7.5° west.
1,000 miles from Azs. 100 miles to Gbr.
Clock changed.
We're on GMT.[10]

Notation entered, Dale sat back and proceeded as usual to scan the dial listening for marine traffic. His heart jumped. He heard, "·- ·-·· ·-·· ---," (ALLO) followed by a profusion of dashes in a triplet pattern — a warning as attention getting as SOS. He waited for the location. It came, "Cape Spartel." Dale phoned the bridge. "Submarine in our front yard, Cape Spartel."

"Which side?"

"Didn't say."

---

[9] Karl Baarslag, *SOS to the Rescue*, first Edition, (New York: Oxford University Press, 1935) p. 230.

[10] Clemons, diary.

He'd barely hung up the phone when it rang. Captain Ryan's voice sounded strained, "I want to check chronometers again before we enter the Strait. When can you get me a time signal?"

"Paris gives signals hourly."

"Set it up. We'll soon have our headland, Cape Spartel in sight."

"Yes, sir."

At 3:55 PM the phone rang again. "We're ready for clock check."

"I have Paris. Counting down. Minus 5 seconds. Start, NOW!"

Eyes closed, Dale concentrated on the monotone rhythmic sound of the time signal. Beep, beep — the clock's tick counted down the seconds of the final minute. Suddenly he felt a sharp jolt and heard a dull thud. "What was that?" No answer. He rushed on deck, phone cords trailing. The British freighter just behind the *Vigo* had been hit. Heeled to one side, she was falling back, her bow enveloped in black smoke, a huge column of spray descending.

Torpedoed! Everyone was shouting, running. The *Vigo*'s whistle was blaring. Transfixed, Dale watched the wounded freighter begin to right herself.

> First glance at the ship astern showed her entire fore part enshrouded in smoke with a huge column of smoke and spray coming down over her. She had heeled over to starboard and was just swinging back to an even keel. Her engines had stopped and she was turning slowly toward her attacker. Her single gun was banging away at a tiny whitish feather far off and which disappeared in a few seconds. Our old ship was turning off to starboard . . . [11]

Baxter yelled at him, "Get back where you belong."

---

[11] Clemons.

Her funnel belching black smoke, the *Vigo* picked up speed, fleeing for her life. Following the prearranged plan, the convoy scattered. Dale thought, *Rules or no, it's inhumane to leave the crew of a sinking ship to fend for themselves.* But there was nothing he could do but listen.

Returning to his desk he switched to the 600 meter wave length in time to hear the freighter's wireless open up with "SOS *Knowsley Hall* torpedoed [the cipher jumbled somewhat], position Lat. 35.40N Lon. 6.10"W." The message was repeated twice, then the transmitter was silent. Too long a silence. There was no reply. *Don't stop! Keep sending, Buddy. Can you? Are you injured? Tell me!* The frantic call resumed "SOS SOS *Knwsly Hall* torpedoed. Position . . ." Then silence. Finally an answer, a painfully slow response. *The fellow must be falling asleep at his key.* Impatiently, Dale copied the message: "*Knowsley Hall* yours received. Gbrltr." Then, again, silence.

"Is that all?" In frustration Dale talked to thin air. "'Yours received?' Tell the poor guy help is coming. Or not coming, but tell him something, you lazy lout." His fist itched to say what he thought. So strong was the urge that he left the radio room and went on deck. There he saw the gunnery crews firing frantically at nothing. Chris whirled the stern gun from starboard to port spraying the ocean, blindly keeping six water spouts standing on the surface. He kept it up until Baxter called, "Cease fire."

By then Ryan had rounded up all available crewmen and repeated his standing order, "Watch for a moving periscope. Looks like a white rooster tail."

Dale returned to his post. Later Andy Wagner poked his head inside the door. "Come have a look."

There, to the eastward, coming up in a tornado of black smoke that hugged the water, came two destroyers climbing huge bow waves.

> While they were a quarter mile away we could hear the drumming, roaring sound of their fans and engines which were beating the water into a small turbulent mountain astern. A rim of reddish

A British destroyer racing to the scene. Note the bow wave more than half way up the side of the hull.

> and blue haze whipped and curled back from their stubby funnels. As they drew past us British tars pulled themselves along her decks by hand guideropes, their shirttails snapping and fluttering in the forty knot breeze as they rushed on.[12]

That's more like it, Dale thought. Heaving a sigh of relief, he returned to his post.

The *Vigo* moved closer to Cape Spartel. Still in full daylight, the lighthouse beacon did its work sweeping a grey, empty surface. Seeing the lonely landmark sent an icy chill down Dale's spine. They were entering the narrow Straits.

Ryan used the risky strategy of running the *Vigo* close to the coast of Africa, not wanting to leave room for a submarine to hide submerged between him and shore. They were entering the Strait at a dangerous time of day; U-boat attacks were known to occur most often at dawn and dusk. *Hurry, darkness.*

Night was descending when Merrick entered the radio cabin. Dale handed him the latest radio report of enemy locations but Merrick barely looked at it. He'd come to blow off steam, "He won't let go of the helm." Dale knew he was talking about the captain.

"What's wrong with that?"

"He's going to run us aground. The man acts crazy. He says he'll ram any submarine he sees."

The phone rang.

---

[12] Clemons.

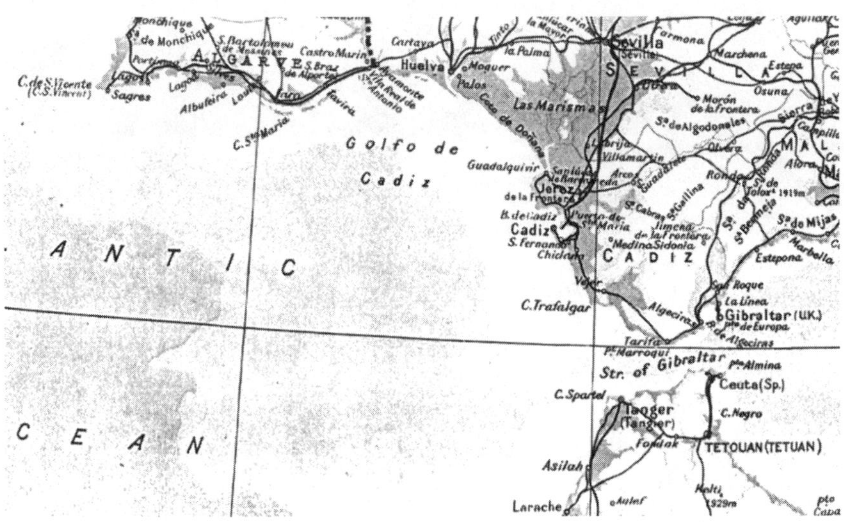

Gibraltar, the entrance to the Mediterranean and crossroads of the world. Note the locations of Cape Spartel and Tarfia. Taken from World Atlas, *Montréal: Geographic International Inc., 1979.*

"Strange ship approaching to port." Dale scanned the wavelengths, heard a radio signal and quickly called the bridge.

"Just heard a Telefunken open up. The operator of that passing ship reported our position." He repeated the position to the chief mate. The bridge officer chuckled "He's wrong by five miles." So far so good.

A corsair, an ancient lateen-rigged sailing vessel common to the region, approached dangerously close. *Vigo* lookouts scanning the vessel found it loaded with goats and sheep and manned by men wearing robes and turbans. Among them, however, Ryan spotted a blonde-headed observer with binoculars. Without hesitation or warning he turned the *Vigo*'s helm hard over, cutting across the path of the oncoming boat. Capt. Ryan hollered into the speaking tube, "Pour it on down there, we're almost through," as the corsair veered away to avoid collision. John Reynolds doubled the number of men heaving coal and the *Vigo*'s French engines pounded louder and harder, producing the best speed logged since leaving New York. From the bridge Brennan sang out, "Eight knots."

Lookouts strained to see through the deepening darkness. They watched for colored lights to show them the channel through the narrowing waters near Tarfia, Spain, knowing that at any moment a torpedo might come streaming through the darkness. Dale's radio screamed SOS calls, and he received a warning of a submarine. The *U-52* was active off Cape Spartel. At the moment he finished copying the information, an explosion rocked the *Vigo*.

Dale was thrown out of his chair onto the floor. Everything went dead. The engines stopped. The lights went out. The radio went off. In total darkness, disoriented by the fall, Dale was lost in his own cabin. He could hear himself breathing heavily and felt panic begin to well up in his throat. "Are we sinking?" He couldn't find the door and briefly forgot where it was. He remembered being aboard the *Pennsy*, hog-tied by his own antenna wires.

"Help!" he shouted, grunting with each breath. Frantic, groping about in the darkness, he tried to find the battery-powered emergency transmitter. Nothing felt familiar. His hands grew numb and stiff, frozen with fear, as if life was ending. At that instant an inner voice came to his rescue, as it had when, exhausted, he tried to get into the boat at Storm Lake, many years before. It spoke softly, calmly, reassuringly, *You'll be all right. Don't give up. Keep trying.* Strength came. Still in total darkness, Dale reached out and found his chair and from memory began to move switches, turn knobs, find plugs. He put on the head phones, ready to signal, when the door swung open.

"Dale!" It was Brennan. "Are you all right?"

"Yes. What happened?"

"Boiler explosion. Bring the medical kit."

Men from the engine room had moved the injured man inside the gangway where oil lamps dimly lit the rust-streaked walls stained brown by perpetual wetness from leaking pipe joints overhead. Crouching down by the flickering light of a lantern he recognized Tony.

"Oh, no!"

The towel around Tony's neck came off taking skin with it. Chest and arms badly burned, he lay quietly, eyes opening slightly from time to time, barely conscious. Tony Campagna, the young man from Italy who was working his way home, unable to afford the price of passage. He would have to leave the ship at Gibraltar. Everyone was concerned. No one aboard was more liked nor would be more missed than cheerful Tony — the stranger from "the black gang" who sang like an angel at midnight.

Angrily, one of the crew swore at the *Vigo,* calling her a "coffin ship."

Dale knew what the term meant. He'd heard the story of Plimsoll marks from a British officer on the *SS Colusa* and from that day on knew to appreciate seeing the mark painted on the hull of merchant ships, to show the legal load limit. Plimsoll, an Englishman, fought for the safety of victimized British seamen who unknowingly signed aboard what came to be called "coffin ships" — merchant ships that were meant to sink. They were old, unseaworthy vessels loaded down with cargo and sent to sea by unscrupulous owners who stood to profit from the insurance covering both ship and cargo when they sank. Plimsoll got the practice outlawed and ships' hulls were required from then on to display a load line on the hull.[13]

What about the *Vigo*? She was badly overloaded. If she had any marks on her hull they were completely submerged. But that didn't prove ill intent. All eastbound freighters were low in the water, weighted down with cargo to aid the war effort. Still, Dale had to wonder. *What about these boiler breakdowns?* And more to the point, *Why was a ship this old snapped up by American owners a month after submarine warfare started?*

Forget it, Dale. Can't be true. She must have passed inspection. Besides, no one would be dumb enough to mount Navy guns on a ship that's not seaworthy.

---

[13] David Masters, *The Story of the Plimsoll Mark*, London: Cassell & Co. Ltd., 1955.

Repairs completed, the *Vigo* got underway again and in the dead of night she cleared the Straits unscathed.

May 31 Gibraltar.[14]

Search lights swept down from high above illuminating the harbor of Gibraltar, a natural fortress in friendly British hands. The *Vigo* arrived just before dawn, delayed, but still afloat and moving under her own power after being stalled without an engine for three hours while boiler repairs were completed. Thankfully, her sails and a favorable current kept the antiquated freighter moving.

The miracle of their escape wasn't grasped right away, not even when Dale emerged from the radio cabin with news of another narrow miss. A U-boat was active in Gibraltar harbor just a few hours before their arrival. "And we're safe. How do you figure that?" No one answered.

Exhausted officers and men gathered at the rail. No one thought of sleep nor did they object to more delay awaiting permission to enter and the arrival of a pilot to escort them to a recoaling berth. They watched a small British navy launch draw alongside. The port officer spoke through a megaphone, "I say, old man, what patrol boat are you?"

The captain answered, "What sort do we look like?"

"Coming in I thought you to be a cruiser. Now I'm not sure."

Pleased to hear that answer, Captain Ryan slid down the ladder and handed the British Navy officer a fresh Havana cigar. They chatted quietly while the combined crew of civilian seamen and Navy sailors lifted the stretcher over the railing and transferred Tony into safe hands on the launch.

"He'll receive the best of care. I'll see to it personally," assured the port officer.

---

14 Clemons, diary.

The launch moved ashore just as daylight gradually revealed a rocky fortress jutting into the air like the prow of a ship — the rock of Gibraltar.

As they eyed the rock fortress, Chris approached Dale. The sailor had sworn not to shave until the *Vigo* passed safely through the Strait. Now he scratched his extra growth of beard and let off a whistle of relief.

"Did we dodge a torpedo? Or were they aiming at the other ship?"

Chris shrugged. "Forget it, Dale." His face brightened. "The rest will be easy. Now, we know what to expect."

There was no real explanation for their good fortune. And no one took credit for their safe arrival. But one by one, the men of the *Vigo* made it a point to give Mutt, their ship's mascot, an extra pat on the head.

14

The Rock

"Station KMC shutting down!" said Dale, methodically flipping switches. He'd been a captive listener for three days, doing double watches, sometimes wearing the radio earphones while asleep. It hurt to remove them. He rubbed the sides of his head with both palms to restore circulation, then massaged his scalp where the hair was mashed down. Yawning and stretching he leaned back in the swivel chair relaxing for a moment, then suddenly he remembered. *Gibraltar!*

While in port, by order of the British Admiralty, each merchant ship's antenna had to be lowered so that the transmitter couldn't be used. It was a regulation he welcomed.

The *Vigo* had shifted to the re-coaling anchorage and awaited delivery. With the radio shut down, all Dale needed was permission to go ashore. While waiting, he joined the men at the rail watching the ship chandler's launch approach. Even before the heavily laden craft arrived alongside, a thick scent of citrus cloaked the *Vigo*, emanating from the piles of oranges covering the deck. The crew and officers leaned over the rail, money in hand, calling, "Here! Over here!" Spanish oranges by the dozens were handed across, tied together with hemp cord. Dale devoured half a dozen on the spot, their juices running down his chin. More citrus came aboard in crates, then other foods. The floating store moved away, depleted, but the *Vigo*'s cold storage room was now stocked with fresh milk, eggs, meats and fruit.

Training his pocket telescope on Gibraltar, Dale saw a surprisingly small city of light-colored buildings crammed into a narrow stretch of land. It ended abruptly at the base of the vertical rock face. The Rock was barren. Its chalky white heights were honeycombed with caves for guns and storage. At the very top stood the arc lights which illuminated the harbor brilliantly at night. He felt safe, protected.

> First time I ever saw real castles in the air; there are several in the back country perched atop craggy peaks, with a vast array of Moorish viaducts and white roadways threading lacelike in interconnecting patterns. The Phoenicians, Carthagenians, Romans, Moors, — all in sequence — have once trod and fought over these hills and valleys through the ages, and probably we shall see it fought over in the future too, for whomsoever holdeth Gibraltar and Ceuta will control the Mediterranean, the Garden Spot of the World.[1]

Many merchantmen lay at anchor, some coming to Europe, others soon to leave the war zone, all doing their best to avoid destruction.

Someone nudged his shoulder. He jumped. Chips patted his back, "Easy, lad," then asked, "Can I borrow yer glass?"

Not interested in modern freighters, Chips searched the wooden hulls of old sailing ships which served as floating coal bins, reading the faded names carved into their transoms.

---

[1] Dale Clemons, "Armed Merchantman," 1940.

"Dismasted." Chips concluded about one of them, studying a splintered stump. Then, handing the glass back to Dale, he pointed, "That one, the *Soldere,* goes back to Nelson's day. Shows you they knew how to make ships in them days. Yep. Made of teak planking. Last more'n a century."

Although once fascinated with old sailing ships, Dale was no longer interested in them. They weren't reliable. He wondered why Chips showed concern for them. Like everyone else aboard, the man often swore at the *Vigo*'s "bad boilers" and carped about "filthy coal dust gettin' inside fresh-washed britches." But instead of bragging up the newest oil-burning turbine engines, Chips looked back at these relics almost tearfully. Dale sighed. He was tired of listening to history and the ruminations of old men. In leaving home, he'd committed himself to the future.

"Go ashore, Dale," Captain Ryan said on his return. His voice sounded urgent. "There's a message waiting for you at the Marconi office."

Several armed guard sailors had lowered a boat and were about to row ashore. "Wait! I'll come with you." Dale hurriedly put on his uniform jacket and cap, then shoved a few dollar bills and some change into his pockets.

In the boat he hardly recognized Chris. His beard was gone and someone had cut his curly brown hair so poorly it stuck out in some places, while in others his scalp showed. Dale tried not to laugh, but sputtered a chuckle as he asked, "What happened to you — a shell backfire?"

Chris frowned and boomed in a deep voice, "He who laughs at a gunner's mate gets tattooed. Them's the rules of the road."

"You don't get your grimy paws on my hide," Dale said, scrambling onto the dock as soon as they were alongside. Then he broke into a run, leaving the sailors to ship their oars and secure the boat.

A cobblestone street faced the harbor. Shipping row. Ship chandler's. Steamship company offices. The house flags of various steamship companies flying below the Union Jack made it clear he'd found the right street, and it was distinctly British. Each establishment was identified by a sedate but rich looking sign with a polished black background and fine gold lettering. Eventually he found Lloyd's of London and finally Marconi's Marine Wireless Telegraph Company Ltd.

"I'm told you have a message for me. Dale Clemons?"

"Yes. A cablegram from New York."

The look in the fellow's eyes made Dale uneasy. Sweat forming on his palms, he looked at the envelope wondering, *what can be this important?*

He saw that his marine office in New York had forwarded the message by trans-Atlantic cable. It was from Guy, dated May 14. The message read:

PAPA DEAD STROKE
MAMA WELL SENDS LOVE
GUY

"Will there be a reply, Sir?"

Dale looked up blankly, confused by the question. Without answering he left the Marconi office in a daze. Turning into a narrow alley, he came face to face with a wall of tall, dark-faced men dressed in long, flowing white robes, carrying rifles and curved daggers at their waists. Sidestepping into a stall he was greeted by a man in a black suit wearing a red fez adorned with a bobbing tassel of black silk. The merchant bowed, pulling on Dale's arm. He offered tea, and pawing, tried to sell him "a tapestry or ivory carvings or perhaps a knife."

Dale backed out and trudged farther up a narrowing incline, finally emerging from the alley and feeling the sun on his face. He stumbled up a winding foot path which grew steeper at every turn. He was only faintly aware of climbing the Rock of Gibraltar.

Uniform tunic unbuttoned, shirt open, hat in hand, he sat down on a rock, frantic to remember. *What was the last thing Papa said to me?* He remembered their final parting and recalled feeling awkward. So he pretended to be leaving just for a weekend. "Right after breakfast he gave me a gift, this gold watch fob. But what did he say as he turned and walked off? Why can't I remember?" Dale ran through it again. Waldo seemed quiet that morning. Distant. "I talked about the future. He never even raised his head — avoided looking at me. Oh, my God." Dale stood up. "Papa knew he was going to die! And I thought it meant . . . " He broke down and cried. He sank to the ground and sobbed and didn't stop until forced to stand to make way for a string of pack mules. When they were past he stood listening to the jingling bells dangling from the leader's neck, gradually fading in the distance. Then, he resumed his ascent. Plodding along, staring at the ground, he heard someone call his name. Looking back, he saw Chris running up the path, waving.

They climbed together. There was no mention of Waldo's death, and Dale was relieved not to have to talk about it. From time to time, they stopped to read one of the numerous small sign posts marking the spot where a British soldier had fallen to his death building the trail.

"A lot of sacrifice!" exclaimed Chris.

"No sacrifice. They died by accident."

"What's the difference?"

They continued to climb while Dale thought about that. "The difference is knowing what it will cost you."

"But who ever knows what it will cost?"

They arrived at a plateau. The view was spectacular. The Mediterranean was clear and calm, with a gem-like blueness.

"Hey, Magellan, look around. We're on top of the world. There's Africa and that's Europe," said Chris, gesturing grandly.

"My father died."

"I know."

"Who told you?"

"The captain. He sent me ashore so you wouldn't be alone."

"Chris, the worst of it is," Dale cleared his throat, and spoke in a wavering voice, "I've said my last word to him and it wasn't enough."

"Let's walk." The sailor changed the subject. "Say, Dale, know what's on the other side of this mole hill? They built a big cement slide and a basin to catch rainwater."

"I've read about it."

"Well, tomorrow we'll sail close enough to see it."

"Tomorrow? Not much time." Dale broke into a run.

"Where ya going?"

"Home!"

The wirelessman didn't look back. His mind made up, he returned to the Marconi office and asked to see the manager. While waiting, he collected his thoughts and steeled himself for an argument. He expected to hear of rules "with no exceptions" and be reminded of the legal document — the Ship's Articles he signed and possibly the threat of jail. Instead, he was greeted politely by a soft-spoken, middle-aged man, offered a comfortable chair in a quiet office, served refreshment and given a choice of a "bracing cup" of tea or Scotch Whiskey. Declining the offer, Dale explained what happened and said, "I'm needed at home. Please arrange replacement."

The refusal came in the form of simple facts showing how extreme the shortage of wirelessmen had become. The British had been at war for two-and-a-half years. At the outset there were only 1,000 operators available for British merchant ships. "The number tripled in two years, to three thousand wirelessmen and that's still not enough to go around."[2] Because of submarine attacks, the British government had seen fit to install apparatus on small ships without passengers. "Besides that, we now know that it takes two men per ship to maintain a constant vigil. We

---

[2] H. E. Hancock, *Wireless at Sea, The first Fifty Years*, (London: 1950) pp 88-90, 96-108.

simply haven't enough men. And they know it. I've seen chaps brought ashore from torpedoed vessels coming in here to request reassignment. Other young men like yourself are working alone, Mr. Clemons. Such courage and dedication will not go unnoticed."

Dale looked down. He had nothing to say. But he didn't give up.

Upon return to the *Vigo* he went directly to the captain's cabin. "Captain Ryan, I'm sorry but I have to go home."

"What did the office say?"

"He claimed there was no one else to take over. I don't believe that. What if I got sick or fell off the Rock, hiking? They'd have to find someone. Sir, please tell them to start looking. I can't do this work alone. Especially now. Damn it! I'm needed at home."

"Dale, I know what you're going through. Been there myself." He paused to light his pipe, then continued. "I don't think going home would make much difference. Unless..." He studied Dale's face. "Is that what your father would expect of you?"

"I don't know." His eyes welled up, "I can't even remember the last thing he said to me."

"And you probably never will."

A pause. They looked at each other without speaking.

Dale sighed deeply. Chest heaving, he looked down at the deck, then back at Ryan. "Tell me what to do."

"What you have to do is make your own peace wherever you are."

After dinner that evening Chris came to Dale's cabin, carrying a package. He said, "Sparks, you need to stop goin' around this ship looking like an undertaker. We're headed into summer weather." He handed Dale a bundle and walked away. The package contained Navy dungarees: shirt, pants and a white sailor's cap. Dale put on the comfortable Navy work clothes and packed away the black Marconi uniform in a drawer out of sight.

At dusk he went on deck to use his pocket telescope for one last look around the harbor, focusing on the wooden hulls of sailing ships. There were ten survivors of that bygone age. Now Dale sensed profound loss. He recognized one name — *Three Brothers*. She was once a speedy Cape Horner. Her graceful figurehead was still poised, eyes gazing seaward as if in readiness for the race.

There were no sails and where her masts once rose tall and proud, a windmill stood turning in the breeze, quietly pumping out her bilges. *Chips was right. She deserves the dignity of a burial at sea.*

15

Running the Gauntlet

Capt. Ryan looked at the officers seated around the saloon table. "The *Vigo* has crossed the Atlantic and survived the Straits. What lies ahead is a grueling nine hundred eighty mile passage to Genoa. Double watches will be required. From here on, we'll be lucky to sleep four hours at a stretch."

Four hours, for you, thought Dale, *radio never sleeps.* He was prepared for an endurance test the day he signed on, but the situation had changed. News of his father's death smothered his sense of purpose. He felt numb. *How many days can a person stay awake and still function?*

Captain Ryan was still speaking when Dale, seated at the far end of the table, opened a book in his lap and read at random from Joseph Conrad's *Mirror Of The Sea.*

> The sea has never been friendly to man. At most it has been the accomplice of human restlessness, and playing the part of

> dangerous abettor of world wide ambitions. Faithful to no race . . . receiving no impress from valor and toil and self sacrifice, recognizing no finality of dominion, the sea has never adopted the cause of its masters . . . The ocean has no compassion, no faith, no law, no memory.[1]

Dale closed the little leather-bound book — one of those that had drawn him to ships, as a boy. Now its magic was missing. Yet, for him, there was a message between the printed lines. *Do your job and don't say you can't.*

"Grab that end, Dale." The captain unrolled a chart of the Mediterranean Sea. Coffee mugs were set on the corners to hold it open. Running his hand over the surface he showed their route along the coastline of Spain, a distance of 600 miles.

"I want to stay close to shore all the way up to latitude forty-two North, just below Palamos. That's where we break away from Spain and begin our dash across the Gulf of Lyon. Then we pick up the coast of France again at Toulon and start our 150 mile run to Genoa."

Some of the officers questioned the route, unsure of Spain's position as a neutral. For that reason, Baxter expressed more faith in the open sea than a coastal routing. Merrick didn't understand the argument. "Spain is neutral."

"About Americans?" The Navy Chief sneered. "They lost Cuba and the Philippines to us." He turned to the captain, "You think those Spaniards don't remember who sank their battleships?"

Captain Ryan didn't blink. He answered with finality, "Neutral is neutral!"

Saturday, June 2, 1917. Gibraltar to Genoa.
980 miles to go.[2]

---

[1] Joseph Conrad, *Mirror of the Sea*. (Garden City, New York: Doubleday, 1905) p. 135.

[2] Dale Clemons, diary.

Her flags flying, the *Vigo* rounded the Rock of Gibraltar. Crewmen gathered on the well decks like tourists, eager to see Point Europa loom into view. Then, in silence, they watched the rugged landmark slip out of sight as the *Vigo* continued east.

Hugging the coast made sense. The waters were too shallow for a U-boat to submerge and the *Vigo* could outrun most submarines as long as they were on the surface. Also, according to the ALLO warnings, the region around the Balearic Islands was an area to avoid.

On the bridge, Brennan acknowledged Dale's latest reports and grunted, "Looks to me like the only safe place is dry dock."

It soon became apparent that other merchant ships had tried the same route. Some failed. They encountered the beached wreckage of torpedoed ships all along the coast as the *Vigo* rounded Cabo de Gato and headed northward around the south eastern corner of Spain. In some places rusting rib remnants of ships protruded from sandbars. It reminded Dale of the coast of Oregon. But here there was more than nature at work.

They passed a stricken vessel half-submerged with part of her superstructure showing, flags still flying high and dry.

Brennan asked, "When in hell did that happen? Looks recent. Still got her flags up."

To Dale it was a reminder of his responsibility. He committed himself to constant radio watch.

Sunday, June 3, 10 PM. We're blacked out.
A steamer is following us. She's all lit up.[3]

Lights ablaze, the Spanish passenger ship took up position half a mile off the starboard side and abreast of the *Vigo*. In an uneasy radio silence, the parallel course continued for an hour. Men off duty gathered on deck, speaking in whispers. From time

---

[3] Dale Clemons, diary.

to time, a sailor sang out depth readings from the foredeck, tossing a lead line into the waters ahead as smoothly as if fishing for trout.

Everyone wondered why they were being dogged so closely. Then the ship bumped twice and came to an abrupt halt, propeller racing. The *Vigo* was aground!

"Shit!" Ryan shouted as he swung the engine room telegraph from "Slow Ahead" to "Stop." Then, with fingers crossed, he rang "Full Astern."

The ship didn't move. The iron hull had dug itself into a submerged sandbar jutting out from shore near Aguilas. Ryan turned to the chart to examine that region of coastline. Merrick was already there scratching his head. The captain's index finger pointed like an arrow to the warning word VIGIA. "Why didn't you say so?"

Merrick shrugged. "Sure, I saw that. Vigia means a hidden danger, usually a submerged shoal. I even know in Spanish it means 'look out.' But I thought we were already beyond that hazard."

The captain walked away in disgust with Baxter hot on his trail, blustering about the deep water advantage.

Calling everyone out on deck, Ryan stood on the wing of the bridge and blew a referee's whistle. "Listen. We can stay here and rust or work together and move ahead. Pass the word. All hands aft, on the double."

The crew was assembling when Dale's wireless receiver came alive:

YOU AMERICAN SHIP AGROUND
OFF AGUILAS YOU NEED HELP?
WE SEND TOW BOAT
EEQ

Told the message, Captain Ryan ordered Dale to break radio silence.

"Tell him to shut up. If he doesn't, let me know."

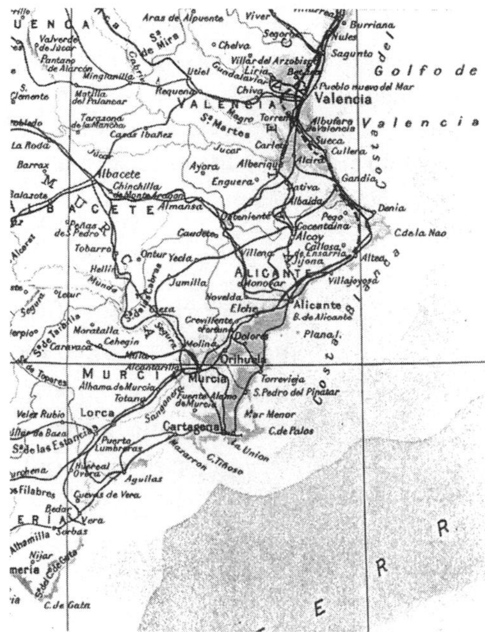

The southeast coast of Spain. Aguilas, where the Vigo *went agound, is west southwest of Cartagena. Taken from* World Atlas, *Montréal: Geographic International Inc., 1979.*

While Dale ran back to the radio cabin, Ryan gathered the crew close together along one rail of the ship and instructed them, at the sound of his whistle, to run to the opposite side, port to starboard and back, hoping to rock the ship enough to break the suction grip of the sandbar.

Dale felt the rocking motion as he answered the Spaniard. His message was brief.

EEQ · · --·- [call letters of the *Muero Cete*]

TTT - - - [the preamble for storm warning]

QRT --·- ·-· - [stop transmitting]

He repeated once, then snapped the antenna coupling back to receiving position. His heart sank. The Spaniard's wireless continued.

Dale hurried out to find the captain, reporting, "He didn't stop. He's giving us away."

"Damn it! Send him another warning and so will I." He gave the order to Baxter, "Fire a shot across his bow."

A warning shot roared out and exploded in the water beyond the *Muero Cete*. Moments later a boat arrived to protest the shooting. An angry Spanish officer shouted at Ryan, waving his arms. "You fired at a neutral."

"Is that so?" An inflamed Captain Ryan leaned over the rail.

> . . . and gave their officer merry hell for advertising to the German Navy all they needed to know to make an historic killing. They had come to protest the shooting but couldn't get a word in edgewise. The ship was the *Mouro Cette* and Capt. Ryan told the Spanish officer to inform his captain to stand straight out to sea for one half hour and not follow us or he'd shoot him up as sure as hell.[4]

With increased urgency, the crew's boat-rocking effort intensified. Working in unison, the armed guard sailors joined the seamen as they moved in a body, locked together, arm in arm. Chips, sensing the rhythm, set the tempo by calling out the verse of a sea chantey. The crew joined in, their voices ringing out:

"Oh I wish I was a bosn a-board a man-o-war.
Sam's gone away aboard a man-o-war.
Pretty work, brave boy, pretty work I say.
Sam's gone away aboard a man-o-war."

It ended with cheers as the ship floated free and further cheers when they saw the Spanish steamer disappear over the horizon.

Gloved in darkness, the *Vigo* continued her coastal passage on through the night, her entire crew too excited to sleep.

Dale copied the midnight press quickly so he could tune back to the marine frequencies where real news was happening. Ship losses seemed to be on the increase. Six, seven, sometimes ten merchant ships a day were reported sunk. Others were fired upon and fighting back. Again and again, in Morse code, he heard the action unfold bit by bit. Cessation in mid-sentence meant the end — an unknown end for someone. Listening was not easy. But listen he must.

> Heard two SOS's almost simultaneously . . . have hardly had the earphones off for four days now. My ears ought to flatten out

---

[4] Dale Clemons, "Armed Merchantman," 1940.

> pretty soon . . . five pins stuck in [the chart] along the Spanish coast, three in the sea lane between Marseilles and the route to Algeria, one off Sicily, two off Genoa . . . they seem to free-lance around in likely places, pick off a ship or two and then reappear somewhere else . . . the *Seeadler* is still being reported . . . [5]

> **June 4 Monday Noon.** Crossed 0° longitude. We're half way up the coast of Spain. Now in the latitudes 39° and 40° North just off the Balearic Islands.[6]

Staying awake was becoming impossible. No amount of coffee delivered at midnight by the messboy could do it. He fell asleep sitting up, until Tom came to deliver food and hot coffee. While Dale devoured a sandwich, the youngster, age fourteen, noticed ALLO in large print on a note pad and asked, "What's that?"

"I'll show you," Dale said, getting an idea. Several times during the voyage, Carr, the short-fused cook, had come after the boy with a meat cleaver over some minor kitchen mishap. Tom had to be alert just to stay alive. He was definitely the right choice. Dale explained his plan. More than willing, the boy asked, "When?"

Dale answered "as soon as I get permission from the captain."

The idea was proposed to Capt. Ryan in the chart room. Dale admitted to falling asleep at the key and said, "I believe I can train young Tom to listen so I can sleep for a few hours. SOS and ALLO warnings are easy to recognize. Tom can wake me in time to copy locations."

Unfortunately, Chief Baxter was within hearing distance. He stepped out of the shadows and said angrily, "You can't put our radio in the hands of a messboy. A kid fumbling around could give us away. Radio is no toy!"

---

5 Clemons.

6 Clemons, diary.

Radio is no toy. Dale's own words came back. He remembered the unending arguments with his father.

Baxter broke through. "Radio is now under the control of the United States Navy."

Dale bristled. Fists clenched, he said, "That's right. And they trusted ME to be responsible."

"Then do it!" snarled Baxter, "We're all missing sleep but we keep going."

Dale looked to the captain who said nothing. *Why are you silent? You knew this job was too much for one man. I told you that in New York. And now I have proof. Careful, no shouting. Say it quietly, like he would.* Dale looked down, pacing himself, then responded calmly, "When you file your report to the Navy Department, let them know that the British now maintain round-the-clock radio coverage. They place two wirelessman on a freighter this size." Then, turning to the captain, Dale asked "Am I denied help?"

Captain Ryan's mouth fell open in surprise. "No," he answered, shaking his head. "If you trust Tom, so will I. Name your hours, Dale. I'll tell Carr."

When Tom showed up in the radio cabin, Dale was again so punchy he had to ask "What day is it?" and with great relief learned it was still Thursday, June 6th. "Tom, I need sleep, just an hour or two." He placed the earphones over the boy's head. Tom pulled away, saying, "I don't know how."

"Sit here." Dale showed him the tuning dial. "You'll hear lots of noise. It's nothing." He yawned while drawing the dots and dashes of SOS and ALLO on paper. "Listen for this pattern — dit dit dit dah dah dah dit dit dit!" He finished groggily, "WWaake me if you hhhear either kind." The wireless-man turned away and flopped face down on his bunk, asleep.

Later, Dale woke up, suddenly clearheaded. Tom was still listening. "You didn't wake me? Hear anything?"

"Plenty of dits and dahs but not like them." He handed Dale the earphones. "It's terrible hard on my head," said the boy pushing away the note pad. Then grinning, showing several teeth missing, he said, "I guess that's how come you sleep like a drunk in a gutter."

Dale nodded and resumed listening, thinking, *It's good Tom doesn't understand what all this 'noise' is about.*

The radio was a window opening on warfare worse than Dale ever imagined. A German submarine torpedoed a British Hospital Ship, the *Dover Castle*. At first he refused to believe the report. Now he was less sure what to think. Wireless telegraph, an invention intended to serve the good of mankind, was being put to evil use. An SOS signal was blocked by a screeching Telefunken which opened up full power on the same wavelength. The operator depressed his telegraph key, held it down, then ran the pitch of his transmitter up and down creating a ghoulish wail that didn't fade until the *Vigo* moved out of range. No rescuer would know where to look for that ship's crew.

As the *Vigo* moved farther into the waters off France where the battle raged on land, radio traffic increased, one outrage fading as a new danger approached.

At dusk a fleet of Spanish fishing boats passed the *Vigo*. Dale heard a Telefunken transmitter, strong and very close, open up with no preamble. He warned the captain.

The *Vigo* had not yet reached latitude forty-one north when Capt. Ryan decided to break away from land and begin the *Vigo*'s dash across the Gulf of Lyon.

Ryan hollered advance warning into the speaking tube to the engine room before moving the signal lever to "Full speed ahead." Speaking to his friend, the chief engineer, he said, "This is it, John. Give me all you got." With twice the usual number of firemen heaving coal, the *Vigo* responded. Gaining speed, the old ship shook like an aspen leaf. After veering to starboard, she plunged headlong through moderate swells venturing forth into the wide open Mediterranean Sea.

Signs of war were all around the *Vigo*. The waters churned with small motorized torpedo boats buzzing back and forth like agitated wasps guarding their nest. From overhead came a different sound. A large dirigible with French markings on its tail materialized through the overcast, moving so slowly it seemed motionless until it dipped lower on a submarine search over the Gulf. The sailor on watch near Dale's cabin said that Germany was using air ships like that one to bomb London. Dale stepped into the doorway and looked up. "That's a Zeppelin? Looks like a child could down the thing with a dart."

An oil tanker, not moving, rode so high in the water by the stern that her half-exposed twin screws thrashed. A gaping wound in her side gushed oil as the *Vigo* steamed past.

Fearful that a U-boat was still in the area, Captain Ryan called to the engineers, "Pour it on down there." That meant feed more coal to the fires to build more steam pressure in the boilers to produce greater speed. The move ahead came not a second too soon.

"Torpedo coming, starboard side," shouted an observer on the stern. In silence, frozen in place, the men on deck watched the streak of white foam race through still blue water towards their ship. The gun crew stood ready for orders. The streak disappeared in the ship's wake.

"Where's it now?" Dale called to the nearest lookout. There was no answer. "We're clear," shouted the lookout in the crow's nest. "Port side. Moving away." It had barely missed the stern but was out of sight by the time Dale got himself unplugged and moved out on deck to the rail.

"Land Ho!" came the welcome call. The *Vigo* had crossed the Gulf. However, the strain of high speed steaming and fear of the unknown took its toll in the boiler room.

> Carranza, a big heavy fireman went crazy this morning. Ran up out of the boiler room and into the galley, seized a huge butcherknife, ran forward into the well and turned, announcing to all and sundry people that he was going to carve all of us into tiny pieces. Ryan went after him with a machine gun, drove him to the well deck railing where he almost jumped overboard. Instead he threw away the knife and fell on his knees crying and sobbing. Poor

> fellow, three days straight without sleep or rest. Captain Ryan put his arm around him and brought him into his own cabin where he was fed well and put to bed in the captain's bunk. Then, Joe, another of these gnomes of Vulcan refused to work any more. Just sat down and wouldn't budge. Instead of being put to bed, this fellow was given a job of coiling rigging on deck.[7]

"That's enough," announced Capt. Ryan. Within hours, the anchor was dropping in the quiet little cove of Ville Franche where Ryan issued the order, "Swim. Eat your fill and sleep. We'll wait until after dark before we go on."

Dale wearily pinned the last submarine locations on his chart. The nearest was eighty miles to the southeast. The array of pins showed plainly that U-boats had hop-scotched their path since leaving Gibraltar. He counted five red pins for as many sinkings along the coast of Spain. Three bristled around Italy — one far south, just off the island of Sicily — two in the Gulf of Genoa ahead. He drifted to sleep wondering who would make use of the crated Hudson auto chassis, the barrels of benzol, the bales of cotton, the bags of sugar and the many other goods consigned to the *SS Vigo,* most of it destined for Milan by way of Genoa.

> **June 9, 6 AM.** Genoa ahead. It's foggy. We slowed down and are waiting for a pilot to take us in.[8]

One hurdle remained. The law required all inbound ships to take on a pilot before entering a busy harbor. The fog lifted. The *Vigo* slowed to almost a standstill, drifting with the current just outside the harbor entrance. Genoa in sight, Capt. Will Ryan paced impatiently back and forth on the bridge.

Merrick asked nervously, "Where's the pilot?"

"How the hell do I know? Fire another flare." With binoculars both men scanned the harbor for a response. Ryan

---

[7] Clemons.

[8] Clemons.

waited a full five minutes, looked at his watch and announced, "That's it. I'm taking her in."

"You're what?" Baxter grabbed his arm. "The harbor is mined." The captain pulled away and gave the order, "Ahead half speed. Keep her to the right of that buoy." Then to Baxter he said, "It's this or wait to be torpedoed. Now would you please go help the lookouts?"

The *Vigo* plowed forward picking up speed.

"Patrol boat, port bow," a sailor sang out. "Coming fast." At that moment a warning shell exploded near the bridge. While the ship slowed down, the crew waved their arms and shouted, "Don't shoot. Americano!"

The patrol boat put aboard the pilot, an officer in the Italian Navy, who took command. His first word was, "Halt!" The excited young officer spouted something no one understood until he said "Idiot! Mines!!!" and pointed aft with a sweeping gesture. Ryan feigned innocence. "Didn't see 'em."

All was quickly forgotten as the *SS Vigo* steamed into port. Sailors and seamen climbed the rigging like monkeys. The city of Genoa beckoned under the bright sun.

The infernal trek ended a month and two days after it began. And to the shout "Hit the beach," another crew of an armed merchantman invaded Italy. Come morning, someone else would begin the tedious job of unloading the freighter's cargo, valued at $600,000. Dale watched a port official seal his radio cabin. As a finishing touch, a little green ribbon was placed on the door lock and secured with a glob of hot sealing wax, then imprinted with the ornate seal of the Italian Government. He was free to go ashore and stay for the nine days it would take to discharge the cargo.

The *Vigo* looked deserted, just as it had when he first saw her. He was somewhat surprised that his feelings about the old iron-hulled vessel had changed to a reluctant fondness.

16

Italia

Genoa revealed itself slowly as the morning sun dissolved a thin veil of fog, then added its brilliance to the colorful port city. Rich in seafaring history — the home of Christoforo Colombo — it was shaped like an ancient amphitheater, rising in tiers with crescent-shaped arms enfolding the bay in a welcoming pose. Like a mother protecting the ships gathered there, it forever welcomed her sons and all weary mariners back to her breast for comfort and nourishment.

Dale leaned against pillows in a long narrow water taxi and listened to the lap of water against the thin hull, enjoying the nearly soundless motion. A good oarsman himself, he admired the exceptional skill of the Genoese boatman who stood propelling his sleek craft over the water as swiftly and smoothly as if under sail.

A stone stairway led up from the taxi landing. The steps were deeply worn in the center and the edges smoothly rounded

R. DOGANA DI GENOVA

VARCO FEDERICO GUGLIELMO

N°

Si attesta che il Sig. ... *è entrato da questo varco portando seco dalla città i seguenti generi :*

Addì ... *19* ... *ore*

IL CAPO POSTO
delle Guardie di Finanza

L. S.

This customs receipt allows the bearer to transport items made of alabaster from the port ot Genoa.

by centuries of use. From the harbor Dale walked along a main street barely wide enough for two ox carts to pass. The sides of the street were enclosed by the walls of churches, buildings and enclosed courtyards. Here was a walled mansion, there an ornate palace once owned by a revered maritime family with the melodious name Andrea Doria, dated 1528. Marble statuary in lifelike poses gazed down at Dale, the awed American, who felt compelled to touch the veins carved into the back of an outstretched hand as thousands of admirers had done before, smoothing the surface to a glassy sheen.

> The architecture and statuary are quite beyond description. The famous "praying monk" surprised me; didn't know about it until suddenly I stood beside the most lifelike work I ever saw. In white marble, now yellowed with age, and ivory-like where thousands of hands have touched the brow, it stands apart beside a column, leaning slightly as though to catch the ray of light streaming into the alcove. The veins of his brow were traced so delicately, and the expression of the eyes was so realistic as to take one's breath away on first sighting the piece.[1]

---

[1] Dale Clemons, "Armed Merchantman," 1940.

Two of the many exquisite marble statues Dale saw in Genoa. Carpaneto monument, right, sculpted in 1886, and Lavarello monument, below, sculpted in 1890.

From the solemn drone of prayers echoing in a church, to lively conversation in the streets accompanied by exaggerated gestures and outbursts of hearty laughter, Genoa presented a maze of moods. He noticed the numbers on cornerstones of buildings built centuries earlier, the oldest from 1109 and 942. It was like retreating into an age which seemed even more foreign than the lyrical language spoken by the handsome, friendly people.

He entered a small shop to ask for directions, fumbling through the pages of an Italian dictionary given him at the Marconi office where the manager scribbled the name and address of a small, inexpensive hotel. The reader nodded, exclaiming recognition and pointed and pantomimed the way.

Looking forward to soaking in a tub of hot water, then sleeping in a bed with clean sheets, a feather down pillow to cushion his still-throbbing head, Dale followed his directions to what appeared to be a private home. He entered a tiny lobby and was greeted by a very large woman seated in a rocking chair, fanning herself. She called out something in Italian. A man came through drawn curtains, wearing an apron, his mouth full. Nodding, he moved his arms in a welcoming gesture as he finished chewing and swallowed. Dale showed him a note which explained what he wanted. Then he counted out lira in the amount agreed upon for a week's rent of one small sleeping room.

The stairway was steep and narrow. It ended at a door so low Dale had to bend down to enter. Inside was an attic room just large enough for a small bed, a chair and a writing table. It appeared dreary and dark, a garret tucked under a steeply sloping roof. Then his host flung open the window shutters. They revealed a breathtaking array of color. Red tile roofs arched over window boxes filled with fuchsias spilling over in bouquets of brilliant color. In the background the Mediterranean was a pure, glistening, peacock-blue with a clear, bright sky mirroring its airy essence. "*Grazie! Grazie*," he exclaimed to the departing owner, gesturing expansively, trying to show satisfaction.

Dale took out the letter from home he received at the Marconi office. Hands trembling, he ripped into the envelope and sat on the edge of the bed near the window.

The letter was from Guy and was full of life, with news of Dale's nephew, Roger. The three-year-old was already building sand castles on the beach and loved boating on the lake. It was a relief not to have to read about his father's funeral. Dale's smile changed to surprise at his sister Athie's decision to become a school teacher. She might attend school in Valparaiso and had "been invited to live with Pauline, that music student you met at that potluck with Mr. Dodge. Remember her, Dale? Pauline remembers you, fondly."

"Really?" Dale answered out loud. "Figured for sure she'd be engaged by now."

He flopped down on the bed and continued reading. On the very last page, in one small paragraph near the bottom, Guy told about the day Waldo died.

> I'm sorry you weren't here to see for yourself, Nibs. Papa felt fine, full of vinegar right up to the last hour of his life. Strange that he should pick that day to unbox the Panama hat. He looked very distinguished. People at church and on the way there noticed and remarked about it. And he told everyone: "Dale bought this for me." Then his eyes would brighten at the excuse to say again, "My son saw the Panama Canal!"

Dale lay back, eyes closed, and drifted off to sleep. In the quiet of the small room, sea breeze bathing his face, he slept through the sunset and all night. He awoke the next morning with a new sense of purpose. Dressing, he hurried into the street, eager to see people.

At a restaurant he asked for, "Coffee, please. Yes, cream. And sugar." He didn't know the word. Someone at a nearby table overheard and said it for him. The waiter bowed, opened a leather pouch which hung around his neck, and, using silver tongs, withdrew a sugar cube which he briefly immersed in Dale's cup of coffee then placed back in the pouch. Seeing this made him glad that the *Vigo* was at that moment unloading 1,000 bags of precious sugar.

He'd almost forgotten the war. Genoa looked undamaged. There was surprisingly little evidence of the fierce fighting reported elsewhere. Here, as in New York harbor, goods were piled high on the docks. He struck up a conversation with the American seated nearby and learned that Italy's fighting front lay even farther north, up in the Alpine region along the boundary where Italy rubbed shoulders with Austria. Dale thought Genoa fortunate to be spared and described the shelling damage he saw while passing the coast of France. Nice, a beautiful, luxurious resort town, appeared deserted with its hotel windows boarded over. And every building facing the Mediterranean bore the blackened scars of shelling by enemy ships. The man told him that Italian military leaders were worried about "aeroplane bombardment." Arc lights were in use all night sweeping the sky and Army officers on patrol blew sirens to clear the streets, warning that bombs could fall at any second.

"Didn't bother me last night" said Dale cheerfully. "I slept through it all."

He was advised that this was not something to joke about. Venice was recently bombarded. In fact, the man was a museum curator from the United States who had just come from Venice where sand bags and hastily-erected brick walls protected priceless art treasures from bomb damage.

Sobered, Dale unfolded a map of Italy. Venice was noticeably close to the field of fighting.

"What about this town? I need to visit some people who live on a farm near Piacenza. How can I get there?"

"Try the train north to Milan. It should stop there. You'll probably have to ride a donkey or walk to the farm. What's the family name? I'll write you a note asking for help."

"How much time should I allow?"

"Charles Dickens made it up there in two days."

"That was long ago."

"True. But a person can still do as well today," he smiled. "By rail it only takes a few hours, IF you can get on a train."

Piacenza. The sign on the station loomed into sight in the train's window much sooner than Dale expected. With a few lira and his note he hired a driver and a mule-drawn wagon.

The Po River valley was as beautiful as Tony had described. Green slopes on both sides of a deep valley were dotted with rocky crags where goats grazed. A winding dirt road led to a shaded plateau with a grove of olive trees. He saw strange-looking rock houses. Barns and homes had open space between them but were joined by a common roof.

Genoa, Italy and the French and Italian Rivieras. Note Piacenza to the northwest of Genoa and Carrara just below Spezia. Taken from World Atlas, *Montréal: Geographic International Inc., 1979.*

Cordial neighbors guided Dale to the Campagna farm. Tony's family knew nothing of his accident but Angelina, Tony's sister, understood English and told her parents that their oldest son was alive and recovering. Brothers and sisters and grandparents rejoiced together. Said Angelina to Dale, "What a fine friend you are! Come sit at our table." He instantly felt part of the family. Farm sounds, cow bells, chickens clucking, goats bleating and the smell of moist grass in the air soothed his soul.

After the meal, Angelina and Dale went for a walk through the orchard and down a hill towards a tiny village on the banks of a rushing stream.

Angelina confided that her parents refused to move south, away from the fighting. She said, gazing at the snow-capped Alps in the distance, "I want to stay here and wait for my husband Emilio to come home."

"Well," said Dale, "I don't think Tony knew what I just learned. Genoa may not be any safer than where you are. Airplanes are dropping bombs on cities."

"I'm glad to know that. We should stay here." She stopped and turned to face Dale and said anxiously, "Tell my brother. If Antony comes home, he'll be put in the Army and sent to the Alps where men are freezing to death from sleeping in snow." Her large brown eyes looked desperate.

"Your Emilio is there?"

"Yes." She sobbed. "They let him come home once. He said the soldiers don't have enough warm clothing. We gave him all the blankets he could carry back to the front. I pray for him."

Continuing their walk, they came upon the village church and went inside together to pray. She and Dale lit candles. Kneeling beside her, Dale couldn't help noticing the angelic features of her face. She was beautiful with a lace shawl draped over her dark hair. She smiled at him, and love shone in her large brown eyes. Suddenly Dale felt free to speak from his heart, "You remind me of someone. Someone kind — Pauline — a music student I met in Valparaiso. She plays the piano — beautiful music. I'm going to marry Pauline." Surprised at his own words, he said, "That's where I'm going. Valparaiso. I'll teach radio."

He took her hand and they walked along a stream, not speaking for some time. Then Dale sat down on a foot bridge and dangled his bare feet over the side in the cold water.

"Your brother wanted me to come here. Now I see why."

"Tell me about your home, Dale."

"I grew up in farm country, too. My father owned a general store." Dale didn't mention Waldo's death but did want to talk about their parting. "It's hard to go against your father's wishes. I had no choice, Angelina. We didn't agree about the war. My mind was on people being killed at sea. He thought the real victims were farmers."

"Victims? I don't understand."

"Wheat tripled in price but not a cent came into the growers' hands. Greedy businessmen, who never even saw wheat being planted or lifted a finger to help with harvest, made millions of dollars shipping wheat to Europe. No one should profit from the misery of others, we agreed on that. The break came over my work on ships. He thought I'd be helping the war profiteers."

Among Dale's pastimes in Genoa was a concert at the Apollo Theater.

Dale shook his head and said, "He was wrong. I work for the Marconi Company."

Angelina recognized the name, "Guglielmo Marconi!" she exclaimed excitedly, "He was born not far from here. He grew up on a farm outside Bologna, in hill country like this."

Going back to town Dale was embarrassed to remember how often he dreamt of one day meeting the great Marconi and shaking his hand. How foolish it now seemed, a boy's lofty illusion of receiving a silver medal from the inventor of wireless in recognition of bravery at sea. He cared nothing about medals now, but his respect for Marconi had deepened. Here was someone renowned throughout the world, a great man with humility, loyalty and courage enough to return home and join a losing Italian Army.

On the train, southbound to Genoa, Dale saw the wounded, dazed-looking soldiers hobbling along on one leg or missing an arm or being led blindfolded. His only wish now was to get back to New York alive and whole.

In the ensuing days he experienced Genoa and the nearby towns and villages. One afternoon he heard singing nearby and found lace makers at work in a small factory, their fingers flying as they accompanied themselves with folk songs. Another time he passed under the imposing city entrance archway, stood at the base of the monumental figure of Columbus, then watched the local fishermen land squid from their boats while he sipped red Bolo wine in the shade. A special day trip was to Carrara, the stone quarry south of Genoa where Michelangelo selected marble for his sculptures.

> Visited a marble cutter's establishment to see how fine statuary is carved. Was surprised to see apprentices, mere kids, roughing out marble, some doing beautiful work. Others polishing nearly finished pieces. I'm unable yet to understand how these artists can cut a nearly detached figure that seems to be suspended in space as though floating along effortless in the heavens. Centuries of experience equip these naturally talented people very early to achieve marvels.[2]

But, best of all was Portofino, a colorful fishing village of beauty beyond description.

A knock on the door of the garret sleeping room awoke Dale at dawn. "Mr. Clemons, are you in there?" He opened the door a crack, "Who wants to know?"

It was Andy Wagner, of the Armed Guard from the ship. "Captain Ryan sends this message. 'Officers report to your ship. Now.' He knows it's a day early."

Dale hated leaving so abruptly. Nearing the harbor, he looked for his ship. The whole world seemed to have sent ships to Genoa. There was no difficulty spotting the *Vigo*. He merely had to scan the forest of masts and find the American flag. He stopped and stared, moved by the sight of the Stars and Stripes streaming in the wind. *No other flag looks like that. So much alive! Prettiest work of art in Genoa.*

---

[2] Clemons.

The water taxi pulled away from the landing with Dale looking back toward the city. He watched the oars silently slice through the water at measured intervals, then turned to face forward and gasped. Directly ahead lay an oil tanker with an enormous hole right through it. "Go closer," he said to the boatman. The huge hole was easily entered. The boatman obligingly rowed through the ship, in one side and out the other. The hull had been crumpled inward from the impact of a torpedo, steel plates bent like tin. Inside Dale saw daylight above in dozens of places where metal was blown upward penetrating the deck.

He looked back at the hull and recalled the story told by a wirelessman one evening in a waterfront bar. The man was a survivor of another sunken tanker, the *Moreni*.

"We weren't torpedoed. All gun fire. Guess the U-boat Commander knew being a tanker, fire would finish us. Damn near did. Burning oil everywhere. I had to swim under it." A trembling hand tried to light a cigarette. Help came from fellow wirelessmen all around the table. Wide-eyed, blinking, they waited for him to continue.

"How did you know to quit sending?"

"No choice," he spoke in a whisper. "A shell passed clean through the radio cabin . . . took the aerial but missed me."

"What about your assistant?"

"Curran, poor devil, drowned.[3] He'd gone on deck to help pass shells. An explosion uprooted the gun. Everyone dove overboard including me." He crushed out the cigarette and took a long drink of water.

"How were you saved?"

"Saw a boat. Swam toward it. The ship upended, propellers still spinning. Hung there then slid down through her own debris and burning oil. Fuel meant for the Italian Army went up in smoke."

"Then what happened?"

---

[3] Karl Baarslag, *SOS to the Rescue*, First edition, (New York: Oxford University Press, 1935) pp. 296-97.

Typically U-boats used their deck guns to shell merchant ships, trying to take out the radio shack with their first salvos, or if the prize was valuable enough they would torpedo it. This painting depicts the ship sinking, the crew at the lifeboats, and the submarine crew watching the ship go down as a shell explodes. From Francis A. March, History of the World War, *Chicago: The United Publishers of the United States and Canada, 1919.*

"Thought sure we were next. The submarine turned toward us but didn't fire." The wirelessman told of encountering a German U-boat captain who spoke perfect English. Leaning from the conning tower, he asked survivors the name of their ship, then invited them aboard the submarine where he personally dressed their wounds, gave them dry blankets, hot coffee and biscuits. Bewildered, the men listened to their attacker explain that he used to live in Chicago until called back to Germany for war service.

"We thought we'd been taken prisoner. But he let us go. He said help was on the way, clanged the hatch cover shut and disappeared."[4]

---

4 Clemons.

17

Gearing Up For Departure

"Halt! Who goes there?" Wyman, captain of the forward gun stood blocking the top of the gangway. With a rifle slung over his shoulder and automatic pistol in a holster at his waist, he looked unusually menacing.

"Me. Why?"

"Show me your papers, mister."

"What is this, some sort of joke?" Dale felt through his pockets for his crew identification, "Come on, Wyman. What's going on?"

There was no answer. The sailor glanced at the Marconi Company card then motioned with his shoulder, "Report to the Chief in the Officer's Saloon."

Baxter greeted him with, "When were you last on board? Have you seen any strangers on deck?"

"What happened?"

"Someone tampered with our gun sights. Better check your radio equipment."

The sealing wax on the radio cabin door was intact. Even the skylight seal looked just as it had when Dale left. But closer examination revealed that someone had forced a chisel through slots in the ventilator grill behind the main transmitter. Fortunately the coil was undamaged. Dale tested everything, using a dummy load on the transmitter. It all worked. He reported his findings to Baxter then went to the engine room to find out about the ship's main generator.

As he descended the metal ladder his footsteps echoed in the unusual quiet. The air smelled of coal, old smoke and oil. The light from the skylight above cast an eerie glow outlining the two mammoth sleeping boilers. "John," he called out.

"Around here," the answer reverberated in the silent air.

Crossing a catwalk Dale looked down to see John at work oiling bearings and tightening bolts. "Any damage down here?"

"No. He didn't get us."

"Who do you suppose it was?"

"That fireman who replaced Tony. They say he was hired by someone in Gibraltar to do whatever he could to hurt any eastbound merchant ship he could sign on. Got caught red-handed up on the quarter deck, messin' around your cabin. Didn't Baxter tell you?"

"No."

"Well he's in irons in Genoa by now."

"Wonder what else happened while I was ashore."

"Word is some food got stolen. Someone traded some hams and cases of lard over the side for fish."

"Fish? Great gobs of fat, we don't need anymore fish."

"What we need is to get underway, Dale. That's the nub of it. Too much port time ain't healthy."

Walking back to his cabin, Dale wasn't so sure there was such a thing as "too much" port time. He yearned to be back there now, for one more visit to the Olympic Cafe where music echoed in the rafters and the air smelled of perfume.

He searched out Chris. "What happened to your gun sight?"

"Nothin' permanent. Say, you missed a good performance last night."

"How's that?"

"We went to that waterfront bar — the one off that alley, that hole you don't like. Must have been a hundred sailors crammed in that place, crews from every ship in the harbor. It started out right friendly, except for the usual elbowing for space. Then someone figured we should have a contest. A guy from each ship was s'posed to get up on the bar and do some sort of stunt. Our man was Brennan. We told them, 'He's the toughest first mate in Italy.'

"But, how could we win? See, that was the thing. There was so much talent up there. Hell, a Russian did one of those sit-down dances, got going really fast, whirling around on a beer slick bar 'till he fell off. The next guy was a Spaniard wearing a gold earring and a long stiff mustache twisted to points. He was a knife thrower. Put a dagger blade right between a guy's fingers planted flat on the far wall. Then up steps a Portuguese, hitched up his pants and did the same thing, but he pulled the dagger from over his shoulder. Moved so fast I never did see it happen."

"What did Brennan come up with?"

"The best he could do was stand on his head for the count of ten. Hell, that didn't seem like much even three-sheets-to-the-wind like he was. But he gave it his best. Stood on his head all right, balanced on two fingers stuck inside empty bottles. That was my idea."

"Did he win?"

"We thought so. Then up steps this big Swede, blind drunk. Takes a beer mug, lays it sidewise on the bar and mashes it with his fist. Those things are thick. That's hard to do even with a sledge hammer. Everyone was too stunned to clap. So he started eat'n the glass and declared himself the winner. That did it. The place exploded."

"You look pretty good, considering."

"I got out early. Climbed through a back window and collected our boys as they crawled out the front door. Dale, you should-a seen Brennan. He comes tripping along barefooted, hummin' to himself, happy-like. Didn't even know his two front teeth were gone or notice both fingers still stuck in the beer bottles."

The vision of Brennan stumbling through the dark with bottles on his fingers was too much for Dale. He laughed, and laughed, unable to stop. Eyes closed, his face red, he doubled up, tears streaming down his cheeks. The laughter was contagious. Chris started. Unable to speak Dale stomped one foot on the deck which made Chris laugh more. Neither could stop. When the laughter began to die down, all one man had to do was hold up two index fingers and it started again.

Finally Dale collected himself enough to ask, "Are they still stuck?"

"I didn't finish. Brennan took off all his clothes, climbed to the top of a pole at the end of the quay and did a swan dive into Genoa harbor. He must-a gone clear to the bottom cause he came up sputterin', coated with oil and muck, smelling like garbage. But the bottles were gone."

The only man late returning to the ship was Mr. Merrick, who didn't show up until dawn. Captain Ryan made it known that he would be docked two days' pay. The crew thought that was mild punishment for someone known to be financially well off. It was meaningless to him and he had enjoyed an extra night ashore with two beautiful women. The crew's rancor was well founded. Merrick knew he was good looking, spent inordinate amounts of time combing his hair and was smug and self-centered. Behind his back they called him "Adonis," with a sneer.

Merrick was last to arrive at the officers' meeting, settling into an arm chair next to Dale at the conference table. Dale wanted to move away but the captain was already speaking.

Captain Ryan announced that as of June 6 the British Navy had begun convoying merchant ships through the Strait of Gibraltar.[1] "But we can't count on Navy escort for the *Vigo*."

"Why not?" asked Brennan.

"Because the *Vigo* is too slow."

"For Pete's sake, that's why we need protection."

"Tell that to the British. Personally I think we can qualify. We need to maintain eight-and-a-quarter knots and come up with short runs of twelve knots. How about it, John?"

The chief engineer's face flushed. "You know the answer to that. Those boilers can't stand much more of this high pressure steaming."

"Come on, John." Brennan cajoled. "Light as we are, empty, we should be able to maintain much better speed than we did coming over."

"I agree. But you can't expect to run hell bent back across the Gulf of Lyon without boiler trouble."

"Why not?"

"Because prolonged overheating weakens metal. Our boiler tubes are wearing thin."

The captain answered calmly, "A good run will earn us the help we'll need to get back through the Straits. You'll just have to plug any firetubes that split and keep us going. A few hours is all we need. And we can use the sails, that should help."

Baxter cleared his throat and stood up, shuffling some papers. "According to the official count, a large number of ships have been sunk by shellfire. Mr. Clemons, you haven't been reporting the causes of sinkings."

Caught by surprise, Dale didn't answer. Baxter went on, "Have you forgotten your official instructions?"

---

[1] John Terraine, *The U-Boat Wars 1916-1945,* (New York: An Owl Book, Henry Holt & Co., 1989) p. 63.

"No, I haven't. The fact is, I seldom know what happens when I receive a distress call. I guess it doesn't matter to the fellow calling for help or maybe they're so busy trying to survive, no one has time to tell the wirelessman why water is rising around his ankles. He's lucky to send his location, much less the cause."

The captain cleared his throat, "Baxter made a good point, Dale. Do what you can." He continued, "As for the *Vigo*, from everything I've heard ashore the SF 11 disguise is still our best ally. Tell the men. This time we'll be loading a cargo of cork in Palamos, just up the coast from Barcelona." Ryan looked at John and smiled, "Enough cork to float us home."

As the meeting broke up, the captain pushed some navigation charts across the table to Mr. Merrick. "All right, Columbus, let's see you find America."

18

Trial By Fire

With engine pounding and black smoke billowing from her funnel, the *Vigo* dropped her mooring lines and began moving. Empty of cargo, the old freighter turned smartly, putting out to sea like a youth seeking adventure.

Mutt barked excitedly as half a dozen of his shipmates secured the mooring lines and hoisted the sails.

As the *Vigo* passed, the crews of other freighters lying quietly at anchor lined their rails, waving and cheering her on. On a British cruiser a brass band struck up. To the waning strains of "Auld Lang Syne" the American merchant ship — boldly marked SF 11 — rounded the last breakwater and embarked on its 4,400-mile voyage to New York.

Before settling down to the radio routine, Dale went on deck for a final look at the serenity of beautiful Genoa harbor. Then he returned to the familiar electric scent of the wireless cabin, cheerful and ready for a fresh start.

To limber up, he practiced tapping out the ship's call letters, KMC, using a disconnected telegraph key while he listened to the familiar frequencies for war news. The first report was the best yet: "General Pershing arrived safely in France. He left the USA on May 28 and brought 1,308 men of the US Army."[1]

"Know what this means?" Dale said excitedly to Merrick who had stopped in to collect news reports.

"Yeah. No convoy for us."

"It means France and Italy have a chance to win the war."

Merrick made a rude gesture and continued looking through the reports.

Dale thought, *The hell with you. Everything's better. We're headed home. This time we're facing the war zone first thing, while we're fresh.*

There was a sudden jolt. Both men froze, open-mouthed, looking at each other. They heard firing. "That's our guns," said Merrick, running out on deck.

"Periscope. Starboard bow!" Baxter shouted to the navigator.

Tethered to the radio, Dale could only listen to a forward gun discharge and hear voices shouting from the bridge, "It's coming toward us."

"Where?"

"We lost it," shouted the lookouts gathered along the starboard railing. Dale heard men racing to the port side. Unable to contain himself any longer, he ran out on deck to join in the search.

"There it is," shouted Chris, pointing off to the left. "Port side. Four points, off the bow."

Immediately the captain gave the order, "Right full rudder," risking showing the sub the ship's broadside in order to bring

---

[1] Holland Thompson, ed., *The World War,* Vol. III, (New York: The Grolier Society, 1920-1921) p. 1102.

The telltale wake of the periscope eye of a submarine just below the surface. From Holland Thompson ed., The World War, *New York: The Grolier Society, 1920*

both bow and stern guns into play. The *Vigo* responded, heeling into a sharp turn. Within seconds, both her guns were firing shell after shell until two furrows of water spouts converged where the sub was last seen.

"Cease fire."

It was obvious that the U-boat wasn't going to surface, nor was it turning to aim its torpedo tubes at the *Vigo*. Instead, the periscope plume was moving out to sea. Everyone cheered.

At midnight Dale entered a new date in his diary. *The nineteenth of June. Why is that familiar?* Then he remembered and said with a tinge of sadness, "That's the day I came home." His mind wandered back to Iowa. He jotted a diary note, "I remember that morning like it was yesterday."

Waldo had insisted on taking Dale for a short ride in his new Model T Ford. They were miles away from home when they came to a deep stream. Rather than turn around Waldo tried to ford the muddy water. In midstream the wheels sank. The engine sputtered to a stop and refused to start. The two of them together, shoulder to shoulder, tried to push the new automobile, all the while sinking themselves deeper into the mud. Giving up on the car, they tried to extricate themselves. Dale's shoes came off but he made it across to the bank, reached out a hand and pulled his father ashore. There they sat on a log pondering their dilemma.

"To think this was the mighty machine that was supposed to replace horses"

"When is that supposed to happen?"

"Not today." said Waldo, laughing. Dale joined in. Despite their predicament, it was the best day Dale remembered with his father.

In the end Dale went for help and the "mighty machine" was pulled home hitched to a plow horse.

Entering the Gulf of Lyon, the teeth-grinding hope was that the *Vigo*'s fire-tubes — the steam generating heart of her boilers — could last long enough to maintain the required eight and one-quarter knots for the ship to qualify for convoy protection once they got to the Strait of Gibraltar.

8 AM. Off Marseilles. Entered gulf. Weather rough, seas choppy but making good speed.
9 AM. We slowed down.[2]

"What happened?" he asked the bridge officer by telephone. There was so much swearing at the other end he couldn't understand the answer. Finally he gave up and went to the bridge to ask in person.

"Boiler tubes split."

Hearing hammers banging, he knew that the black gang was already busily plugging the leaking fire-tubes so boiler water wouldn't drown the furnace fire.

> This requires one man to crawl back over the hot gratings which, a few minutes before, had borne a white hot fire. He requires a stream of water to be hosed over him to keep him from suffocating. His job is to insert a cone of wood or metal and pass a long steel rod. He fixes the nut over the rod end. In this way the rod draws a plug into the ends of the tube and seals it off.[3]

With the damaged fire tubes plugged, that boiler could stay in service and keep the ship moving.

---

[2] Dale Clemons, diary.

[3] Dale Clemons, "Armed Merchantman," 1940.

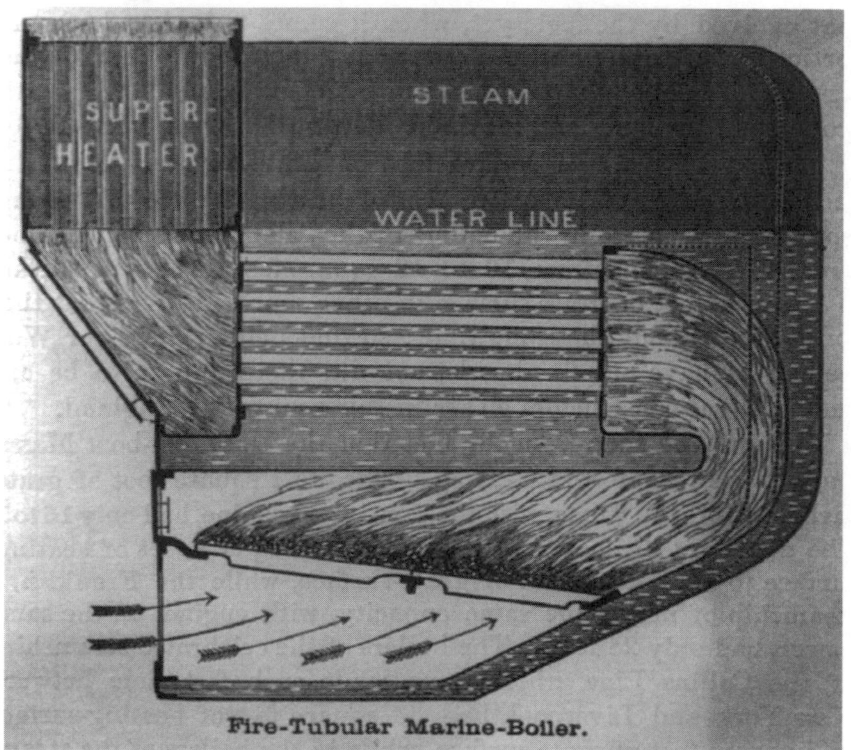

Fire-Tubular Marine-Boiler.

This simplified drawing of a firetube marine boiler (also called a Scotch boiler) is similar to those found on the Vigo. *Note the tubes through which the fire flows and which the crew had to plug to prevent leakage. In actuality there are eighty to one hundred tubes. From* Roper's Engineering Handy-Book, *Philadelphia: Edward Meeks, 1881.*

Ryan's impatient demand for more speed rang out on deck and echoed below. The *Vigo* responded. Approaching the halfway point of the Gulf, the old ship engaged in a race against itself.

> **3 PM.** We slowed down. The plugged boiler gave way again. Can't even give us half speed. More tubes went.[4]

A second boiler began failing.

---

[4] Clemons, diary.

Steam travels from the boiler to the compound engine, shown here, where it pushes the high and low pressure pistons which turn the crankshaft and the connecting propeller shaft and propeller. From Roper's Engineering Handy-Book, *Philadelphia: Edward Meeks, 1881.*

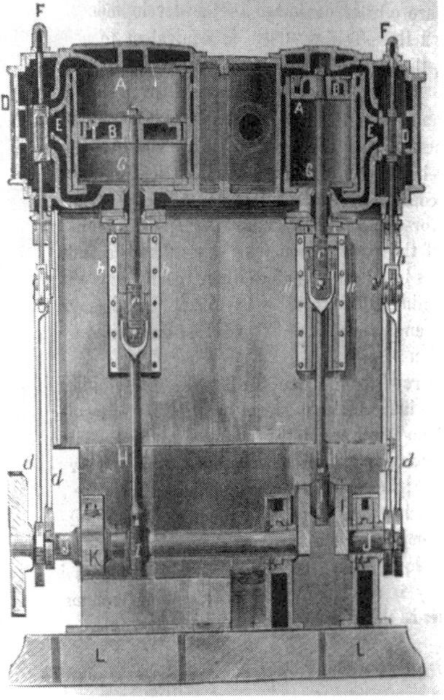

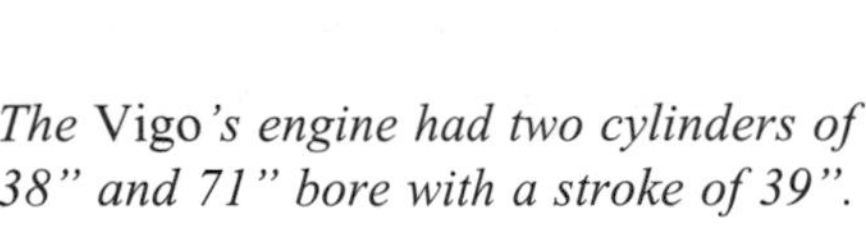

The Vigo*'s engine had two cylinders of 38" and 71" bore with a stroke of 39".*

Engine Room watches were doubled. Every available man went to work nursing the ship's boilers, tightening bolts to stop leaks and provide lifesaving power for the propeller.

> **7 PM.** Holy Jehosaphat! Three of our four boilers broke down. The engineers have used up all of our rods and plugs. Sparse wind. We're inching under sail. Looking for the closest port.
> June 20. Port Selva, Spain.
> Canvas carried us across.[5]

The *Vigo* limped into port at 5:45 AM. Captain Ryan was stomping mad. He spent the night talking to the engine room crew, one man at a time, trying to find out why three of four boilers failed in rapid succession. "How do you account for this breakdown?" he asked, over and over.

The chief mate thought a better question would have been, "How come we ran out of rods and plugs to keep the boilers going?"

Dale wondered, "Why is the ship listing to port?"

Answers would have to wait. Ryan was away in a boat headed for shore before the anchors had time to settle.

One thing seemed clear to the officers who gathered in the galley. "We're finished. Can't make it home on sails alone. There's too much propeller drag." Brennan and Baxter in unison cursed the ship's worn out boilers.

John Reynolds sat silently in the galley, looking dejected. Dale sat beside him. "What's going on? Why did your first assistant go ashore with the Skipper?" John shrugged.

Merrick sauntered in looking for coffee.

"Where's Ryan?"

"In Spain by now."

"Good. Probably trying to sell this rust heap for scrap."

"What we need is passage back to New York."

Gradually the entire crew gathered on deck waiting.

Once again Dale asked the first mate, "Why is the ship listing to port?"

"We dumped the starboard boiler makeup water tank. Captain's order."

---

[5] Clemons, diary.

"Why?"

"Didn't say." Brennan shook his head and swore under his breath while squinting through field glasses. "But in about five minutes you can ask him. He's coming back."

"What do you see?"

"A tugboat pulling a barge. He's bringing water, for God's sake and boiler tubing."

Correcting the *Vigo*'s list was easy. The barge bearing fresh water would fill the empty boiler feed tank and right the ship. Captain Ryan also brought new tubing with the intention of rebuilding the boilers.

But the crew balked. When told to pitch in and help move material aboard, several engineers joined with the black gang and stood together, arms folded. "We're not paid to build boilers."

Captain Ryan turned to his old friend, John, sitting alone halfway up the bridge ladder. The chief engineer's sullen silence was the loudest protest of all. Too much had gone wrong. The engine room crew distrusted the idea of boiler repair being good enough to withstand the 4,000 mile passage to New York. The deck hands added their cause for doubt. "If we break down in mid-Atlantic, this sail rig is too small to carry us back the way we came. We'll be lucky to buck the current."

Dale had his own concern and asked to be included when Ryan and the chief engineer went to the officers' saloon to speak their minds.

The captain began. "Why didn't you report salt in the boilers sooner?"

"The early salt tests came out negative."

The captain wasn't satisfied. "Nagle suspects sabotage. You reported no such thing."

"Will, the damage was from corrosion, plain and simple. When a pinhole develops in a condenser, that's it. Vacuum sucks in sea water fast, and as weak as our boiler tubes are, it didn't take much salt to eat through them." The rush across the Gulf had only worsened the damage.

They looked at each other in silence.

John frowned and continued. "What burns my hide is all of this could have been prevented. Why didn't YOU stand up to the owners and make them install new boiler tubes when we had the chance? Is it costing less time and money and risk here? Speaking of risk, how can you trust tubing any Spaniard would sell to Americans?"

"I don't. That's why I took Nagle ashore. He used to build boilers in Pittsburgh and knew what to look for."

"I didn't realize that." John's tone softened. "I thought he drove locomotives."

"He did both. And by the way, we brought back enough rods and plugs so we'll never have to worry about running out again."

"Just like that. Don't worry. Patch her up and keep going, top speed; `pour it on down there'. If you're wrong, just take to the boats and row away. We're stuck in that hell hole waiting for steam to spurt in our face or a torpedo to bust through the hull. Who needs the enemy? The plating on this old tub is thin enough to throw a hammer through. Want to see?"

Ryan shook his head and grinned as though enjoying the argument. Then he turned to Dale. "What's your gripe?"

"Not a gripe, but I do have a question, sir." Dale talked of hardship, Italian soldiers fighting in the Alps freezing to death for want of warm clothing. "I know we delivered a mountain of cotton. The only wool I saw was one battered box of knitting yarn consigned to some lady in Rome. It made me wonder." His voice dropped, "What good did we do?"

"Good?" Ryan exhaled like an infuriated bull about to charge. "Damn it! Listen to me, both of you. Merchant shipping is a business. The war just got in the way. This is no mercy mission. If it's doing good you're after, then go lower a boat, paint a red cross on the side, fill it with stuff YOU pay for and haul it back to Italy on your own time. Stop carping about owner profit. That's what shipping is about. Always has been and always will be. We're here to make money for the owner. Any ship that stops being profitable gets scrapped. Why do you think those solid teak hulls are growing barnacles in Gibraltar harbor? Good for nothing but coal hulks. Steam pays. Sail doesn't. If the owner doesn't make money, you're out of work. Understand?"

Dale didn't answer. He watched the captain stuff tobacco into a pipe and puff so hard and fast that the match flame rose from the bowl and singed his bushy eyebrows.

Calmed by a few puffs of tobacco, Ryan turned to John. "Unless you got a better idea, we're going to rebuild the boilers. Nagle knows what to do." His voice lowering almost to a whisper, he said, "I'm counting on your help."

"You've got a fire-tube expert. Why ask me?"

"Because the crew will follow your lead."

The meeting ended abruptly with friends still at odds, avoiding eye contact. Finally John stood up, heaved a long slow sigh, repositioned the coal-blackened leather cap on his graying hair and went out on deck.

Dale waited with the captain, watching him pace. Suddenly he stopped, snapped his fingers, and said, "Columbus!"

Calling the crew together on deck, the captain slung a foot up on the lower rail, leaned forward and spoke distinctly. "We did our best to qualify for convoy. We failed. But we're not giving up. We have to figure out a way to go it alone." He paused for emphasis, then said, "As for crossing the Atlantic bucking the current, we won't. We'll head south and pick up the tracks of the real sailing ships. We'll follow the old trade routes home — WITH or WITHOUT boilers! We'll sail home if we have to."

If desperation swung the hammers that rebuilt the *Vigo*'s boilers, the ridiculousness of the attempt raised the spirits of men who, a few hours earlier, would have stood in line for a hand in scuttling their ship. Amid the clanging and banging and shouting intermingled with high pitched swearing, bursts of raucous laughter floated up through the open engine room skylight.

Dale watched the work proceed. Through the skylight he saw the Navy gunners working alongside the black gang. Cheerfully, they replaced boiler tubes, taking orders from the first assistant engineer who knew exactly what to do.

The pounding stopped. The boilers were filled, the fires ignited but kept low at first to assure gradual warming of the new fire tubes.

Meanwhile, Capt. Ryan ordered everyone over the side for a swim. Faces blackened with sweaty grime, the men emerged from the engine room. Looking at the crew covered with engine room soot, the first mate chided, "Ain't it a shame to dirty up such clean clear water?"

"Sure is. We could just fumigate and live with the stink."

Then, laughing and joking, they lined the rails waiting for Brennan's whistle. When it blew they dove in with happy shouts, clothes and all, some head first in a graceful arc, others feet first, holding their noses. After a while the playful splashing and duckings died down; then there was a race to be first back aboard the ship. Wyman started Mutt up the ladder then swam forward in long smooth strokes and climbed the anchor chain back to his post. As their mascot shook himself dry, the seamen and sailors went to work hosing down the deck as they enjoyed the warm sun.

Someone shouted, "Where's the music?"

The deck crew answered with a pioneer song they'd adopted, "She'll be comin' round the mountain." After one verse the seamen added their own words.

She'll be rounding Point Europa
under steam
under steam.
She'll be chasing submarines
out of sight
out of sight.
She'll be running with the dolphins
day and night
day and night.

19

PALAMOS

Cork — the bobber on fishing lines, the flotation of life preservers, the stopper plugs for bottles — grows on trees. Piled high on the dock, ready for loading, were enough bales of cork bark to fill all four of *Vigo*'s holds.

"I never knew where it came from," said Dale. "Did you?"

Merrick combed his shiny black hair with one hand while he smoothed it with the other. "Will you forget about cork? They got wine cellars in caves and maybe a Spanish barmaid or two."

Dale watched the process with a mixture of envy and disgust. Still he felt obliged to pass along the captain's warning, "Loading this cargo won't take much time. You better keep your ears open. Ryan says he'll blow the whistle three longs and a short. That means we sail in ten minutes and he won't wait for anyone."

Ashore, Dale followed a parade of slow-moving ox carts piled high with cork, tracing them to their source. The path winding across the countryside ended at a grove of enormous trees. They looked like any other tree until he got close enough to see the bark. Unlike ordinary tree bark scarred by vertical cracks, the weathered surface of cork trees grows in a pattern of swirls. He watched as men wielding long sharp knives sliced around the tree trunk in two places, then stroked downward, forming a rectangle. Using the blunt butt of the knife, they peeled away a two foot by four foot plank of cork bark three inches thick without injuring the growing part of the tree. Dale found the underside smooth and soft, recognizably cork-like in color and texture.

He heard his name called.

Andy Wagner and Chris shouted across the valley "Ahoy!" and motioned urgently.

Dale trotted over to them to learn they'd discovered a wine cellar set in a dimly lit cave cut into a hillside. Inside, their eyes gradually adjusted to the darkness. It was cool and damp and the air was permeated with the tingling scent of fermenting grapes. Soft rays of daylight entered through openings in the earth above, illuminating a row of huge wooden casks that stood on their sides, each one taller than a man.

They followed the Spanish vintner into the depths of the underground tunnel, tasting as they went. At each stop, the shipmates passed around a drinking cup, noticing less and less of a difference in taste as the proprietor patiently turned spigot after spigot. Soon, the word spigot itself became a tongue twister. This made them laugh and the wine merchant began to look irritated. Hastily Dale pointed at the closest barrel and said, "That one" in Spanish, holding up fingers equal to the number of bottles they wanted.

The threesome pooled assorted coins from their pockets. Uncertain of the price, Chris offered the wine merchant what seemed a generous handful of money. On inspecting the coins, the Spaniard's hospitality suddenly vanished. He threw the coins in the dirt and spat.

"Americano!"

Without comment or consultation, the trio ran to the entrance, reached into bins and grabbed up all of the straw-covered bottles they could carry, then dashed down the hill nonstop to the ship, laughing like school boys. Halfway there they heard four sharp whistle blasts.

Still breathing hard, Dale reported to the bridge. Ryan silently accepted a gift bottle of wine with one hand and pulled the cord blowing the *Vigo*'s whistle with the other. Dale looked around. "Where's Merrick?"

"Late again. Too bad," said the captain. In one breath he shouted the order, "Bring in gangway! Cast off!"

The *Vigo* had moved away from the dock beyond swimming range when Merrick careened around a corner, waving both arms. His desperate pleas changed to an angry string of curses which only widened the smile of pleasure on Ryan's face. Not once did the shipmaster look back. Not only would Merrick be again docked two days pay, but this time he was forced to hire a motor launch to catch up with the disappearing *Vigo*. When Mr. Merrick finally climbed aboard, he was furious. He walked stiffly, digging his heals into the deck and climbed the bridge ladder in three bounds, sputtering and furious. Ryan calmly feigned innocence.

"Why," he answered calmly, "I had no idea our *indispensable* navigator was missing."

Dale shrugged, "Don't look at me."

The icy stare continued.

"That's what's wrong with you," said Dale, pointing his index finger at Merrick's nose. "You got no sense of humor."

No one was sorry to be leaving Spain. There was an obvious animosity toward Americans. When the harbor pilot prepared to leave, the look on his face was clearly unfriendly.

One of the deckhands asked the departing pilot. "What'd we ever do to you?'

There was no answer, only a cold glance. Still puzzled, they quietly watched him leave. Halfway down the Jacob's ladder the pilot's foot slipped and he fell backward into the water. He came up brandishing a fist. Ryan sounded the whistle once. Someone tossed a brick-sized chunk of cork over the rail and the deckhands shouted, "Ole'," as the pilot scrambled into a waiting dory.

That night at dinner Dale asked the captain. "What's going on? We got no quarrel with these people. Why can't they forget the Spanish American War? That was twenty years ago."

"Ah, but think what it cost. More than a few islands. Spain lost her place in the world, Dale. And we took it."

20

Crossroads

The new fire tubes held, bringing the *Vigo* safely to Gibraltar. However, the ship's doddering condition could no longer be denied. Capt. Ryan considered the failure to qualify for convoy a personal setback. Ship masters are accountable to their owners for any added expense or delay. Voyage success depends on speed — the fewer the days spent on a voyage, the greater the profit. Without the safety afforded by traveling in convoy, the captain wouldn't risk his ship and crew by following the sea lanes, a direct route home. He chose a less traveled and longer route.

He minimized the problem when he spoke to the officers over dinner. Doubts were met with ready replies, "We'll burn less fuel under sail. We're lighter. And we'll get a boost from our southerly route, heading west WITH the current and winds at our back." He scooped up a mouthful of mashed potatoes, washed them down with coffee and added, "Of course we'll have

Recoaling in Gibraltar. Coal in baskets is carried and dumped into bunkers on either side of the hatch.

to add more sail. Chips has the plans drawn. We'll re-coal then start construction."

The following day the coal barge was secured on the portside, adjacent to the forward well deck, and the re-coaling operation began. Dozens of barefoot boys and men — each balancing a basket-full of coal on his shoulder — trotted across narrow planks spanning the space between the hulls. The baskets were emptied into a chute opening above the steamer's coal bunkers, forward of the bridge. The basket count was tallied on paper by Brennan and Merrick. On deck, John and his engineers supervised the process, making sure equal amounts were distributed on both sides of the ship. Without pause the coal bearers moved back and forth, until three hundred tons were on board.

Gritty coal dust settled on every surface, calling for a general wash down of decks, masts and rigging. This was followed by a bedding change and clothes-laundering.

The work was finished but the *Vigo* could not sail. The check to pay for the coal had not cleared the bank. "Nothing we can do but wait." Capt. Ryan grumbled.

To keep the crew's minds off the dangerous run through the bottlenecked Strait of Gibraltar, he ordered the exposed decks and superstructure repainted.

"*Poor Butterfly*" slowly died on the windup Victor Phonograph machine. A voice from under the awning erected at the bow gun shouted, "Kill it, Joe. Put on the other one." Voices from the stern gun objected. "Wind it up, Joe. We're sick of the other one." Joe Youhman, a member of the forward gun crew, put on the *Vigo*'s only other record, turned the horn facing aft and raised the volume as high as it would go. A tenor sang, *"I Ain't Got Nobody"* so tiresomely, even Capt. Ryan complained,

Hearing Dale groan, Chris responded, "Cheer up Sparks." The sailor grinned and rubbed his palms together, "Leave everything to the Navy."

An American destroyer, the *USS Chester,* had recently arrived from New York. A trading session was arranged. Each ship carried worn out magazines and newspapers they were willing to exchange for anything their crews hadn't yet seen. The *Vigo*'s gunners gathered trinkets and anything they could think of that sailors fresh from the States might want to buy.

Soon the *Vigo* lookouts announced a contingent of blue jackets was rowing toward the *Vigo*. Boisterous shouting and laughter greeted the gunners from the *Chester* as they shipped oars and tied up alongside. Soon they were aboard, trading stacks of battered magazines and dog-eared books. Some Egyptian trinkets and chipped cameos from Italy found buyers. A handful of Turkish cigarettes went for half a package of American.

Then came the main object of the trade. "*Poor Butterfly*" was put over the side for "anything lively." The record given in exchange had no label, but the crew was assured it was lively. Finally, saving the best for last, the visiting sailors tossed up a mail bag addressed to the Armed Guard of the *SS Vigo*, then shoved off.

Mail sorted, letter reading came first. The merchant crew gathered around the Navy sailors, listening to news from home. Then came the newly-acquired recording. It was badly scratched, like someone had forcibly removed the needle by dragging it across the grooves. "Wind it up," said Wyman. "I'll hold the needle down."

This business card is from one of the shops Dale visited while ashore in Gibraltar.

It opened with rousing martial music but went rapidly downhill. A soldier's chorus was interrupted by a storm at sea, the roar of wind, the splash of waves, followed by a shrill siren with gunfire. Then came the unmistakable swooshing sound of a torpedo coursing through water and an explosion. The ending featured a chorus singing the hymn "Nearer My God To Thee," drowned out by a rushing, gurgling noise. Everyone recognized the recording, "Sinking of a Troop Ship."

Capt. Ryan removed the record and broke it in half over his knee. "That's not funny."

Handing Dale some money, he said, "Go on ashore and bring us back some good music."

The only "good" music Dale could find was operatic. Seeing "La Forza Del Destino," Dale didn't need to know Italian to recognize "The Force of Destiny." *Perfect for us.* But to the seller he made a face and bargained until he paid only fifty cents of the captain's dollar.

Before returning to the ship, he stopped by the Marconi Office to check for mail from home. His last stop was the Harbor Master's office with a note from Capt. Ryan. The message said that the sailing delay was due to failure of a check to clear the banks in New York or London. Ryan wanted to know, "Is there any way to expedite payment of money owed on 300 tons of coal?"

The answer was simple, "No." But hearing the name *"Vigo"* jogged the harbormaster's memory. Opening a file drawer, he shuffled through stacks of papers until he came across a cablegram from the Vigo Steamship Company. He said, "This came to me some time ago. Your captain should read it."

Dale carried the cablegram back and gave it to Captain Ryan. Dated May 23, more than a month earlier, it was addressed to the Port Authority, Gibraltar.

> According to rumor, our ship, the *SS Vigo* was sunk. Please confirm.

The inquiry was signed by an attorney for the SS Vigo Steam Ship Company.[1]

Capt. Ryan slammed his fist on the table so hard the inkwell jumped out of its hole and spilled. Ignoring the black stain rivering across one of the navigation charts, he handed the message to Dale, saying, "Read this." Neck muscles bulging, Ryan said through clenched teeth, "They want to collect the insurance money. What do you think of that?"

Dale grabbed the chance to ask, "Captain Ryan, was this ship <u>supposed</u> to sink?"

"Who knows what those greedy bastards want? They stand to profit off of our misery one way or another.[2] Well, we'll see." He nodded and said, "The *Vigo* is MY SHIP. And come hell or high water, <u>she's going home</u>."

The big, square, Viking-like sail planned for the foremast would take days to construct. Everyone knew it wouldn't come into play until the *Vigo* got beyond the Strait of Gibraltar but their efforts in sail-making kept the crew busy and their minds off the bottleneck ahead.

---

[1] US Navy, CNO, official correspondence, June 7, 1917.

[2] A freighter bound for Europe was chartered for as much a month as it could have been sold for earlier the same year. Thomas Caldecot Chubb, *If There Were No Losses*, (New York: Chubb & Son, 1957) p. 28. The insurance value of the vessel, if sunk, was proportionally high. Ed.

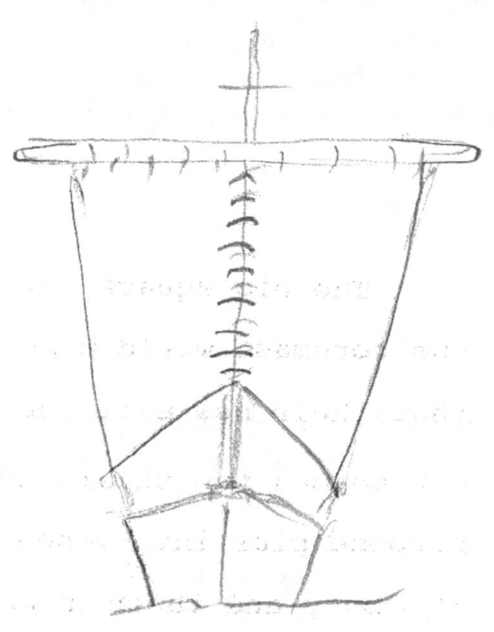

This sketch shows the two gaff sails rigged upsidedown, as viewed from forward looking aft. Credit William L. Olesen, Los Angeles Maritime Museum.

Chips, the carpenter turned sailmaker, came into his own. His plan was to create the sail using two gaff sails sewn together along their luff edges and mounted on the foremast upside down. For a yardarm two cargo booms were swung out, one on each side of the mast and secured athwartships. Block and tackle rigging completed the skeleton to which the canvas skin would be attached.

The gaff sails were hauled out of the locker and unrolled on deck. Use of their existing grommets and lacings simplified joining them together along their former mast-meeting edges or luffs. Mounting the new sail upside down would place the former foot of the sail up under yardarms, while the sail peaks, pointing downward, would serve as tacks to anchor the huge wind bag on deck, allowing it to fill with following wind.

Raising the outstretched cargo booms with a curtain of canvas attached took careful preparation and more than simple manpower to accomplish. The *Vigo*'s old cable laying fixtures, posts and winches and a donkey steam engine were overhauled and put to work. The deckhands put on a show worth watching. Barefooted, bare-chested, trousers rolled to their knees the men of the fo'c'sle showed their skill as deepwater sailors, scampering aloft, handling the running rigging as Chips gave the command,

"Haul around!" Slowly and steadily, the canvas sail went up. Below, feet planted firmly on the deck, Chips sang out orders. Like a mother hen clucking over her brood, he oversaw the handling of braces and halyards as the monstrous canvas swayed up the yard. The words were familiar to him for they came easily, but to Dale they sounded like poetry. "The upper block hooks to an eye bolt; the lower block hooks to a thimble in the strap."

The new sail was a beautiful sight, filling the crew with hope even if, at the moment, it was empty of wind and useless at anchor. Clewed up to the yard it gave the *Vigo* the appearance of imposing strength.

The only complaint was from Baxter who objected to the removal of the crow's nest to make room for the sail. "My observer's platform is gone."

Ryan had a ready answer. "Your observer can station himself on the truck[3] of the mast and really see what's going on out there."

The idle waiting continued.

July 3rd. Two months ago today, I signed on the *Vigo*.
We're stuck in Gibraltar waiting for clearance.[4]

Tony, the fireman, returned. Declared well enough for light duty, he was released from the hospital. A crowd gathered around the rail to greet him. The men on duty the day he was burned recounted what happened. Tony had chased everyone away with a shovel, then stepped in and cut out the bad boiler himself. Now there he was, still heavily bandaged, looking thin and weak but smiling as broadly as ever, glad to rejoin the crew.

Same old self; smiling, and wants to go to work. Ryan says he will serve as an oiler hereafter on the engines and stand half watches

---

[3] The truck is the highest point on the mast.

[4] Dale Clemons, diary.

> awhile. We gave him as good a reception as anybody who ever came aboard . . . We lined the rails, gave him three cheers and presented him with a silk shirt, silk scarf and a pipe.[5]

Eventually Tony worked his way to where Dale was standing and asked about Italy. Dale conveyed the family message, "We're safer staying on our farm."

Tony exclaimed something in Italian, then said, "It's good they agree." He'd already decided not to go home. "Here is my place. Right here at sea," he gestured with both hands forming a cornucopia, "bringing to Italy things they need."

Dale hesitated for an instant, then nodded. "Glad you're back, Tony. I know now what you meant. Your country, your family and Genoa are all `superb.' My visit was well worth the voyage."

Wednesday, The Fourth of July, 1917. Clearance!!![6]

The fires were started. Slow warming of the boiler tubes gave the crew time to celebrate the Fourth of July. It started with good news brought by the ship's agent. The captain called out through a megaphone, "General Pershing landed in France. And right now, 15,000 American soldiers are parading through Paris.[7] In other cities of Europe the people are dancing in the streets. Even in London they're celebrating our Independence Day."

A cheer went up. Every flag on board was run up until the ship was festooned with color from stem to stern. Bells rang out. Other ships caught the spirit of '76 and chimed in. The *Vigo*'s crew sat down together on deck and feasted on a special dinner.

---

5 Dale Clemons, "Armed Merchantman," 1940.

6 Clemons, diary.

7 S.L.A Marshall, *The American Heritage History of World War I,* (New York: Dell Publishing Corp., 1964) p. 264.

> Had beets, corn, fried chicken (Spanish, with drumsticks as big as turkeys'), squash, prunes (known as Ward Line cherries to seamen), cake mit raisins, coffee, ice cream, and subsequently, a stomach ache. We brought in our chef, complimented him . . . so tonight we're full of Spanish chicken and beets.[8]

Dusk came. The party was over. Laughter and joking gave way to wondering. "When do we sail?" The crew saw other cargo ships leaving followed by the *USS Chester*.

"What are we waiting for?"

"Can't be darkness."

The sun had set. A full moon was on the rise. The boilers were ready, and still Captain Ryan waited. Finally at 9:10 PM the *Vigo* got underway. Heading south at first, she then turned, approaching the Strait of Gibraltar.

As always, the *Vigo* was blacked out. Dale turned off the radio cabin light and opened the window and shutters. He was struck by the glow of a full moon. The hills of the African Coast shone brightly. The water sparkled and danced. Waves cast shadows. *If a fish jumps we'll see it. A submarine is sure to see the Vigo*. Dale thought, then closed the shutters. *We should have followed the others. Why didn't Ryan just fall in behind?*

From his own plotted times and locations of enemy action it was no secret that dawn and dusk were the most dangerous times of day. *So he let dusk pass. Fine.* As for location, U-boats seemed to hang around prominent points of land. Lighthouses loomed as favored lairs.[9] Here a U-boat could lay in wait for merchant ships to pass, knowing they needed the landmark for accurate navigation. Cape Spartel, a cliff projection at the western end of the Strait, was a prime trap and the one spot they all dreaded passing.

---

[8] Clemons.

[9] RADM Gordon Campbell, *My Mystery Ships*. London: Hodder & Stoughton, Ltd., 1928.

There's no way around. Dale wound his watch. After some hasty calculations, he estimated the time remaining. *At this speed, we should be out of range by 3 AM.*

Midnight came and went. The sandwich and coffee were pushed aside untouched. With his eyes closed Dale sat listening intently to the radio, half holding his breath. Slowly scanning the frequencies he heard the pop and crackle of static mixed with the solid, reassuring sound of Morse code as ships in the far Atlantic exchanged routine information. Minutes became hours. The clanking rhythmic engine noise seemed to grow louder and louder. Unwelcome thoughts rippled through his mind. He stood up and threw open the shutter. Then he noticed. "It's getting darker," he said aloud. "The moon must have slipped behind a cloud." He looked up through the skylight. There were no clouds. Nevertheless, the moonlight continued fading. Opening the door, he went out on deck to see the moon disappearing. Capt. Ryan had timed the *Vigo*'s departure to coincide perfectly with a total eclipse of the moon.[10] Gloved in blessed darkness, the *SS Vigo* slipped by Cape Spartel unseen and unharmed.

The next day he copied a British destroyer transmitting to Gibraltar and learned just how fortunate they were. In his diary he wrote:

> **July 5.** Sub active off Spartel last night.[11]

[10] 2 AM GMT, July 5th, 1917. Duration 31 minutes. *Lloyd's Callendar 1917*, (London: Lloyd's, Royal Exchange, 1917) p. 3.

[11] Clemons, diary.

21

Save Our Ship

The *Vigo* had escaped the bottleneck. Germany's proclaimed "war zone" lay somewhere safely behind. The mood of the men settled into a peaceful routine. Those off duty slept. For those awake the only question was, "How many days before we get to New York?" No one knew the exact answer but two weeks now seemed a likely estimate. The boilers held. The sails helped, and soon they'd benefit from a change of course to a more southerly route, gaining added thrust from the trade winds. Bypassing the Azores was welcome news to the crew — the prospect of hitchhiking the Equatorial current homeward, then gliding up the eastern seaboard in the Gulf Stream seemed certain to stretch the coal supply, perhaps even enough to carry the *Vigo* all the way to New York.

> Guess Mutt still carries his charm. He is very proper and correct now; clean and glistening in his coat of black and white. Scratches at doors politely and proceeds down to his sand box at the base of

> the foremast, where he investigates diligently his cairn for whatever it is that a doggie checks on during his routine of life. When the gong sounds for dinner he files in with us, sits upon his canvas padded bench studying avidly the faces of the men, watching all the goings-on, probably sizing up the prospect of a big juicy bone being set aside for him, smart and shining in his polished, brass studded harness. On the bridge he paces alongside the officer, and when the latter levels his glasses to study some object on the water far off, Mutt rears up, places his paws on the railing to look also, but with his nose, which twitches and bobs for any telltale scent of interest.[1]

The *Vigo* was on course, moving along well south of the Azores in fine weather when Dale began feeling uneasy.

> **July 8.** Arlington faint. Fades in and out. Too quiet!!![2]

During the night a strange premonition crept in. Dale sat up in bed, perspiring, sensing something wrong. Indeed, it was. The next morning there was a discouraging announcement.

> **July 9. Monday.** Engineers say coal won't last. May have to stop at the Azores.[3]

Ryan was angry. "What are you talking about? We got plenty of coal, three hundred tons, ordered, paid for and delivered in Gibraltar."

"We were cheated," said John. "This stuff burns too fast or not at all. We've got pieces of shale mixed in with it."

"Rocks? Damnation!" Capt. Ryan thought a moment. "All right. We'll burn cork, even woodwork if we have to. But we are NOT changing course."

The situation grew worse. The ship began losing speed. Dale guessed from experience what that meant. The only bank

---

1 Dale Clemons, "Armed Merchantman," 1940.

2 Dale Clemons, diary.

3 Clemons, diary.

of fire tubes which the crew hadn't replaced was beginning to leak and needed plugging.

Dale continued his work, listening for SOS calls. His mind needed distraction. He doodled, sketching out an idea for a submarine engine detecting microphone, suspended from a kite, flown behind the ship. Yet his premonition of something seriously wrong persisted.

July 10. Tuesday. Trouble.[4]

During the night, the *Vigo*'s engines stopped dead. Dale awoke with a start. Then he heard someone on deck shout, "A leak in the engine room."

He followed Ryan down the metal ladder into the engine room. They stood on a grating looking down at water spouting under force from a massive intake pipe.

"Jes-sus" Capt. Ryan exclaimed, "That's sea water."

Between the ship's hull and the main circulator pumps was a sixteen-inch cast bronze inlet manifold. When they increased speed after repairing the blown boiler tubes, the bronze manifold developed a two-foot crack, spewing salt water in a torrent. Dale remembered when they were eastbound, the engineers had the floorplates up watching that same manifold.

John Reynolds explained the situation. "We need that water going to the circulating pumps. They pump sea water to the condenser where it acts as a coolant. Can't make steam without it. Even if we manage to stay afloat, we can't steam ahead without our circulator pumps operating. And right now that leak is so big they have nothing to pump."

The engineers managed to open an alternate sea-cock, then, working against the force of the incoming water, shut down the main intake valve. This stemmed the flow of water enough for them to try re-enforcing the manifold. John and his assistants worked frantically all night forging bands and clamps to fasten around the break.

---

[4] Dale Clemons, diary.

For hours the *Vigo* moved ahead under sail only, bleeding from an internal wound she could not stop.

Dale took to writing across his drawing paper, recording events in bold strokes. "The main sea valve and adjacent inlet flange has also split and is working loose from the hull.

"4 PM. Steering engine broke down. We are now steering by hand, using auxiliary wheel on deck above the rudder.

"9:20 PM. The big sea valve let go. Water's coming in fast.

"Cork or no cork we don't like it. The hull could collapse.

"Midnight. We turned back. Trying to make Azores."

All nonessential engines were shut off to give all of the steam power the boilers could muster to the ship's main engine. Jury-rigged pumps were set up in the engine room, hand-operated by teams of volunteers from the deck crew.

> July 12. Thursday. Still underway, very slow, possibly 3 knots. Water gathering below. Auxiliary pumps needed to keep the incoming cold water away from our boilers.
> Our refrigeration quit. Food is starting to rot.[5]

Failure spread like tumbling dominoes. Would the ship's generator be next? Worried about the loss of electrical power, Dale made sure his battery-operated emergency set was in good working condition. Then he listened for the upcoming time signal to be sure of the *Vigo*'s exact position in mid-Atlantic should the worst happen.

Friday the 13th. 1:05 AM.[6]

Captain Ryan opened the door looking pale and exhausted. "All right, Sparks. Tell the world. We're a hundred miles from Port Fayal, making three knots, sinking. Need help fast."

---

[5] Clemons.

[6] Clemons, diary.

The lifeboats were already swung out. Most of the crew was in life preservers. Extra hands were below helping in the engine room. Dale threw the antenna switch down to engage the transmitter. Tuned to the 600 meter band he struck the telegraph key and sent a series of electric signals screaming into the night.

"··· S --- O ··· S [3 times]

"*Vigo* need tow.

"29° 2'W, 36° N."

Then he threw the switch up and listened.

The air was silent.

In the deathly stillness, he could hear his pulse pounding. An eternity passed as he wondered, "Should I try again or wait?" Just then an answer came through his earphones.

"*Vigo*, *Empress of Australia* answering. Coming to your assistance f.a.c. [fast as can] Est. 6 or 7 hours. Hang on, old man."

His hand was poised to answer when another wireless cut in:

"*Vigo*. Repair tug *Emanuel* on the way from Fayal. Repeat your location."

Was it really a repair tug or an enemy trick?

The sound of the tugboat's Marconi built transmitter was familiar and friendly. He answered, repeating their position. Transmitting felt so good, he wanted to keep the conversation going, but remembering the submarine threat, he sent the *Vigo*'s call letters and signed off.

"There's a tug on the way," he reported to Capt. Ryan. Smiling, the captain thumped the bulkhead with his fist, "Good work." Glancing at his watch he said, "Six hours, eh? Pass the word. Help is coming."

The wirelessman made the rounds of the ship then returned to his post. He saw fear in the eyes of many brave young men and wished it would all go away, just vanish like a bad dream.

The terrible uncertainty made waiting alone in the radio cabin difficult, but he knew it was worse for the men below, sentenced to a windowless prison.

He found excuses to go on deck hourly, to inquire about the ship's speed, present location and, once, to peer into the open engine room skylight. It was reassuring to see the pumps controlling the water level, the ship's furnaces still glowing.

7:00 Tow ship sighted.[7]

Soon, workers boarded the *Vigo*, greeted with handshakes and welcome smiles. Shipyard engineers went below to assess damages while the tug crew hooked the towing bridle to the *Vigo*'s massive anchor chains.

Finally, the towing master gave maneuvering instructions to Captain Ryan and the deck officers, then departed. The slack was taken out of the towing lines by a winch on the tug and a green flare announced, "ready to tow." The *Vigo* answered in kind and her forward motion increased, leveling off at five and a half knots.

7:40 AM. 74 miles to go.
The *Empress of Australia* sent greetings.[8]

The danger wasn't over. At any moment the added stress of towing might cause the old iron hull to collapse. Then incoming water would kill the ship's fires, causing the boilers to explode. That would finish the ship too fast for even the wireless to be of use.

Halfway through the night, John appeared on deck carrying a chair. He sat down on the quarter deck near a lifeboat, arms folded.

Dale scribbled out his thoughts,

> John has no desire to be next! So there he sits, not a quitter, a good man, an engineer who's given his all to a 2,500 ton freighter of no real value to anyone except miserly owners whose greed has

---

[7] Clemons, diary.
[8] Clemons, diary.

> no code in this wirelessman's book of sinking causes. Let Brennan object. Let Baxter fuss, more worried about bad examples than the rotten shape we're in. Ryan, bless him, stood up for John. Just now he said, "Let him be!"[9]

The *Vigo* rounded Ribeirinha Point, Fayal, limping and listing but still moving ahead under her own steam. At 8:30 PM the anchor was dropped.

Preparations had already begun. The crew shifted ballast and movable furniture, creating an intentional list of thirty degrees. Then the ship was towed up the channel at Fayal into shallows so that she could be beached, tilted to one side. Shoreside carpenters carved a sixteen inch disk-shaped plug from a block of teakwood. Then they plugged the sea gate inlet so the faulty bronze casting could be removed for repair. Within hours it was lifted out of the engine room with heavy-duty cranes and set on a waiting rail cart. Then it was rolled into a nearby machine shop.

The work proceeded as though such things were routine. To Dale it was all new. Before going ashore, he climbed inside the engine room, working his way up the inclined cold metal flooring for a close look at the site of the damage. The wooden plug leaked driblets of water, a tiny reminder that it was holding back an ocean. He was never more glad to set foot on land.

> Fayal. Crazy. We didn't expect to return. Then thought we couldn't make it back. But we did and we found mail waiting.[10]

Ashore, Dale sat down on a stone wall and again read the disturbing letter from Athie.

His father had died in debt. Suddenly, he understood. *That's why Papa wanted me to stay home. He hoped I'd take over the store and work off the debt. Mama is hoping the same thing.* He stopped reading and sent a cablegram to his mother.

---

[9] Clemons, diary.

[10] Clemons, diary.

DO NOT DELAY. DO WHAT IS BEST FOR YOU.

That was easily said. But the news could not be dismissed with a cablegram. Nor could he disown the sense of responsibility felt for his parents. He carefully reread what his sister had written.

> You remember, Dale, how Papa always used to say to people, "pay when you can." Well people never did pay him the amount he owed on those goods. Guy and I agree Mama should sell the store. She has an offer of $60,000 which is more than enough to cover his debts. But Mama won't do anything. She says "Dale is my only flesh and blood son. I have to know his wishes.[11]

He hopped off the wall and walked further inland. Along the way he saw a Portuguese farmer walking behind some cows, keeping them in line with the light touch of a long bent stick with a bit of string dangling from the tip ready to tickle the leader's nose.

Reminded of home, his daily chore of walking milk cows to pasture, Dale suddenly felt frantic. *Papa didn't tell ME he was in trouble.*

He found his way to Miguel's farm and stopped to deliver the promised shoes from Italy. The barefooted farmer looked pleased and spoke words of gratitude but carried the shoes as he walked beside Dale down the rocky path leading to the village.

Dale entered a church, drawn there by the smell of candles, remembering Italy, the comfort of being among the faithful. He wasn't Catholic, although he carried a St. Christopher's medal given him by Angelina. He sank to his knees. "Everything is coming apart. I don't know what to do, Lord. Please show me the way."

---

[11] Athie Clemons to B.J. Clemons, 1974.

22

A Stern Chase

Stubbornness, ingenuity and hard work put the ailing *Vigo* back on her feet within a week. The repaired bronze manifold was stronger than ever. The boiler tubes and steering gear were made good. And as insurance against additional food loss, crates of live chickens were purchased and secured on the cargo deck aft of the bridge. Only one problem remained. The bunkers were filled with coal but the quality was poor. "It's better than nothing," John explained, "There's a shortage of coal everywhere."

The captain nodded, "Keep a watch on it. We'll do what we have to."

The crew had ample time to blow off steam ashore and most of them were on board well before sailing time on the evening of July 21. As the *Vigo* got under way, Dale leaned on the rail enjoying the gentle evening air. He watched the sun sink below the horizon, the sea glistening like silver. In the distance,

Pico, a beautiful volcanic island, glowed brilliant pink, holding the sun's rays after the lower nearby islands took on the dark blue cloak of dusk.

At midnight, Dale copied the press with greater than usual interest, having been out of touch during the week the ship was repaired.

> Russian soldiers are in retreat, laying down their guns going home to join the revolt.
>
> German Chancellor Bethman-Holweig has resigned.[1]

Then came the day's sinking reports. "U-boat active west of Horta." He noted the latitude and longitude and phoned the captain. "Two merchant ships were sunk west of Horta. Isn't that where we're headed?"

"No. We're sticking with the original plan. Head south, pick up the current and trade winds. That way we can use the sail and burn less coal."

Time passed slowly. Favorite subjects, shore leave and women, gave way to ship talk.

Chips lit a clay pipe, "Some ships last and last and never break down."

Dale thought of the *SS Colusa*, the most reliable ship he'd ever been on.

Chips continued, "And some ships are bad tempered, cranky from the day they're launched. They suffer mishap after mishap and sink early. The battleship *Maine* was like that — plagued from the day her keel was laid.[2] Then there's the touchy ship, the kind that only responds well to one captain and will do anything for him. That's what I think we got here. Ryan really is Master of the *Vigo*."

---

[1] Francis A. March, *History of the World War,* (Philadelphia: The United Publishers of the US and Canada, 1919) pp 732-33.

[2] John Edward Weems, *The Fate of the Maine*, New York: Henry Holt & Co., 1958.

"Tell us about the *Great Eastern*. Wasn't she haunted?" Dale knew the answer but enjoyed listening to Chips recount the story of the troubled trailblazer. The enormous iron-hulled steamer, a paddlewheeler, was built to carry passengers across the Atlantic. On her maiden voyage people heard hammering on the hull, especially at night. Years later, when she was finally broken up for scrap, they found the skeleton of a workman who disappeared during construction."[3]

"There, you see?" said Granle, the third assistant engineer. "Everything has an explanation. You just need to know the facts."

"On land, maybe so. Out here things can happen that don't make sense. Stay long enough and the sea will make you a believer." Chips pointed an index finger to the heavens.

Granle studied the old weather-worn face for a moment, then asked, "What was your worst experience?"

Chips chuckled, "Hasn't happened yet. I thought I was finished, once, though." He shook his head, puffing on his pipe. When the ashes began to glow, his face lit up and the years disappeared, "Back then, every one of us was a sailmaker. And I was learning sail-handling from the best. I wanted to do it all. Got careless. I was only fourteen at the time. Bound for China, we rounded the Horn. Guess I fancied myself an old salt by then and the captain decided to teach me a lesson. I was ordered out on the bowsprit to help stow the jib and fore stays'ls which were down and dragging in heavy head seas. I was standing on the chains, doin' my part, when suddenly the ship yawed. I came up rolling in her wake. Mates saw me go. They heaved a line and some wood over the side but by the time I got a-holt of it, the wind had carried my ship away."

"So what happened?"

"I started praying. Tried swimming but that was useless. Waves were so high I couldn't see my ship. But I hung on,

---

[3] James Dugan, *The Great Iron Ship*, (New York: Harper & Brothers, 1953) p. 267.

praying for dear life. Rising on a crest, I saw sails and a man waving his arms. Might have been good-bye except the man was my brother, the ship's mate. The captain gave the order to turn back and look for me. Next thing I knew I was being rolled over a barrel. I woke up in warm blankets, being spoon fed hot coffee by the skipper himself. When he knew I could hear he gave me the words we all live by. 'One hand for the ship — the other for yourself.'"

> **Tuesday, July 24.** Weather great. Making best speed of the voyage. 10 knots!
> **Wednesday, July 25.** Ho hum.[4]

A bored crew began looking for things to do to pass the time. Some whittled ship models, others joined together to build a castle of cork like the turreted bastions seen along the coast of Spain.

Forward on the fo'c'sle, Sanderson, a sailor from Wyman's crew had built himself a cart out of an empty ammunition box. Fastened with sled-like runners on the bottom, it slid back and forth across the deck as the ship rolled.

> . . . guided by a stick dragged astern. In rough weather when he is off watch, he climbs in the box and slides from one side of the ship to the other as she rolls, which she does accommodatingly enough these days. On one of these high speed round trip excursions from hence to thence his carriage struck one of the deck plates just at the peak of the roll. The box stopped abruptly, Sanderson went right on through the broken-out end, acquiring a liberal assortment of splinters in diverse tender parts of his anatomy and several deep cuts from the nails in the side boards, which scraped the hide loose as he went through in transit from starboard to port. I thought it proper to douse him liberally with iodine . . .[5]

---

4 Dale Clemons, diary.
5 Dale Clemons, "Armed Merchantman," 1940.

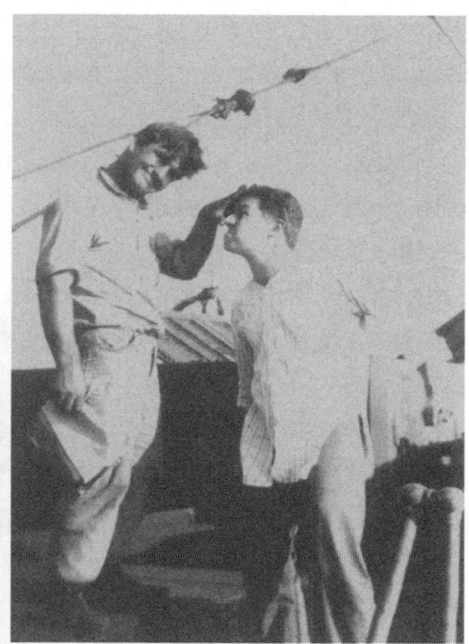

Clowning for the camera. Above Chris (left) and Dale in a carefree moment. Left, Dale feigns seasickness.

Nearby, Wyman was engaged in hypnotizing a chicken by stroking its beak along a chalk-line drawn on the deck, while a buddy kept Mutt, the barking mascot, under wraps.

Dale was just returning to the radio cabin when he heard the lookout stationed at the truck of the foremast sing out, "Smoke on the horizon."

After a few minutes the lookout reported, "Steamer, one point abaft the starboard beam, turning toward us."

On the bridge, Dale asked Baxter, "What is it?"

"Funny lookin' steamer. Low profile. British flag."

Dale ran to the radio room and put on the earphones. He heard the distinctive sound of a Telefunken transmitting close by and reported to the bridge, "I hear a German set transmitting near at hand and it's getting louder!"

"SUBMARINE!" shouted Baxter. At the same instant the British flag came down; up went the black, red and white double eagle of Germany. The *Vigo*'s alarm clanged on deck and Ryan worked the engine room telegraph lever back and forth, signaling an emergency, before signalling "Full Speed Ahead." He hollered into the speaking tube, "Sub on the surface. Give all you got."

A shell screamed through the air and landed off the starboard side with a loud explosion. Ryan ordered the helm hard over to port to present the narrowest possible target.

Baxter shouted, "You're moving the bow gun out of position."

"A stern chase is a long chase and I aim to outlast him."

Feeling the *Vigo*'s stern gun return the fire, Dale climbed to the roof of the radio cabin, heart pounding. He knew they always try to hit the radio cabin first. Looking forward, he saw the big Viking sail on the foremast belly out full as the ship rose up on her haunches, gathering power. It could never add enough speed to win the race with a submarine on the surface, but in light trim, the extra canvas gave the old freighter a fighting chance.

Dale returned to his post. He heard the incoming scream and explosion of shells nearby and the jolt of the *Vigo*'s stern gun responding.

He phoned the bridge. "Are we gaining?"

They weren't sure. The shelling continued. Dale kept his right hand on the telegraph key, ducking with each explosion. On it went, a dead heat race. He heard excited voices on the bridge through his telephone receiver.

"Why no torpedoes?" asked the captain.

Baxter answered, "I think they want us to surrender."

Ryan rang the radio room, "Keep your ears open, Dale. This submarine is acting like a surface raider. He may be trying to catch up and capture our supplies."

"For what it's worth, they stopped transmitting."

The firing continued. The armed merchantman and the submarine engaged in a running gun battle that lasted twenty-five minutes. Then suddenly, the firing stopped.

"Maybe she's out of ammunition or low on fuel or broke down." Whatever the explanation, the impossible had happened. The captain announced, "All clear."

Dale emerged from the radio room to see for himself. The U-boat had turned away and was now a black smudge fading on the horizon.

"Are you sure that was a U-boat?" asked Brennan, "What about the smoke?"

"They may have been trying to mislead us," replied the captain. "Raiders have been known to do that."

"No." Baxter shook his head, "She was a sub, all right. I saw a conning tower and smoke coming from an exhaust pipe."

After dinner that evening, everyone off watch gathered on deck below the bridge. Heads bowed, they gave thanks.

John opened his Bible and once again read aloud his favorite verses from Psalm 107:

"1. Oh Give thanks unto the Lord, for He is good; for His mercy endureth for ever.

2. Let the redeemed of the Lord say so whom He hath redeemed from the hand of the enemy.

4. They wandered in the wilderness in a solitary way; they found no city to dwell in.

5. Hungry and thirsty, their soul fainted in them.

13. Then they cried unto the Lord in their trouble; and He saved them out of their distresses.

14. He brought them out of darkness and the shadow of death, and brake their bands in sunder.

23. They that go down to the sea in ships, that do business in great waters.

24. These see the works of the Lord, and His wonders of the deep.

23

Last Leg — Last Straw

Baxter was concerned. During the battle, it was very clear how easily an incoming shell could sideline enough men to put a gun out of action.

The captain agreed and sent out the order, "Starting now, I want every man-jack crewman and officer on the list to take part. Break'em loose. The best will be selected as the *Vigo*'s auxiliary gun crew."

Exercises commenced immediately and finally Baxter posted a list of the chosen. It included John, the chief engineer, and Carr, the cook.

The passage from Gibraltar to New York, normally two weeks, took the *Vigo* more than a month. In that time the ship backtracked to the Azores and was forced to stop at Bermuda to take on more coal. She had burned too much in her high speed escape from the surface raider.

While in the Azores, Merrick gave away the ship's only phonograph record to get a room reserved just for him in the local bordello. He recommended a hotel to Dale who paid good money to rent a room infested with bed bugs. He spent the night curled up on a marble-topped table, trying to avoid the creatures but was soon met with an army of biters hungry enough to crawl up there after him.

Back underway, there were no more problems and in the Gulf Stream the ship's speed increased from 8 to 9-and-three-quarters and sometimes even 10-and-a-quarter knots. The saving grace was her huge Viking-like air scoop sail on the foremast which had pulled her out of range of incoming shells.

August 8. 185 miles to go.[1]

The last chicken had been eaten. They were down to a diet of beans and hardtack with a concoction of dried apples, raisins and molasses for dessert. Once again, the crew had to bathe in sea water using a special soap that was gritty enough to holystone the deck. But talk was not of food, nor of the war, only of home.

Chris and Dale talked about how much there was to see and do in New York, but Chris shook his head. "No shore leave for us. We're a month late. Soon as we drop anchor it's back to the Brooklyn Navy Yard."

The subject changed to the most recent episode of food thievery. Four hams were missing. Chris learned that Merrick made a deal with Carr for a little "shore trade."

"Trade for what?"

"To get laid. What else is worth four hams?"

"So he not only traded our only record for a private room, the bastard stole our food to get himself laid?" asked Dale.

"Yep. That's the way I heard it."

---

[1] Dale Clemons, diary.

"And I spent the worst night of my life ashore because he recommended a hotel full of bedbugs."

"That's why you should sleep in a hammock."

At that point the door opened and in walked the opportunity for sweet revenge.

Marshall looked unsettled, his complexion was pasty. "I must have dyspepsia or something. Must be the food. I keep tasting onions."

"Show me your tongue," said Dale, taking out a tongue depressor.

The navigator complied.

"WOW. Look at that, Chris!"

"Whaaa?"

"He is sick," Chris agreed.

Dale and Chris thumbed through the big medical book that came with the ship's medicine chest. Sorting through bottles of elixir and assorted pills, they selected Croton Oil, a powerful laxative, as the best remedy .

"We're in luck," said Dale. "I have that. A sure cure for what ails you." He found the bottle and poured a generous overdose into a glass then filled it with water. He handed the glass to Marshall saying, "Drink up."

Together they watched the navigator swallow, his Adam's apple bobbing slowly. Croton Oil ran down his chin as he finished the overdose and burped.

Dale said, "Keep the glass, or better yet, throw it overboard on your way out."

Marshall-the-Magnificent was due on watch that evening. He didn't make it. All his time on watch was spent in the head. Dale fell asleep that night laughing to the music of the navigator's pounding feet.

Around noon the next day, Marshall beat on Dale's door, angrily demanding to "see the book."

Dale smiled, "Sorry, you're too late, Mister Marshall. That's been sealed with all the medicine in the captain's locker. Customs regulation, you know."

August 9th, 1917. 4 PM. Hours away.[2]

Approaching New York, the big canvas sail was taken down. The cargo booms were lowered and put in readiness for their ordinary work. Then came the eagerly-awaited cry, "LAND HO!"

The excited call brought everyone to the railing. Suddenly a shell screamed out from the battery protecting the Jersey coast and roared over their heads. Another followed. The ship slowed. The lookout reported a small, fast Coast Guard cutter dashing out from shore, signalling an identity challenge by flag and blinking light, "What ship."

The captain said to Brennan, "Run up our numbers." The *Vigo*'s code flags were raised on the signal halyard.

The Coast Guard cutter approached warily, the crew manning their guns. A young officer boarded. "We have no record of the 'SF 11.'"

"I know that," said Capt. Ryan. He handed across proof of the freighter's American identity.

The Lieutenant handed it back. "No," he said, "the *SS Vigo* was listed as missing weeks ago."

Meanwhile, on the main deck, the *Vigo*'s sea-weary sailors, hoping for news of home, were greeted with scorn. "What'd ya do to get stuck on this old rust bucket?" And about the SF 11 marking, "What do you think you're pretending to be?"

Baxter stepped forward. There was no mistaking his United States Navy uniform. "No one's pretendin'. THIS is an armed merchantman back from the war zone."

Finally convinced, the Coast Guard gave permission to proceed.

A pilot came aboard to guide her around Sandy Hook. The Armed Guard sailors changed into crisp white summer uniforms. Hats cocked low over their foreheads, they stood, feet wide apart, arms behind their backs, manning the rails on bow

---

2 Clemons, diary.

and stern, as she steamed through the narrows in sight of the Brooklyn Navy Yard.

Spontaneously, the crew of the *Vigo* added a final verse to their chantey, and sang out,

"Oh! She's coming around the mountain
on her own
ON HER OWN!"

24

LETTING GO

We are off Stapleton for the night. Now dark, but can enjoy the millions of twinkling lights ashore, the soft night sky and bask in the freedom symbolized by the Statue of Liberty . . . All this, our own United States, means so much to us all who have been away for awhile, particularly in foreign lands full of glamor and foppery, where our idea of life cannot seem to find root, and cannot be appreciated. We always feel this way on returning from long voyages. And now our last voyage is over. Our part seems so very, very small and insignificant, but we have the comfort of knowing that quite a healthy sized cargo was left in a place where it is vitally needed by many people abroad. I suppose these are the days when wars are won by millions of people and machines each having merely a number. All soldiers and sailors seem to feel that way; that their individual parts are so useless and much less than they would like to do individually.[1]

---

[1] Dale Clemons, "Armed Merchantman," 1940.

Chris and Dale sat together in silence on the ladder leading to the bridge, high enough for a good view of their surroundings. Their paths would soon separate. Dale's final voyage was over; Chris belonged to the US Navy. Yet a brother-like bond had been forged.

Dale wanted to thank Chris for his friendship but found himself at a loss for words. "Here, it's yours," he said, handing Chris his pocket telescope. "Keep an eye on the sea for me."

"How you doing . . . about . . . your father?"

"Still wish I'd been there."

"Why is that?"

"So I could talk to him. We argued. That's no way to part company. I wish I could stop feeling bad about leaving."

"You think staying home would have made a difference? Seems to me, you had to be out here to see for yourself what counts."

"He was in trouble and didn't tell me."

Chris nodded, "Hey, let's go find that screwdriver I borrowed."

They walked aft to Chris's sea chest near the stern gun. While he searched, Dale announced, "I've decided one thing. I want to teach radio. Watching you teach your crew was an inspiration."

Chris found the screwdriver, handed it to Dale and said, "Let me see your watch fob."

"Why?"

Dale removed the medallion from its chain. Chris held it up to the light, then asked "All right if I engrave this?"

"No. My father gave that to me. It's gold."

Chris looked at it closely. "Dale, this is not gold. It's shiny bronze, and that's better. Bronze is tougher than gold. I'll be right back," Chris walked away with the medallion.

Left alone on deck, Dale remembered receiving that precious parting gift from Waldo, a watch fob on a chain of gold. He visualized their parting and suddenly understood. "PAPA!"

he said aloud. "Now I understand. You didn't tell me because you knew I would stay."

Chris returned and showed Dale the engraving on the bronze medallion: "Italy SS VIGO Marconi Co. 1917"

Dale took the medallion and ran his finger over the engraving, "I just realized silence can be a message. My father did approve."

"Glad you figured that out."

"Thanks, Chris." They parted with a handshake and a promise to meet again and some day go sailing on Lake Michigan.

The next morning, August 10, before being cleared by port authorities, a priest came aboard to bless the ship. Navy officers in gold braided uniforms walked around the deck, interested in the *Vigo*'s disguise. This time there were no disparaging remarks about the ship or its civilian crew. The mock guns were impressive and Baxter, acting as guide, proudly displayed them.

Front and back of Dale's watch fob with Chris' inscription, above.

The bell clanged, summoning the crew to line up on deck for health inspection. An officer from the Public Health Service looked at tongues and eyes, and asked if any illness had occurred during the voyage. Benzol poisoning didn't count. He was there to stop any communicable disease such as cholera from being carried ashore. Examination complete, the *Vigo* was given "a clean bill of health."

Captain Ryan handed out pay envelopes to his officers and crew, asking Dale to wait until last. The envelopes contained a war bonus — extra money for hazardous duty — and the men happily counted their money, shook hands and left. Then the captain walked with Dale to the radio cabin before giving him his envelope. Inside was $120, far less than he expected. "Where's my bonus? I'm supposed to get a hundred percent war bonus like the rest of the crew."

Ryan shook his head, "Read the note." The message from the ship's owner said, "This man works for the Marconi Company. No bonus required."

"Can they get away with this?" asked Dale.

"They say it's Marconi Company policy."

Dale's shock turned to anger. Left alone, he fumed. Standing at the wash stand, Dale dashed cold water on his face and confronted himself in the mirror. Two wirelessmen had walked away from this job, refusing to work alone. *Well, I did the job, damn it!*

He felt cheated. There was a principle involved.

Dale put on his uniform, shined his shoes, polished the brim of his officer's cap, settled it low on his brow, and went to find the captain.

He found Capt. Ryan signing papers in the chart room. He waited for him to look up, then began, "Sir, I need to talk about my bonus."

"It's out of my hands, Dale. Talk to Marconi."

Dale waited for a moment, then said. "Capt. Ryan, do you think extra money is why I volunteered? I never heard of a bonus until you mentioned it. What I don't like is being promised one thing, then dealt another."

Ryan looked up, brow low, jaw set. He pointed at Dale and said in a low voice, "Don't press me. I'm in no mood to give a rat's ass what they did to you. They're threatening to bleed me for expenses they owe if I refuse to go out again on this coffin ship."

Brennan opened the door. "Owners are in your cabin, asking . . ."

"On my way!" Ryan gathered up some documents and stormed off the bridge.

Dale heard shouting. He went down the ladder and stood outside the captain's cabin, eavesdropping.

Brennan came out, winked and said, "He's telling 'em plenty."

Through the open door, Dale caught a glimpse of three large balding men dressed in shiny business suits, gold watch chains draped prominently across their fat bellies. Puffing on cigars, heads shaking, they took turns trying to get a word in as Capt. Ryan's tirade continued. "Go right ahead and do that," he shouted. "I'll put in a formal protest. No judge could excuse what you did to us. Profit is one thing. Pig-trough-wallowing greed is another. You're worse than the enemy. You took advantage of your own people. Shut up! Here's the log, not that you'll read it. I suggest you sell this worn-out ship for scrap. Either way, we're finished. Me and my chief engineer have berths on a two-legged nine-knotter. You have a gripe? Tell it to Ryan Brothers Shipping Company's lawyer. All I got left to say is God have mercy on your next crew."

Dale ran forward. Feeling avenged, he leaped up and swatted the ship's bell as he passed underneath.

Later, as he was packing, the captain knocked on his door. "We didn't finish our talk."

"Sir, I've been thinking. A volunteer is a volunteer."

"I'm not here about money. I know why you signed on. And I know why you're leaving. I just wanted to say that a year from now you'd never remember how you spent those extra dollars. But you'll never forget what you did here and neither will I."

Moved, Dale silently handed the captain the key to the ship's radio room, the wirelessman's last official duty. The captain nodded, gave him a steady look and said in a low voice, "For as long as I have a ship, you have a berth." It was the greatest compliment a ship master could pay a crew member. They shook hands. The captain smiled, took hold of Dale's shoulder and said, "Steady as you go."

Dale packed his Marconi uniform jacket in his Gladstone bag and snapped it shut. He took off his officer's cap and from a celluloid liner removed the folded up magazine advertisement for the wireless school and read it again.

ATTENTION ADVENTUROUS YOUNG MEN.
Here is your chance to earn money in a new and growing field
while traveling the seven seas.

That is exactly what it was. Folding it back carefully, Dale placed the ad inside his wallet. Then he walked out on deck to the railing and stood there for a moment, hat in hand.

"Papa," he said, as though Waldo could hear. "I had to do this." He hesitated. "But not anymore." He sailed the Marconi wirelessman's cap out into the wind, watching as it skimmed through the air and sank into the sea.

With mixed feelings Dale watched the crew disperse. No matter how many times he went through it, it was never easy. It was like a family scattering. He watched as, with shouts, the Armed Guard sailors departed, showing the same enthusiasm they had coming aboard. Then the merchant seamen, shore bags balanced on their shoulders, leaped over the side into waiting launches. Dale knew they would blend into the population of the city, briefly, then grow restless, impatient to go out again — feeling at home only at sea, whatever the ship or destination.

The *SS Vigo* now seemed deserted, just as she was the day he first came aboard. He looked at the lifeboat, no longer swung out in readiness for instant use, and saw *Vigo* painted in black lettering on the transom.

"Never did find out what *Vigo* means." Dale felt compelled to make some sense of it in order truly to let go. Then he thought of a longer, softer-sounding Italian word. "Vigorosa means strength. That's what WE gave her. And, come to think of it, that's what I gained in return."

Dale paused at the railing for one last look back. Mutt, the mascot, came loping toward him, ears flapping. Tom appeared on deck carrying a bucket of dishwater. He walked to the rail to dump it overboard. Shaking his head, he said, "Me 'n Carr ain't even close to leaving. We're still cleaning the stove. But when I go ashore, I'm joining the Navy. Wyman says I look old enough."

"Decided to be a gunner, huh?"

"No sir. I want to be a wirelessman, like you."

-•-• •-••

[C L = I'm closing my station]

73

[Best regards]

EPILOGUE

"I'm sick of this war!" was Dale's final diary entry. When he left the *Vigo,* he left the Marconi Company and returned to Dodge's Institute of Telegraphy to begin teaching radio. But fate intervened. He had registered for the draft and was taken into the Army in 1918, serving as Master Sergeant Electrician in the 209th Field Signal Battalion stationed at Camp Sheridan, Alabama. There he taught and worked with radiotelephone voice transmission, including some of the first ground to air radio communications. Training completed, his unit was ready to embark for France just as the war ended.

In 1919 Dale married Pauline B. Sayler. After their marriage, he taught radio at Dodge's Institute. During those years their two children, Thomas R. and Bette J., were born.

In 1925, while still teaching, Dale constructed a broadcasting station, WRBC for the Immanuel Lutheran Church, now recognized as Valparaiso's first modern radio station. The station was built to broadcast church services to shut-ins. Dale functioned as both engineer and announcer.

By 1927 the commercial radio operator's license certificates of Dale R. Clemons reflected a then-rare fourteen years of varied radio experience. Despite the lack of a high school diploma, he passed the stringent test and became a licensed professional electrical engineer and went to work for the Western Electric Company, Hawthorne Plant, Chicago. Pauline and Dale made their home in Riverside, Illinois from 1927 to 1960. Initially in capacitor development, Dale ended his thirty-three year engineering

Dale and friend, taken while he was in the U.S. Army Signal Corps in 1918.

career in the semiconductor division. A number of his original ideas were granted patents.

On his retirement, Dale and Pauline moved to Phoenix, Arizona. Dale's interest in scientific progress never waned, his boyhood love of amateur radio lasted a lifetime. Assigned call letters, W7AE, his "key fell silent" April 28, 1968.

Dale never forgot the *SS Vigo*, a ship he referred to as "that witch riding a broom." What happened to the *Vigo* defies logic. She survived the First World War. Breakdowns continued, nevertheless, she completed six more voyages to Italy. Then, at war's end, the defiant forty-four year-old steamship of obsolete design continued to elude the scrap heap. She was sold in 1919 and renamed *Katingo A Lemos* after her new owner, a Greek shipper. Finally in 1920 she met her end at sea. En route from Tees, England to Baltimore, heavily burdened with iron ore, the antiquated freighter sprang a fatal leak and sank like a stone off Cape Finisterre. Ironically her grave lies at the bottom of the Atlantic Ocean not far from a port city — Vigo, Spain.[1]

---

1 John L. Lochhead, Mariners Museum, Newport News, Virginia to B.J. Clemons, Jan 5, 1971..

Dale Clemons at his radio station WRBC, taken in 1925.

After the war, on November 20, 1919, the Marconi Wireless Telegraph Company of America dissolved.[2] It was replaced by the Radio Corporation of America (RCA).

It is still possible to see vestiges of the early days of wireless. If you drive out to Point Reyes, California, the bleak cliff-walled outreach of land where a lighthouse continues to warn mariners of rocks to the north of the Golden Gate, you will find a winding rural road that passes an odd configuration of old telephone poles. Arranged in a pattern close together, they are the weather worn masts of the original trans-Pacific Marconi Station, inaugurated on July 27, 1915. Nearby is the modern RCA Marine Coast Station where satellite discs silently face the sky, engaged in global communications.

Born at sea, wireless radio formed the basis of electronic communications development and thus reshaped the pattern of our lives. The original usefulness continues. Enticing words meant to advertise the Marine Services of RCA hark back to the beginning and the dreams of pioneer wirelessmen like Dale Clemons,

"Your route to the seven seas."

---

[2] The parent company lives on today as the Marconi International Marine Communications Co. Ltd.

Appendix
About the Author
Bibliography
Index

Appendix

The United States in World War I

After being caught unprepared to counteract a new form of warfare — the sinking of merchant ships on sight — the United States rose to the challenge. Within the brief period of eighteen months the U.S. government managed to mobilize and transport a two million man Army to Europe with war-winning effect.[1]

Although shipbuilding was delayed by the need to build shipyards, the acute shortage of ships — resulting from submarine warfare — was overcome. Germany's large, fast passenger liners lay hidden away in neutral ports where the crews had damaged their engines by cutting a piece out of the pistons. Our government commandeered those ships and repaired them. A new technique, electric welding was pressed into service to restore the damaged pistons.[2] The result was, ironically, that Germany's own merchant ships (with the 54,000 ton, twenty-four knot *Leviathan* being the most notable example[2]) played a major role in transporting the U.S. Expeditionary Force.

---

[1] Josephus Daniels, *Our Navy at War* (New York: George H Doran Company, 1922) p. 70.

[2] Thomas G. Frothingham, "American Transports," *The Naval History of the World War*, Vol. 3, (Cambridge: Harvard University Press, 1924-26) p. 175.

At sea, unrestricted submarine warfare which aimed to destroy merchant shipping and win a stalemated land war, nearly succeeded. Counteractive measures had to be developed. Implementation of the convoy system demanded cooperation on both sides of the Atlantic by nations unaccustomed to being allied with each other. For months on end, sinkings continued unchecked until convoy protection of merchant ships was implemented on a grand scale.

The arming of American merchant ships began in March of 1917 because ship masters demanded protection and refused to leave New York Harbor.

War was declared April 6. Rear Admiral William S. Sims of the U.S. Navy was sent to England to assess the situation. He recognized a crisis and asked that all available destroyers be sent to England where he strongly advocated convoy adoption.[3]

Britain's destroyers were in use guarding the battleship fleet or out hunting for submarines in an assigned thirty mile region. Admiral Sims argued that merchant ship convoys escorted by fast moving Navy craft offered offensive advantage, that the convoy system would force submarines to risk destruction as opposed to lying in wait at almost no peril.

Convincing experiments concluded, the convoy system was put into effect on a massive scale, region by region. The first regular convoy was established at Hampton Roads, July 2, 1917; followed by Sydney, July 10 and convoys began leaving New York on July 14.[4] Last of all the Mediterranean Sea was taken under the wing of convoy protection in October-November 1917.[5]

Aggressive defenders (destroyers, sloops, patrol boats) scurried around slow-moving freighters or troop ships watching for the wake of a torpedo, then followed it to the point of origin and circled the spot dropping a new weapon — depth charges. A

---

[3] William S. Sims, RADM, *The Victory at Sea*, (Garden City, New York: Doubleday, Page Co., 1920) pp. 1067-1093.

[4] Frothingham.

[5] Patrick Beesly, *Room 40, British Naval Intelligence 1914-18*, (New York: Harcourt Brace Jovanovich Publishers, 1982) p. 240.

listening device developed late in the war undermined the enormous advantage of the submersible enemy.

April of 1918 is a recognized turning point when more ships were being built than were being sunk.[6] By mid-1918 the submarine campaign had been defeated.

Every convoy had a Commodore sailing in a ship equipped with wireless and a Navy signalman (for silent ship-to-ship communication). Wireless warned of enemy location thus entire convoys could be diverted in a moment's notice.[7] As Admiral Sims himself pointed out, wireless telegraphy (radio in its infancy) helped accomplish a hard won victory at sea.[8]

---

[6] John Terraine, *The U-Boat Wars, 1916-1945,* (New York: An Owl Book, Henry Holt & Company, 1989) p. 127.

[7] Beesly, p. 261.

[8] William S. Sims, RADM, "The United States Naval Forces in European Waters," *The History of the World War*, Vol. 3, pp 1072, 1081, 1083.

ABOUT THE AUTHOR

On the night of her birth in 1925, Bette Clemon's father, Dale, was busy broadcasting at the radio station he built in Valparaiso, Indiana. Two years later the family crossed the state line and settled in Riverside, Illinois, a suburb of Chicago. Dale's creative ideas had attracted attention at Western Electric Company and he was hired as an electrical engineer, but radio and he were never far apart.

As a child, after dinner the author liked to peek into the doorway of Dale's basement laboratory to watch her father. Seeing her, he would pause and motion to her to come near. "I'm talking to another ham." Then he'd slip the earphones over her head and say, "Listen."

One summer day near the end of the Great Depression, Dale took the family on an all-day excursion across Lake Michigan aboard a steamship. It was the largest ship young Bette had ever seen. The weather turned nasty and many of the passengers took cover. But Dale stayed on deck, leaning into the wind. Looking back, he urged her on. "You'll get your sea legs!"

Then, ignoring chain-barriers and "No Admittance" signs, he led her into the depths of the ship for a glimpse of the coal-burning engine. From there it was up to the top deck where they found a small, dimly-lit room. The warm air was tinged with a familiar scent. Bette heard the musical mix of wireless telegraph messages in the background while her father and a stranger wearing earphones talked like brothers. Her father turned to her, "This is what I used to do."

Bette graduated from the West Suburban Hospital School of Nursing in Oak Park, Illinois and got her Registered Nurse's license in 1946. She worked as an emergency room nurse for nine years, then took a post graduate course at Cook County Hospital in Chicago to become an operating nurse.

Moving to Phoenix in 1956, she worked in the operating room at Good Samaritan Hospital. She was invited to join a gifted team of cardiovascular surgeons and served as their operating room nurse from 1960 to 1968. During this time Bette developed and patented a holder for suction tubing.

Her writing career began with the winning of a national essay contest open to operating room nurses. From 1965 to 1985 Bette was published a score of times in nursing, hospital and medical journals. She also worked as a freelance writer doing library research and as a ghost writer.

Retirement in 1987 freed Bette to turn her attention seaward. The posthumous find of Dale's sea diary, old letters and snapshots reawakened her love of ships and sealore. But it was the lingering curiosity of the child who watched her father talk to the world from his basement laboratory which fueled the research underlying this recounting of a young man's adventure as a wirelessman aboard a merchant ship in wartime.

BIBLIOGRAPHY

CITED REFERENCES

Annual Reports of the United States Navy Department for Fiscal Year 1917. Washington, D.C.: Government Printing Office, 1918.

Archer, Gleason L. *History of Radio to 1926.* New York: The American Historical Society, Inc., 1938.

Baarslag, Karl. *SOS to the Rescue.* New York: Oxford University Press, 1935. Reprint as *Famous Sea Rescues.* New York: Grosset & Dunlap [1946].

Beesly, Patrick. *Room 40, British Naval Intelligence 1914-18.* New York: Harcourt Brace Jovanovich Publishers, 1982.

Bone, David W. *Merchantman-at-Arms.* London: Chatto and Windus, 1919.

Bucher, Elmer E. *Practical Wireless Telegraphy.* New York: Wireless Press, Inc., 1917.

Campbell, Gordon Vice Adm. *My Mystery Ships.* London: Hodder and Stoughton, 1928.

Conrad, Joseph. *Mirror of the Sea.* 1906. Reprint. Garden City, New York: Doubleday Page & Co., 1923.

Chubb, Thomas C. *If There Were No Losses.* New York: Chubb & Son, 1957.

Cornwell, E. L. *Illustrated History of Ships.* New York: Crescent Books, 1979.

Cranwell, John P. *Spoilers of the Sea.* Freeport, New York: Books for Libraries Press, 1940. Reprint. New York: W.W. Norton, 1970.

Daniels, Josephus. *Our Navy at War.* New York, George M. Doran Co., 1922.

Dugan, James. *The Great Iron Ship.* New York: Harper & Brothers, 1953.

Frothingham, Thomas G. *The Naval History of the World War.* 3 vols. vol. iii 1917-18 Cambridge: Harvard Univ. Press, 1924-26.

Hancock, H.E. *Wireless at Sea. The First Fifty Years.* Chelmsford, England: Marconi International Communications Company, Ltd. 1950.

Horn, C.F. and W. F. Austin. *Source Records of the Great War.* (Vol. V -- 1917) Indianapolis: The American Legion, 1930.

Howe, Hartley. *The Compact History of the United States Navy.* New York: Hawthorn Books Inc., Publishers, 1967.

Hoyt, Edwin P. *The Phantom Raider.* New York: Thomas Y. Crowell Company, 1969.

Kennedy, David M. *Over Here.* New York: Oxford Univ. Press, 1980.

Lloyd's Calendar 1917. London: Lloyd's, Royal Exchange, 1917.

Lloyd's Calendar 1954. London: Lloyd's, 1954.

March, Francis. *History of the World War.* Philadelphia: United Publishers of the US and Canada, 1919.

Marconi Wireless Telegraph Company of America. *Traffic Rules and Regulations.* New York: Wireless Press Inc. 1917.

"Marine Services." New York: RCA Global Communications, Inc. [n.d.](circa 1986).

Marshall, S.L.A. *The American Heritage History of World War I.* New York, Dell Publishing Co., 1966.

Masters, David. *The Story of the Plimsoll Mark.* London: Cassell & Co. Ltd., 1955.

McCullough, David. *The Path Between the Seas. The Creation of the Panama Canal 1870-1914.*New York: Simon and Schuster, 1977.

O'Brien, Francis William, ed. *The Hoover-Wilson Wartime Correspondence.* Ames: Iowa State University Press, 1974.

"Recently Equipped Marconi Apparatus." *The Wireless Age.* (Feb. 1917) 361.

Roper, Stephen. *Roper's Engineer's Handy-Book.* Philadelphia: Edward Meeks, 1881.

Schubert, Paul. *The Electric Word. The Rise of Radio.* New York: The MacMillan Co., 1928.

Sims, Williamm. S., RADM. *The Victory at Sea.* New York: Doubleday, 1919.

Sims, William S., RADM. "U.S. Naval Forces in European Waters." *The World War*, Vol 3. New York: The Grolier Society, 1920.

Terraine, John. *The U-Boat Wars. 1916-1945.* New York: An Owl Book, Henry Holt & Company, 1989.

Thompson, Holland, ed. *The World War.* Vol. III. New York: Grolier Society, 1920-21.

Van Der Veer, Lt. Norman R. *The Bluejacket's Manual United States Navy.* 5th Ed. New York: Military Publishing Co., 1917 (rev. 1916).

Verrill, J. H. *Harper's Wireless Book.* New York: Harper and Brothers Publishers, 1913.

Weems, John E. *The Fate of the Maine.* New York: Henry Holt and Comp., 1958.

The Yearbook of Wireless Telegraphy and Telephony, 1914. London: The Marconi Press Agency Ltd., 1914.

Non-cited References

Babcock, F. Lawrence. *Spanning the Atlantic.* New York: Alfred A. Knopf, 1931.

Baker, W. J. *History of the Marconi Company.* London: Methuen & Co. Ltd., 1970. Second printing 1984.

Beck, Horace. *Folklore of the Sea.* Vol. VI. American Maritime Library. Mystic, Ct.: Mystic Seaport Museum, Inc., 1973-85.

Benson, Brian. *Ships.* New York: Grosset & Dunlap, 1974.

Benson, Wm. S. *The Merchant Marine.* New York: MacMillan Co., 1923.

Brown, Raymond. *Phantoms of the Sea (legends, customs and superstitions).* New York: Taplinter Publication Co., 1973.

Bullen, Frank T. *The Men of the Merchant Service.* London: John Murray, 1900.

Clark, Arthur H. *The Clipper Ship Era 1843-1869.* New York: G.P. Putman's Sons, 1910.

Collinder, Per. *A History of Marine Navigation.* London: B.T. Batsford Ltd., 1954.

Couper, Alistair. *Times Atlas of the Oceans.* New York: Van Nostrand Reinhard Co., 1983.

De Kerchove, Rene. *International Maritime Dictionary.* New York: D. Van Nostrand Co. Inc., 1948.

Earle, Ralph. *Naval Ordinance Activities, World War 1917-18.* Washington, D.C.: Government Printing Office, 1920.

Hawkins, N. *New Catechism of the Steam Engine.* New York: Theo. Audel and Co., Publishers, 1904.

Hilbrink, W. R. *Who Really Invented Radio?* New York: G.P. Putnam's Sons, 1972.

Hoeling, A. A. *The Great War at Sea.* New York: Thomas Y Crowell Co., 1965

Hoy, Hugh Cleveland. *40 O.B. or How We Won the War.* London: Hutchison & Company Ltd., 1934.

Kane, Robert S. "Genoa." *Italy at its Best.* Lincolnwood, Illinois: Passport Books, National Textbook Comp., 1985.

Kemp, Peter, ed. *Encyclopedia of Ships and Seafaring.* New York: Crown Publications Inc., 1980.

Knight, Austin M. *Modern Seamanship.* 10th Ed. New York: D. Van Nostrand Co., 1942.

Round, H. J. "Direction and Position Finding." *Journal IEE,* vol. 58, (1920), 224-57.

Sprout, Harold & Margaret. *The Rise of American Naval Power 1776-1918.* Princeton, New Jersey: Princeton University Press, 1939.

Stevers, Martin D. and J. Pendleton. *Sea Lanes. Stories: Man's Conquest of the Ocean.* New York: Minton, Balch & Co., 1935.

Taylor, A. J. P. ed. *History of World War I.* London: Octopus Books, 1968.

Tryckare, Tre. *The Lore of Ships.* New York: Holt, Rinehart and Winston, 1963.

Wheeler, Harold F. B. *Daring Deeds of Merchant Seamen in the Great War.* London: George G. Harrap and Co., Ltd., 1918.

Whitney, Marvin E. *The Ship's Chronometer.* Cincinatti, Ohio: American Watchmakers Institute Press, [undated].

Index

E

F

G

H

I

K

L

M

N

P

R

S

T

U

V